THE STORY OF
BRACKNELL
BEFORE THE NEW TOWN

ANDREW RADGICK

First published 2024

The History Press
97 St George's Place, Cheltenham,
Gloucestershire, GL50 3QB
www.thehistorypress.co.uk

© Andrew Radgick, 2024

The right of Andrew Radgick to be identified as the Author
of this work has been asserted in accordance with the
Copyright, Designs and Patents Act 1988.

All rights reserved. No part of this book may be reprinted
or reproduced or utilised in any form or by any electronic,
mechanical or other means, now known or hereafter invented,
including photocopying and recording, or in any information
storage or retrieval system, without the permission in writing
from the Publishers.

British Library Cataloguing in Publication Data.
A catalogue record for this book is available from the British Library.

ISBN 978 1 80399 587 8

Typesetting and origination by The History Press
Printed and bound in Great Britain by TJ Books Limited, Padstow, Cornwall.

Trees for Life

Contents

Preface		5
Introduction		7
1	Before Bracknell was on the Map	11
2	Bracknell up to 1800	29
3	Before the Railway	45
4	Victorian Times	73
5	Brickworks in Bracknell	109
6	Before the War	133
7	The Effect of the First World War and its Aftermath	163
8	Life Goes On	189
9	Second World War and the Coming of the New Town	209
Postscript		239
Acknowledgements		241
Bibliography		243
Endnotes		245

Preface

'Bracknell is a New Town – why do we need a History Officer?' This was the question I was asked when I took over the role for the Bracknell Forest Society.

I was born in Devon, but moved to Bracknell in 1974 when I started work. The New Town was still being built, with the estates of Hanworth and Birch Hill under construction. The town centre ended at Stanley Walk (it would be another ten years before Princess Square opened) and you picked your way across rough ground to reach the train station. That was the original one, built in 1856, but demolished just after I arrived (to stop me leaving?). There were other changes – a Health Centre at Skimped Hill, social housing at Boyd Court, the Wilde Theatre at South Hill Park. While I had a passing interest in history, I was more concerned about earning a living and enjoying myself.

I was forced to give up work in 1996 due to ill health, giving me more time to pursue my hobbies. Family history already interested me, and when I joined the local branch of the U3A, I enrolled in the local history group as well. It was a close friend who asked if I would be prepared to take over the role of History Officer for the Civic Society due to the current incumbent having been diagnosed with a serious illness, and I attended my first committee meeting in that role in May 2011.

One of the tasks I took on was answering historical queries, submitted via the society's website. These were very varied and led me to research Heathfield School, the old Primitive Methodist chapel burial ground, Bracknell brewery, the 'chalk factory', Priestwood House, Bullbrook School, VE Day celebrations in 1945, Lily Hill Poultry Farm, the formation of the original Bracknell Social Club, and a local army camp for Dutch soldiers during the Second World War, as well as many other topics. Each new query widened my local knowledge.

When the centenary of the First World War approached, I took on the task of researching the local men named in both Bracknell and the other parishes in the borough, publishing the results in three volumes in 2014. This gave me a wider understanding of life and the social history of the period.

Far from having no history, Bracknell has a wealthy back story, all the way back to the earliest inhabitants in the Iron Age and the Romans. It was part of the royal hunting grounds of Windsor Forest for centuries. There were changes brought about by the turnpike road and later the railway, the brick industry that thrived until the Second World War but which has now disappeared completely, and of course the arrival of the New Town.

I have been aware for some time that no one had written a history of Bracknell. Eileen Briggs wrote about growing up in the town, and Colin Hickson published a book of old photos, but there was no fully documented version. When the country went into lockdown in 2020 due to the Covid pandemic, there were no external distractions or temptations to prevent me from starting one. From online resources, conversations with older residents, local newspapers, miscellaneous books and other publications, and others with specific interests who were able to add their knowledge and expertise, I have been able to write this story: the story of Bracknell.

Introduction

Ask most people what they know about Bracknell, and they will tell you it's a New Town. They might even remember the Met Office used to be here. But what was here before the New Town? How long has Bracknell been a place, and how long have people lived in the area? How did we get from being a clearing in Windsor Forest to a bustling commuter town?

Bracknell was located in Swinley Forest, a name dating back over 1,000 years, an adaption of swine-ly, indicating the presence of wild pigs in the area. The land was used as a hunting ground for royalty for several centuries, with deer present in large numbers. The shallowness of the topsoil meant the land was sparsely vegetated, mainly covered by heather, with occasional gorse bushes and clumps of trees. Samuel Pepys thought the area 'gloomy' while Daniel Defoe called it 'a black forest'. William Cobbett, writing in the 1820s, described Windsor Forest as 'bleak ... barren, and as villainous a heath as ever man set his eyes on'. A similar landscape can still be seen today at Chobham Common. It was only in the twentieth century that the area was deliberately planted with trees, completely changing its appearance.

While Easthampstead, Warfield and Winkfield appear in the Domesday Book, Bracknell does not appear on a map until the beginning of the seventeenth century (although Braccan Heal is mentioned in documents nearly 700 years earlier, a copy of which is held at the British Library). The area had been created from the clearance of woodland during the Saxon period, around AD 600 to 700, and the manor of Winkfield, covering about 150 acres, granted to holy woman Saethryth, and then to Abingdon Abbey.

The name of the town, meaning a hidden place where bracken grows (an earlier suggestion that it meant land belonging to a person named Bracca has now been discounted) has evolved over time. Early records mention Brackenhale (1185), Brakehal (1224), and Brackenhal (1241). In 1285, there is the first record of a highway from 'Brackenhale to Reddinge', while a Goring charter of 1463 refers to Brackenale. The names Old Brecknoll and New Brecknoll first appear on a map in the early seventeenth century, the former straddled a road down to the Downmill River (now culverted under the Southern Industrial Area), while the latter lined the current High Street. Brecknoll had become New Brackenwol in 1758, and Bracknel Street by 1787, Bracknel in 1805, and Bracknall in 1832. But perhaps journalists were more literate than cartographers, as the name Bracknell appeared in the *Reading Mercury* newspaper as early as 1770.

The *Wokingham, Bracknell and Ascot Times* described the town's origins:

> Bracknell was first known as a small settlement at a crossroads in the forests which were a favourite hunting ground for many English monarchs. To the north was farmland, and it was due to the local farmers rather than the patronage of visiting royalty that Bracknell first developed ... A quiet market town whose trade revolved around the individual shops in the High Street, it catered simply for the needs of the small community living here and for the farmers nearby ... The traders almost invariably lived on the premises. They were all known by name to the residents, and equally, they knew all their customers by name. Shops were local meeting places for swapping gossip and matters of community interest. C. Smith's *New Map of Great Britain and Ireland*, of 1802, and the First Series Ordnance Survey Map in 1805, both depict Bracknell as a small aggregation of houses along the High Street.

While Bracknell was connected to Reading with a road by the late thirteenth century, both Ascot Heath to the east, and Bagshot Heath to the south, were frequented by highwaymen during the seventeenth and eighteenth centuries. With mostly ineffective parish constables and the absence of a police force, detection and arrest were 'very difficult'. Bracknell's location at the south-east extremity of a 'safe' travel area limited its development.

The building of a turnpike road in 1759 started the village's development, a process accelerated when the railway arrived in 1856. Now goods and people could be transported anywhere on the country, and utilising Bracknell's natural resource of clay, brickmaking became the major employment in the area. Despite two world wars, Bracknell plodded on as a sleepy country town, but change was in the air. The creation of New Towns, and specifically one in Berkshire, led to unprecedented upheaval and change.

Much of the information for this book has been garnered from the newspapers of the time. Initially much of Berkshire, including Bracknell, was covered by the Reading newspapers. The *Wokingham and Bracknell Gazette and County Review* started in Wokingham in 1903. Newspaper reports used language that would not be considered acceptable in today's times, but the original entries have been used to illustrate the attitudes of the day.

Introduction

Bracknell residents have been caught up in external events over the years. There were two world wars and other conflicts, some still remembered but others forgotten, such as the employee at Bracknell railway station who died when an Isle of Wight steamer hit rocks in 1899.

Bracknell has a unique history, and this is its story.

Note: To avoid lengthy repetition, the following abbreviations have been used for the names of councils:

BCC – Berkshire County Council

ERDC – Easthampstead Rural District Council

1

Before Bracknell was on the Map

The earliest evidence of human activity in the area is at Amen Corner. Numerous flints have been found between Moor Lane and the A329 (as well as on the Wokingham side of the road). The earliest dates from between 12,000 and 10,000 BC, soon after the end of the last Ice Age. It consists of a flint blade, part of a reusable knife, which would have come with a wooden handle and a scabbard. Prior to this, flint tools were used once and then discarded, so this find is not only important in illustrating human development, but is also extremely rare. At this time, Britain had a scattered highly mobile population living a hunter-gatherer lifestyle, following herds of animals. Aurochs (wild cows), elk, wild boar, hares and rabbits, and red deer were hunted in a landscape of birch, pine and alder trees, shrubs, and grasses. The other flints found are mainly blades and scrapers, and date between 10,000 and 4000 BC. Finds from the Neolithic Era, 4300 to 2000 BC, were also found when the A329 flyover was constructed. After this period, farming using more fertile land became more common as the population increased.

An Iron Age enclosure (1200 to 600 BC) existed to the north. There is also evidence of Roman activity, possibly iron smelting and pottery production. The land at Amen Corner later belonged to Buckhurst Manor (now St Ann's Manor in Wokingham), and medieval ridge and furrow field systems can be seen. A medieval frying pan has also been found, along with a silver shilling minted during the reign of George III.

Probably the best-known evidence of early settlement in the area is Caesar's Camp, a Scheduled Monument just to the south of Nine Mile Ride, thought to have been established between 3000 and 500 BC. It is said to be the best example of a true Iron Age contour fort in the country. The hill fort itself covers an area of more than 17 acres (7 hectares). The defensive banks and ditches closely follow

A selection of flints found at Amen Corner. The oldest is from the Late Upper Palaeolithic period, 10,000 to 12,000 BC.

Caesar's Camp is an Iron Age fort constructed between 3000 and 500 BC. The photo dates to the early part of the twentieth century.

the contours of the hill, resulting in a plan that resembles an oak leaf, but 'this is probably more due to the geography of the site than a conscious design with special significance as suggested in some sources'.[1] The site's name was given by eighteenth-century antiquarians in the mistaken belief that it was a Roman camp left by Julius Caesar after his campaign of 55–54 BC. Although a little way off the Devil's Highway, it is probable the Romans used Caesar's Camp as a vantage point. Mr Narrien from the Royal Military College in Sandhurst reported in 1818: 'On the north side *there* appears to have been once a considerable pond which is now dried up,'[2] while George Martin Hughes wrote in 1890: 'It was also well supplied with water, a large pond existing to the northeast side of it, which is now nearly dried up.' He also referred to it being 'encroached on by recent planting *of trees*'.[3]

Although there was a well outside the enclosure, the soil here is not suitable for farming. Its huge outer walls and rampart, 1 mile (1.6km) in length, suggest that it was used as a safe haven in case of attack. Despite the later plantings of trees, central Bracknell and Crowthorne are still visible from its highest points on clear days.

From a coin discovered in the interior, the site appears to have fallen under the rule of Cunobelin, king of the Catuvellauni tribe in the first century AD.[4] No archaeological excavations have been made at Caesar's Camp, but Iron Age pottery, Roman coins, various ornaments, household utensils, and earthenware jars have been found in the area, along with evidence of both wooden and brick buildings.

To the north is a gully, supposedly cut at the beginning of the eighteenth century for Queen Anne, enabling her to follow hunts in a coach when she became too infirm to ride. Many new rides were also being cut through the forest in the 1780s for George III for similar reasons. The remains of a redoubt, roughly 40m across, have also been found within the hill fort.

A now demolished woodsman's cottage was built inside Caesar's Camp in the second half of the nineteenth century, possibly with a cistern to hold water as a lined excavation has been found inside the hill fort. The cottage was demolished in the 1960s. A gravel pit at the northern end is also marked on maps in 1898 and 1913. The area was used by Canadian and American troops during the Second World War, while a bomb from the conflict was discovered here in 1958.

In 1949, a resident of Crowthorne 'discovered a line of thirty-four small mounds, ranging between twelve and twenty-four feet in diameter, and running for almost two-thirds of a mile ... roughly parallel with the Upper Star Post Ride'. One of the mounds was excavated and nine small pits found on the inner edge of the ditch surrounding it, each containing charcoal from oak or beech trees. The Wellington College Archaeological Society excavated one of the surviving mounds three years later and found the same layout of pits, 'filled with a mixture of ash, sand and charcoal'. One of the pits also contained 'fragments of early nineteenth century, cream coloured, glazed pottery'.[5] More than half the mounds were lost when the area was cleared and bulldozed for replanting in 1960. The origins and use of the ditch, pits and mounds remains a mystery.

The Caesar's Camp site has suffered significant erosion and some restoration has been carried out since the late 1970s. It is now part of the Thames Basin Heaths Special Protection Area, and is home to ground-nesting nightjars, woodlarks and Dartford Warblers.

'Bowl barrows are funerary monuments dating from the Late Neolithic period to the Late Bronze Age, with most examples belonging to the period 2400–1500 BC. They were constructed as earthen or rubble mounds, sometimes ditched, which covered single or multiple burials.'[6] Bill Hill, near the Horse and Groom roundabout (also known as Beedles Hill and Borough or Burrow Hill in the past), is a Bronze Age bowl barrow on top of a steep-sided hill, with a ditch on the south side. Originally, the ditch would have surrounded it, providing the material for its construction. It is a particularly good example, and was designated a Scheduled Ancient Monument in the 1950s. Many tumuli were disturbed by the early barrow diggers of the late eighteenth and nineteenth centuries, and the hollow in the top of Bill Hill barrow may well have been the result of an early unrecorded excavation of this sort. Several linear banks are visible on the hill; these are probably old field boundaries as identified on an estate map of the area dated 1757, although they may be even older. These boundaries had disappeared by 1841, by which time the area had been forested.

Another well-preserved bowl barrow, probably from the Bronze Age, is situated on the edge of a north-facing ridge of high ground in Swinley Park. The barrow mound is flat-topped, has a diameter of 24m and stands to a height of 1.6m, the top of the mound being slightly hollowed. Surrounding the mound are traces of a ditch. There is no evidence for disturbance of this barrow, 'and [it] has potential for the recovery of archaeological remains and environmental evidence relating to the landscape in which the monument was constructed'.[7]

Near the foot of Woodenhill in Great Hollands are the remains of another mound. The perimeter 'has been reduced by cultivation around its northern quarter so that today it is ovoid in shape … the surrounding ditch has also become partially infilled over the years'.[8] In 1969, a brief assessment of the feature suggested it might be a motte or a mound associated with hunting or game-watching rather than a burial mound as previously thought.[9]

Several archaeological investigations have been made at Fairclough Farm (near the Plough and Harrow pub in Warfield). An Iron Age pit was discovered, and a Middle Iron Age occupation site, dated to the third to second century BC:

> consisting of two roundhouse gullies and ancillary structures, and pottery fragments. Early Roman features, ditches along with a single beehive-shaped pit, indicating a series of minor enclosures or fields with nearby settlement. The

large, unabraded nature of the pottery sherds recovered make it highly likely that there were people living in the very close vicinity. Medieval pottery was also found here, and two contemporary enclosures, ditches, a gully, a posthole and large amounts of pottery were also found during archaeological investigations at nearby West End.[10]

Further investigations at West End in 2020 revealed 'archaeological features belonging to the Early Roman and medieval periods', the latter 'predominantly in the form of an enclosure and paddocks'.[11] At the nearby Warfield Primary School site, 'two adjoining medieval enclosure ditches and a modest amount of pottery ... enough to date the ditches *was uncovered* but the paucity of other finds and absence of other features suggest they may belong on the edge of an occupied area, and may be stock pens'.[12] Archaeological explorations at Watersplash Lane in 2017 and 2018 uncovered both Roman and post-Medieval evidence in the form of a few ditches, sherds, and metalwork.[13, 14]

The Quelm Stone at Lark's Hill was deposited by a glacier in the Devensian Ice Age, about 14,000 years ago, and marks the old Warfield/Binfield Parish boundary. It lines up with the entrance to the communal living hut of the Fairclough Farm settlement with the setting sun on 21 June. Other stones of the same composition were used in the Middle Ages to build parts of nearby churches at Warfield, Binfield and Winkfield.

Another local community was a comparatively large settlement at the former Park Farm in Wood Lane, Binfield. Here, the inhabitants appear to have earned a small fortune from the sale of pottery, and were lately known for processing charcoal, laundering textiles and farming wheat.

On a map dated 1790, the area of Park Farm is indicated as Binfield Common, a more open area than the surrounding woodland. An Oxford Archaeology report from 1990 states:

> Occupation of the site probably started no earlier than the second century BC, and seems to have been continuous up to about the middle of the second century AD. The pottery shards discovered, most of which date from the later part of the first century, point to a settlement of fairly low status. Nearly fifty loom weight fragments were found, indicating that weaving went on throughout the occupation of the site. Evidence of burning was also found, with more than half the samples contained significant quantities of charcoal, the amount of Quercus (oak) charcoal being particularly high, suggesting a non-domestic activity taking place which involved burning. The concentration of artefacts, building material, charred cereals, burnt flint, and charcoal, coincided with three of the four probable houses and indicate a single domestic focus throughout the life of the site. Gullies, post-holes and pits may point to further, unidentified structures.

The most salient feature of the site is its division into north-eastern and south-western sections. To the north-east of a boundary ditch, rectangular enclosures contained very few finds and no burnt flint, while to the south-west, circular enclosures contained rather more finds, suggesting a domestic focus. The protection of at least some of the houses by surrounding ditches suggests that animals were kept on the site. The two groups of enclosures may have served for different aspects of animal management, although the larger, rectangular enclosures may alternatively have surrounded arable plots.

While the Iron Age and Roman remains are small in scale and not widespread, they add to a growing picture of settlement and land use in the centuries either side of the Roman invasion of Britain in 43 AD. It demonstrates that this landscape was far from densely wooded, marginal land. Particularly interesting at West End, was the recognition of a number of late 11th to 14th century medieval enclosures. The enclosure ditches contained domestic pottery, showing that settlement was nearby and that the origins of the hamlet of West End certainly belong to the medieval period.[15]

The closest community to Caesar's Camp, and modern-day Bracknell, was at Jennett's Park. Oxford Archaeology examined the site in 2006 and 2007, prior to work starting on the development there:

> The earliest occupation comprised the small, temporary camp of a band of Mesolithic hunter-gatherers at the top of the southern slope of Jennett's Hill, most likely taking advantage of the elevated position of this knoll overlooking an area of wetland to the south-west. The remains of the camp consisted of a concentration of worked flint recovered from a buried topsoil, and the range of tools present indicated that a variety of activities were carried out here including the processing of hides ... After a hiatus of activity during the Neolithic period, when the site appears to have been little visited, activity recommenced in the middle Bronze Age. Features of this date comprised three burnt mounds, two waterholes, two trough-like pits and a possible cremation burial or deliberately-placed pot, as well as a number of small pits or postholes buried beneath two of the burnt mounds ... Jennett's Park was first used for permanent settlement during the middle Iron Age, when a small farmstead was established. Late Iron Age and early Roman activity was observed to the south-west of Jennett's Hill, consisting of a series of large ditches, probably acting as an enclosure around an area of more extensive settlement, and pottery fragments in this area suggest continual occupation. Finds recovered include pottery sherds, fired clay, and fragments of tegulae (overlapping roof tiles) and brick (although it was suggested these may have been introduced during subsequent cultivation of the fields). There was also evidence for smelting and smithing which continued

through into the Romano-British period. The site was apparently abandoned during the early 2nd century. Some flint-tempered sherds of Late Bronze Age pottery were also recovered at Lovelace Road on the Southern Industrial estate. Two undated parallel ditches may possibly be related, but are probably of a later date.

Further evidence was found at the northern end of the investigations for two definite and one possible curvilinear stock enclosures dating from the late 11th to late 12th centuries, which were superseded by a system of fields and enclosures that were in use until the mid-14th century … their abandonment may have been associated with the enclosure of part of the area during the creation of Easthampstead Park. A post-medieval kiln, probably for lime burning, was excavated. This may have supplied lime for the construction during the 17th century of the first Easthampstead Park House.

Medieval finds included a series of field or enclosure boundary ditches, enclosures, and postholes for a fence line, all of which form part of a medieval field system complex. These date from around 1100 to the mid-13th century. A possible trackway was also discovered, designed to control and direct the movement of animals while keeping them out of adjacent enclosures, which may have enclosed areas of pasture, arable or horticulture. More than five hundred shards of pottery were found, dating from the late 13th to early 14th centuries and all in good condition, comprising of gritty material found locally as well as Surrey white wares. Aerial photographs taken in 1961 showed cropmarks likely to be from the same period.

Two gold half-nobles of King Henry VI (1399–1413) have been found near Peacock Lane. Although in good condition when deposited, they had suffered considerably in the ground, being almost doubled over and seriously buckled; this was probably caused by ploughing. A post-medieval gunflint was found near Ringmead during a fieldwalking survey by the East Berkshire Archaeological Survey.

A post-medieval kiln, built of bricks, was also excavated. This may have supplied materials for the construction first house at Easthampstead Park during the 17th century, either bricks or lime for mortar.[16]

In 2006, prior to the building of The Parks estate on the site of the former RAF College site off Broad Lane, an investigation was also carried out, this time by Thames Valley Archaeological Services. Middle Iron Age (299 to 100 BC) features comprised of pits, ring gullies, ditches and a posthole were discovered:

The ring gullies suggest a large roundhouse and a smaller structure while 65 sherds of pottery found in the pit, along with fragments of burnt flint, pieces of slag and a fragment of burnt clay, suggesting that some ironworking was taking place nearby. More pottery and burnt clay was found in one of the gullies; the pottery, along with charcoal found nearby, was carbon dated to around 200 BC. Environmental samples contained fragments of oak, blackthorn and weed seeds of goosegrass and chickweed. It was concluded that the site comprised an unenclosed settlement with just one, or possibly two, house sites.

A few sherds of medieval pottery were also found, but not enough to point to the site being occupied.

Much more activity was recorded for early post-medieval times, with various ditched boundaries and pits, and an area of industrial activity dating from the mid-sixteenth to seventeenth century which comprised two lime kilns and a well; these may relate to the production of mortar for the construction of a house on the site, the forerunner of Ramslade House which formed the original Staff College.

The dig revealed brick-built structures from about 1600, interpreted as lime kilns, a few sherds of pottery, lumps of chalk, fragments of post-medieval bottle-glass, burnt and struck flint, iron nails, a knife blade, and post medieval bricks and pantiles, and a clay pipe stem ... were unearthed. Animal bones may also indicate the slaughtering of old animals on the site.[17]

Devil's Highway is part of the main Roman road running from London (Londinium) to Silchester (Calleva Atrebatum), the principal route to the south coast and the south-west of England during this period. Romans had invaded in AD 43, and road construction would have been rapid to facilitate the movement of the military, provisions, and goods. It is likely this road would have been in place by around AD 50.

The road passes through Swinley Woods, entering near Rapley Farm on the Bagshot Road (it was still visible here until about 1930), and runs east–west, exiting just north of Crowthorne. In 1783, in a field on the farm called Roman Down, 'the plough came across some crockery, and the poor ignorant farmer merely altered his ploughshare to go a foot deeper and drove through a rich mine of treasures ... Fifty or sixty urns and other pottery were crushed to pieces. Very few fragments were preserved.'[18] The line of the road changes direction just before this point, and both Codrington (1903) and Margary (1955) in their books on Roman roads mention the idea of another road from here, running to Winchester via Farnborough and Farnham, although no trace of the northern end of it has ever been found.[19]

Roman roads were generally constructed in straight lines due to 'the primitive surveying tools available to the engineers'.[20] Routes were planned to avoid bends as far as possible, but they also tried to avoid roads going up and down hills where feasible. Hollows were difficult for carts to traverse and there was always the risk of flooded sections impeding the movement of troops. Bishop Bennet, 'a very early driving force behind the investigation and publication of some of England's Roman roads',[21] recorded its details at the end of the eighteenth century when the surface was still raised, but it was levelled around 1800 when rides were being constructed through the forest. Ivan Margary, the leading authority on Roman roads in Great Britain during the first half of the twentieth century, records the

The Devil's Highway was the principal route to the west of Britain during the Roman period. It enters Swinley Woods at Rapley Farm, and exits on the north edge of Crowthorne.

distance between the small ditches as being 83ft (25m); earlier sources give the width at 90ft (27.5m). Cuttings were made at several points during its construction where the gradient steepens so as to preserve its linear route. As late as 1936, the road was 'still obvious over the greater part of its length' and a walker was able to follow it from Finchampstead to Virginia Water.

In the May 1836 edition of the *United Services Journal*, an account was published of an expedition by officers of the Sandhurst Royal Military Academy to map the route of the Devil's Highway from Silchester to Staines, surveying having started some fifteen years earlier:

> Several portions of the road still exist on the ground northward of Finchampstead church, occasionally deviating in a slight degree from the precise rectilinear direction, in order to avoid inequalities of the ground; but, on descending the eastern side of the ridge of heights, the course of the road is discovered pursuing an unbroken line from thence along a level country to Easthampstead Plain, and bearing the fanciful name of the Devil's Highway. The ascent of the road obliquely along the sloping ground to this commanding plateau may be distinctly observed, with a deep fosse *(long narrow trench)* on one side, and the general eastern direction is preserved quite across the plain. But from this spot, where the road rises to the summit of the plain, on the western side, a lateral branch, which has been carried out in a curvilinear direction, passes by the head of a deep ravine; and then, proceeding across the plain, rejoins the road on the eastern side. At the head of the ravine is an assemblage of aged thorns, which have the name of Wickham Bushes. The spot on which they grow has long been remarkable for the quantities of bricks, tiles, and coarse pottery which have been discovered under its surface.[22]

But later publications clouded the issue, and the straight line of the road we see today was accepted.

Margary carried out investigations in 1955 and reported the raised portion of the road and roadside ditches were visible. Surveys in 1979 and 1989 (the latter when the Crowthorne bypass was being constructed) suggested the road did deviate to the north, although no evidence of road surface was found. Thames Valley Archaeological Services made a more recent evaluation here in 2006, and but only found evidence of the survival of remains of the Roman road in just one trench, where the foundations for a metalled surface were identified.[23] Local historian Richard Brignall has recently traced the eastern section of the road from Rapley Lake for several hundred yards; this has now been cleared of large overgrowth. This follows the line of the road on the Ordnance Survey map from 1872, with tree planting at the beginning of the twentieth century and later having covered parts of it.

The Devil's Highway had become a major trunk road in the seventeenth and eighteenth centuries, and there are many tales of highwaymen along it from that period. And as Richard Brignall notes: 'For those who enjoy such things, there are reports of people hearing the ghostly footsteps of the Roman legions marching along the road at dusk, and the cries of the highwaymen as they went about their business.'

The Wickham Bushes settlement, laid out on a typical grid pattern, is also a Scheduled Ancient Monument. It is about 6 hectares in extent, although other discoveries suggest it covered a much larger area. Wickham Bushes is about 20 miles from both Staines and Silchester, the distance Roman soldiers would march in one day. Evidence of these settlements is very rare (they are usually found either in the north of England, or on the chalk downlands of Wessex and Sussex). It is only in areas with limited, if any, subsequent land disturbance that they can they be found. The town is believed to have remained in existence for a couple of hundred years after the Romans left Britain, having been taken over by the Saxons. However, it had disappeared by the time of the Norman Conquest and is not mentioned in the Domesday Book. The name 'Wickham' is of Saxon origin, indicative of an earlier Roman settlement. There is also a mention of 'The Town' by a local antiquary in 1783,[24] as well as on the earliest Ordnance Survey map of the area, surveyed in the 1820s. A report in 1818 mentions 'a few very old thorn trees which are called Wickham Bushes ... *and* wheel tracks which cross the place'.

The official description describes it as:

A series of archaeological excavations and survey work has demonstrated that the settlement was occupied throughout the Roman period and included a mixture of dwellings, agricultural structures, and small semi-industrial workshops. The buried remains of a number of large, multi-roomed buildings with tiled roofs have been identified. These were first built in the years immediately following the Roman invasion ... it is likely that the settlement expanded because of its association with trade along the road, and it may have had an official mansio building where messengers and imperial officials could stop to rest or change horses. Large quantities of pottery, a brooch and other artefacts suggest a series of successive phases of occupation well into the 4th century AD.[25]

The site has a long history of investigation. In 1783, work had been undertaken by antiquary Rev. Talbot Blakeney Handasyd, assisted by 'a labourer':

At least twenty holes were dug and ... several 'wheelbarrow loads' of material recovered, though the location of the trenches is unknown ... An almost incredible quantity as well as variety, of different kinds of pottery, shards of brick and tile ... with masses of cinders not dissimilar to those of a forge ... and a regular but coarse brick floor, at a depth of eighteen inches below the surface.[26]

Further limited excavations prior to 1800 'resulted in the discovery of some Roman coins and pieces of metal, but not in any quantity', while a dig by:

> one of the Masters of Wellington College, who had been aided in the work of digging by some of the Sixth Form in 1878, found very numerous fragments of pottery, and many specimens of roofing tiles, both of undoubted Roman origin ... and a coin of Probus *(the Roman emperor from 276 to 282 AD).*[27]

Another source claims 'at least one paved floor of small squares of red brick'[28] was also uncovered. Building materials and personal items have also been discovered. Other discoveries included:

> A great number of nails, iron binding, bolts, hinges, and fragments of burnt wood, showing a settlement living in wooden houses. Personal ornaments such as bangles, brooches, a snake-shaped ring, and a small cameo representing Hermes with a cornucopia in one hand and sheaves of corn in the other ... along with household utensils of back Upchurch ware, Samian ware (from central Gaul), and fragments of pale green-blue glass.[29]

A newspaper report from 1913 records that 'one of the stones from a handmill for grinding corn' was displayed in the museum at Wellington College, along with fragments of mortaria (saucer-like vessels in which meat and vegetables could be ground up). As late as 1800, 'some of the old hut-pits ... [were] still visible'. At a meeting of the Berks Archaeological and Architectural Society in 1886, it was noted that 'one coin is particularly interesting because it was almost certainly struck in England, by an emperor who ruled this island alone ... It is a coin of Alectus ... and such coins are not at all common.'

More diggings in 1917 to 1918 'recovered many finds, now lost or dispersed (but catalogued) with no record of where the fieldwork took place'.[30] A report in the *Berks Archaeological Journal* for 1933–34 'noted regretfully that everything that had been given to the College Museum had been lost or disposed of'.[31] When Wellington College received bomb damage in 1940, the display cases in the establishment's museum were emptied and the contents disappeared. Camberley Museum received 'a quantity of Romano-British pottery and tiles found during digging ... near Wickham Bushes' in 1939.[32] More recently, the site has been the venue for trenches in 1973 (but no report on the dig was subsequently written) and topographic observations in 1980, along with assorted metal detectorists.

Bracknell District Archaeology Group conducted an excavation in the mid-1970s that revealed a first-century Roman timber building with sarsen footings and successive gravel floors. Two phases of scientific excavation were carried out in 1983 and 1985 under the auspices of the Berkshire Field Research Group and Reading University. Nearly forty trenches were dug in total within the then extant pine woodland:

> A dense complex of archaeological deposits were recorded with occupation spanning from the earliest Roman period through into the later 4th century, though deposits and finds from the 2nd century were poorly represented. The deposits included buildings represented by robbed out walls and floors, probable buildings represented by beamslots and postholes and various ditches and pits. Quantities of iron slag indicate iron working or production on the site.[33]

After the area had been cleared of trees by felling, Thames Valley Archaeological Services were able to carry out field-walking, geophysical, and topographical surveys in 2005 over much of the area. Some concentrations of brick, tile and stone were found, some of which appear to have been collected into small piles. Small items, such as tesserae and pot sherds, would not have been collected and moved in such a manner and probably reflected something close to their original discarded positions. More than 400 shards of pottery were recovered, almost entirely from the Roman period, but all were in poor condition, 'suggesting they had been lying on the surface, undisturbed, for some considerable time'. Most of the material was local, although a few pieces were of Samian ware, Dorset black burnished ware, material produced in Oxfordshire, plus one shard possibly from the New Forest. Among the vessels identified were a lid-seated jar, various rimmed jars, storage jars, flat rim bowls, straight-sided dishes, flanged bowls, one flagon and a beaker. Although the dates of the material spanned the first to fourth centuries, most came from the latter end of the period, and no pottery of post-Roman date was recovered:

> A large amount of ceramic building material fragments were also found. This mostly included brick or tile fragments, too small to identify positively, but there were also overlapping roof tiles (typical of Roman architecture), some floor tiles and tesserae, along with a small number of pieces of ridge and flue tiles. Four fragments of glass were recovered in various shades of green or blue-green, one of which been partly melted. A single bronze coin, too worn to be identified, and one fragment of an iron blade were also discovered.[34]

More items came to light in the years following this work, including a complete Roman iron linch pin (used to secure the wheel of a cart to the axle), 'its survival is notable as iron objects rarely survive in such good condition *in the local acidic soil*'. Richard Brignall has also identified small pieces of quartz buried in paths through the site. These were used like the cat's eyes in present roads, with the quartz being brought in from outside the area, and indicate a main road passing through, rather than an offshoot track.

The name Braccan Heal first appears in AD 923. The area had been created from the clearance of woodland during the Saxon period, *c*.AD 600 to 700, and the manor of Winkfield, covering about 150 acres, granted to Saethryth, a holy woman, by King Edmund in lieu of rent. The land was then granted to Abingdon Abbey by Saethryth, and a copy of the document describing the boundaries is held at the British Library.[35] The name is soon used again in a Winkfield boundary charter of AD 942. Old Bracknell is mentioned in a Goring charter of 1463, probably the first indication of a settlement rather than just a feature in the forest.

The Domesday Book, dating from 1086, provides 'extensive records of landholders, their tenants, the amount of land they owned, how many people occupied the land ... the amounts of woodland, meadow, animals fish and ploughs on the land ... and any buildings present'.[36] Locally, it included entries for Easthampstead (named Lachenstede), Warfield and Winkfield. The land was partially waste, either due to the invading army having moved through the area, or left uncultivated, and the small settlements were typical of the time.

The first reference to a highway connecting Bracknell to Reading was recorded in 1285, when it was referred to as 'the royal way'[37]. This also facilitated travel to Wokingham, which had gained the right to hold a market in 1219, and Earley. Reading had also become a place of pilgrimage after the founding of its abbey in the previous century. But the nearest settlements to the east were Egham and Staines, both sizeable settlements, but not so convenient to reach. Indeed, the Thames would need to be crossed to reach Staines, a feat that proved tricky when the railway was eventually built.

Although the kings of Anglo-Saxon England were great huntsmen, they never set aside areas declared to be 'outside' the law of the land. All this changed in the eleventh century with the building of Windsor Castle by William the Conqueror. A vast area of Windsor Forest to the south of the castle became reserved by the king for personal hunting, and also to supply the castle with wood, deer, boar and fish, with Forest Laws being introduced. At its greatest extent, the boundary extended to Hungerford in the west, Guildford in the south, and Buckinghamshire in the east. Red deer, boar and wolves were protected, along with fallow deer, foxes, martens, roe deer, hares, coneys, pheasants and partridges. Trout and salmon were also off limits. Commoners were allowed merely to hunt squirrels and hedgehogs, and to fish for dace, grayling and dudgeon. Wild boar, once common (the name 'Swinley' means 'pig meadow'), were hunted to extinction. They were already rare by the eleventh century, but the Forest Law gave them protection from all but the royal hunts. More than fifty were supplied to the royal court in 1530, and James I tried unsuccessfully to introduce them again from the Continent in both 1608 and 1611.

The term 'forest' now refers to an area of wooded land; however, the original medieval sense was closer to the modern idea of a 'preserve', land legally set aside for specific purposes such as royal hunting, with less emphasis on its composition.

Clearing forest land for agriculture, and felling trees or clearing shrubs, was prohibited. In addition, inhabitants of the forest were forbidden to carry hunting weapons, and dogs were banned (except as watchdogs). Payment for access to certain rights could provide a useful source of income for the Crown. Local nobles could be granted a royal licence, in return for a payment, to take a certain amount of game. Common inhabitants were limited to taking firewood, and to cutting turf (as fuel). Poaching was considered the most serious crime, with suitably heavy punishments for offenders. A series of officials and wardens undertook the upkeep and maintenance of the forest, and the apprehension of offenders in special forest courts. By the time Henry VII came to the throne in 1485, Forest Law had largely become anachronistic, and served primarily to protect timber in the royal forests, although there were still harsh punishments for anyone committing an offence. However, by the mid-seventeenth century, enforcement of this law had died out, although many of England's woodlands still bore the title 'Royal Forest'. In 1810, responsibility for woods was moved to a new Commission of Woods, Forests, and Land Revenues, with much of the land being sold off, including Windsor Forest in 1813.

Despite all the restrictions, 'commoners enjoyed a number of rights and privileges'.[38] Sheep and cattle could be kept on the land, peat and turf could be cut (heather and bracken were later added). Two further rights were open to 'interpretation'. Browse-wood cut from trees to provide winter provender for the deer could be taken in the spring, and pigs were permitted to root around under trees for acorns and beech mast 'under certain conditions and at certain times'.

Easthampsted Parke was a royal park in Windsor Forest, conveniently close to Windsor Castle, first mentioned in 1365 as 'a park surrounded by palings ... It was probably a hunting lodge at an earlier date, and the monks of Hurley had a small house here, but now a regular residence was built.' This was situated south of the current mansion on what is now Downshire golf course, and the park 'became a favourite royal hunting ground. There were two buildings arranged about a courtyard. The building to the east was converted from two rooms up and down into eight chambers, and the western building, a single room up and down, was converted into five chambers.'[39] The hall, chapel and kitchen were reroofed at the same time. In 1392 there were references to a great hall, great chapel, and a spicery.

As well as hunting, the buildings were also used for 'the entertainment of foreign visitors on their way between Windsor to the west'. There are records of visits by Richard II, Henry VI and Richard III. Local folklore says Catherine of Aragon stayed here on her way to marry Arthur, the elder brother of Henry VIII. Arthur stopped here on his way to the meeting at Dogmersfield near Fleet in Hampshire in 1501, but there is no record of Catherine at Easthampstead. Arthur died less than six months later, and Catherine went on to become Henry's first wife in 1509. She is also said to have returned to Easthampstead Park in 1531 while waiting for her divorce, although no source has been found to include it. Henry himself often visited Easthampstead Park 'in search of greater game', and was there with Thomas Wolsey (who was attempting to arrange the divorce with the Pope) in 1529. A sweating sickness, often fatal, broke out intermittently across the country during Henry's reign, and it has been suggested that he visited Easthampstead frequently to avoid being infected.

By the end of the sixteenth century, enclosures and the planting of trees had made great changes to the forest. James I came to the throne in 1603 and ordered a survey of the area, carried out by John Norden. Easthampstead is shown on the maps produced by both Saxton in 1574, and Norden in 1607. In the latter's time it contained a moated lodge and enclosed 265 acres of land described as 'very mean, well timbered and stoked with two to three hundred fallow deer'.[40] There were also red deer kept at Swinley. James I enjoyed Easthampstead, and held his court there in both 1622 and 1623. He also enlarged the park, but it had begun to decline by 1629 when his son, Charles I, granted out the property to William Turnbull. Charles was executed in 1649, but not before law and order in the area had started to break down. 'Every village in the forest had some daring spirits to stir up their fellows to revolt', with George Godfrey and the wonderfully named Aminadab Harrison among the 'leaders' at Easthampstead.[41] Despite the best effort of the authorities, things deteriorated with our two local men 'snaring the King's deer', followed by complete chaos during the English Civil War. According to a petition of 1660, all the deer had been destroyed in the conflict and it was impossible to replace them, but Easthampstead survived as an ornamental park. Banks and ditches forming pattern of fields of at least two phases are still visible on aerial photographs. The present house dates from 1864.

The Black Death, a bubonic plague pandemic, reached England in June 1348, and had spread across the entire country by the summer of the following year. There was another outbreak just over twenty years later. Berkshire was badly hit, with an estimated 40 per cent of the population perishing. Warfield and Winkfield churches stand in isolated positions today, but would have previously been at the centre of the villages. Those attempting to avoid the disease moved away from the centre of the outbreak, frequently taking the disease with them. So many people died in Warfield that a plague pit was dug (near the junction of Westhatch Lane and Wellers Lane) to take the dead bodies.

The redoubt within Caesar's Camp probably formed part of the defence line created for military exercises in the summer of 1792. Five further redoubts still exist in Swinley Woods (there may be more to be discovered as a contemporary report talks of ten redoubts),[42] along with a shattered one on the summit of Butter Hill.[43] This one was 'deliberately mined and exploded by engineers as a climax to exercises watched by the Royal party, in order to demonstrate assault and engineering skills'.[44] These all include earthen banks and ditches roughly 50m across and approximately square. They are enclosed by open ditches up to 3m wide and a metre deep (although many are now partly infilled with leaf litter). According to Historic England:

> the exercises were designed to allow the Army to test its new Handbook of Military Manoeuvres, whilst sending signals of strength to continental Europe in the aftermath of the French Revolution. They boosted morale in an Army still shocked by its defeat at the hands of revolutionaries in the American War of Independence, and demonstrated the Crown's ability to maintain order in the event of any Republican unrest in Britain ... the tactics and manoeuvres perfected in the practices were later used successfully by Wellington, notably at Waterloo ... The surviving redoubts are the only documented examples in England of a full battlefield defensive system of the Napoleonic period ... They are therefore all considered to be of national importance and worthy of protection.[45]

A detailed description of the exercises is to be found in the following chapter.

Elsewhere in Swinley Woods, there are concrete constructions associated with the Second World War. Due to its proximity to the military training college at Sandhurst, the area was used as a training ground in preparation for the D-Day landings in June 1944. The innermost of the GHQ stop lines ran through the forest and a number of defensive features such as pillboxes, ditches and other anti-tank features have survived to the present. An arrangement of five octagonal concrete blocks, each measuring 1.6m high and 1.8m wide, and with evidence for timber shuttering, is located adjacent to Lower Star Post, 'although it is probable that they have been removed from their original defensive context'.[46] Archaeological Observations by Border Archaeology, made during water main works in 2015, identified 'a cluster of five possible tank traps associated with defensive works undertaken during the Second World War. The well-preserved base of a possible ... storage tank or similar structure was recorded immediately southeast of the tank traps.'[47]

The paucity of finds shows intermittent activity in the area, but no long-term habitation. The first real indication of the fledgling settlement of Bracknell occurred at the beginning of the seventeenth century.

2

Bracknell up to 1800

Until now, references to Bracknell had been few and far between, and it was no more than a name. All that was to change with the publication of Norden's map of 1607. John Norden was an English cartographer and antiquary. In 1600, he was appointed surveyor of the Crown woods and forests in Berkshire (as well as Devon and Surrey), and seven years later produced a 'Description of the Honour of Windsor', with maps and plans in colour. Between Warfelde Walke to the north and Easthampsted Walke to the south are two small settlements – New Brecknoll and Old Brecknoll:

> New Brecknoll is situated on a crossroads; the track to the north heads towards Winkfeylde, to the east towards Englemeare Ponde, westwards to join another track running roughly north/south towards Easthamsted Parke, and southwards to the west of Old Brecknoll. The latter settlement is represented by a smaller scattering of buildings, but also where four tracks meet; north (by a different route) to Winkfeylde, southeast to Bagshot Parke, in a southerly direction towards Easthamsted Walke, and westwards to again meet up with the track to Easthamsted Parke.

Some of these tracks approximate to modern roads, while the route of others is less obvious.

New Brecknoll follows the line of the current High Street; the settlement is named Bracknell Street on a map of 1787, a name still used by some residents into the early twentieth century. The name Old Bracknell continued to be marked on Ordnance Survey maps until at least 1909 but is absent by 1932, although a road called Old Bracknell Lane still exists. At the start of the eighteenth century, Bracknell was still just a row of houses and shops along 'a narrow cart track'. To the east and south were the wilds of Ascot and Bagshot Heaths, while Priestwood

Common to the west had no road across it and no bridge over the Downmill River (now celebrated by The Bridge pub).

According to the catalogue of Listed Buildings maintained by Historic England, The Bull is the oldest building in Bracknell, originally a hall house from about 1400.[1] The large extension to the rear is the latest in a long line of changes to a building that still manages to maintain an air of history, complete with its resident ghost (a man about to be hanged in Quelm Lane who can occasionally be seen, sipping his last pint). Arguably, the latest changes have saved a building that was in a poor state of repair and in need of extensive renovation. Bull-baiting is said to have taken place outside the building, the main event of the year taking place on Good Friday. It has been claimed, without any evidence, that Henry VIII watched the sport in Bracknell.

The Old Manor at the opposite end of the High Street is a fascinating building. Also originally a hall house from the fifteenth century, it has subsequently been faced with brick and much altered.[2] In Tudor times, it was owned by a Catholic family who hid many persecuted priests in the secret 'priest-hole'. This was discovered above a fireplace in 1969 and is now visible as a 'talking point'. According to some reports, it was also used later by local highwaymen keen to escape from the authorities.

Although Dick Turpin (1705–39) is said to have been active in the area, his haunts were primarily to the east and north of London, and he is unlikely to have strayed this far west. The Hind's Head, at the top of the High Street, was said to be his favoured drinking place, with a tunnel large enough to accommodate him riding his horse, connecting it to The Old Manor (then a private house). It is also claimed he hid in the parish church, a building that was only built more than a century after his death! But two other highwaymen known to have frequented the area were Claude Du Vall (or Duval, 1643–70) who was 'notorious ... his fame resting hardly less on his gallantry to ladies than on his daring robberies'.[3] On one occasion, he was reported to have held up a coach and danced with its female occupant before 'charging' her husband £100 for the privilege of watching (this may have occurred on Bagshot Heath). He was finally caught and hanged at Tyburn in London. William Davies (or Davis, 1627–90) was also active in the seventeenth century. Details are muddled, but he led a double life as a successful farmer who supplemented his income by robbing the passengers of coaches crossing Bagshot Heath. Avoiding jewels and other items that would be recognised, he stole only money, and became known as The Golden Farmer from his habit of paying large bills with gold (he is commemorated by the pub of the same name in Easthampstead). He was eventually caught, and died either at Westminster, or was executed at Salisbury (there are two accounts of his death), and the body hung in chains near the former The Jolly Farmer pub, on the roundabout on the A30 to the west of Bagshot. Thomas Simpson (also known as Old Mob) sometimes operated in conjunction with William Davis. There is a report a newspaper as late as 1785 of a highwayman taking money from a couple on Binfield Road.

There were also many tales of secret tunnels leading from The Old Manor to other parts of Bracknell. The most likely one led from the cellar to The Hind's Head, a hostelry that once stood just 20ft away on the opposite side of Warfield Road; the version that says the tunnel was large enough to ride a horse through is more likely to have been the result of a good evening's drinking! There are also rumours of a tunnel stretching the entire length of the High Street to The Bull (which has never been found despite extensive rebuilding of this part of the town centre). The house remained a private residence (called Studlands) until the 1930s, with the small extension to the side of the main building (now integrated into the pub) housing a shop, variously used by a vet, a basket maker, and a butcher. Since then, The Old Manor has had a variety of uses including a private boys' school, a club, and a residential hotel, before becoming a pub. Again, such an old building with a chequered history has a collection of ghostly residents, including 'Old Fred' (a figure wearing a cowl), and Bert (a regular in the early 1970s who reappeared shortly after his death). There are also reports of a young girl from the Victorian era who haunts The Old Manor, as well as a woman who makes her presence felt in an upstairs room.

The Red Lion has been a prominent building in Bracknell since its construction in the sixteenth century. It served as a coaching inn after the turnpike road was built in 1759. It is now The Blue's Smokehouse. This picture shows the Berkshire Yeomanry passing, just prior to the First World War.

Another building from the same period stands further down the High Street. Now occupied by Prospects estate agents, it is known as 'Ginger's' by many older residents after the delicatessen that occupied it for many years.[4] It is difficult to imagine how it might have looked as it was re-faced in the eighteenth century, before being restored, altered and extended in the late twentieth century. The Old Farm (off Warfield Road) is of a similar age.[5]

The Red Lion (now Blue's Smokehouse) was a prominent building in Bracknell. Standing at the bottom of the High Street (the area was called West End), it was built in the sixteenth century as an inn with stables.[6] To the right of the bay window and central chimney was an opening for a coach and horses to pull off the highway into a rear courtyard. The east end of the building became a shop (and the West End sub post office at the beginning of the twentieth century). It soon became the premier inn and dining establishment in Bracknell, although several landlords went bankrupt while attempting to provide a more luxurious establishment than their income permitted. By the nineteenth century, in addition to travelling coaches, carriers and postal services were running from The Red Lion. Writing in the 1730s, a Binfield resident referred to assembly rooms and a coffee house in Bracknell. Such facilities were usually located in the major public house in the town, so the Bracknell ones were probably at The Red Lion.

Originally a cottage built in the seventeenth century, The Horse and Groom has been a pub for at least 200 years. Like several old buildings in the area, it has resident ghosts, one of whom is fond of spirits.

Mallorys in Broad Lane also dates from the sixteenth century with later alterations (Hill House was built on to the rear of it in the 1920s).[7] It was probably a farmhouse on the edge of Old Bracknell. During restoration work, a child's shoe from the 1600s was found behind some wooden panelling.

The nearby Horse and Groom was built in the following century but has been subsequently much altered.[8] Originally a cottage, it has been a pub for at least 200 years. Two ghostly presences are associated with The Horse and Groom; footsteps of an old woman can be heard as she cleans the upstairs rooms, while whisky is said to disappear from a locked spirits cabinet.

Two other buildings still exist in Bracknell dating from this time. Lynwood Cottage[9] in Goughs Lane is a private house, while Whynscar,[10] near The Old Manor, was extended and re-faced in the eighteenth century. It is reported that a priest hole was also found here.

Two lost buildings also date from this period. The Hind's Head, as already mentioned, was formerly known as The Bunch of Grapes. Dating from the early seventeenth century, this stood at the top of the High Street (part of Bracknell and Wokingham College now stands on its former site). A report from 1772 says it 'stood alone on the dreary heath' – certainly it would have been the first hostelry encountered travelling westwards from Ascot. It had rather a dubious reputation, with links to the local highwaymen. There is also the story of the landlord, one Richard Millard, who would ply guests with drink, before robbing them and murdering them in their beds, then disposing of the bodies. He was caught when a barmaid warned a traveller what would befall him. Millard and his wife were allegedly hanged, although he continued to haunt the pub until it was demolished in the 1960s. But Millard appears in the 1861 census running the Station Hotel (now The Market Inn), and by 1881 had retired and was living on London Road, dying of natural causes two years later. Extra rooms were added to The Hind's Head after Millard's tenure, and the establishment acquired a better reputation, hosting meetings and dinners for several prominent local organisations, including the Royal Forest Agricultural Association. Being the closest inn to Bracknell Market, it was always busy on a Thursday, which was market day.

The Crown Inn was the first documented inn in Bracknell, opening in 1644. It was located next to the current Lloyd's Bank. Next door was a lock-up for local criminals; both were demolished to make way for a post office in 1932 when the 'House of Correction' was described as:

> a stone building consisting of one room, arched over ... It was here the wrongdoers of the parish were incarcerated after a day in the stocks which were situate just outside. Adjacent to the House of Correction was a well providing the water supply for the parish ... The old 'Crown' was situate almost alongside the House of Correction, and when the temporary inhabitant of the stocks

The Hind's Head stood at the top of the High Street. Originally it had rather a dubious reputation with links to the local highwaymen, but later ran a flourishing trade as the nearest hostelry to the weekly Bracknell Cattle Market.
(Photo courtesy of Wendy Wright)

was transferred there for his nightly repose on a bed of straw, he immediately enlisted the sympathies of his friends. They saw that he was plentifully supplied with liquor! A churchwarden pipe was given to the poor inhabitant, and he was able to absorb all the liquid refreshment he needed by the skilful manipulation of this moulded piece of clay. It closed about sixty year ago.[11]

The article remarks that many prisoners came out of the House of Correction more drunk than when they went in! The Crown, along with an old forge that stood opposite The Red Lion (opened in 1680, it was demolished to make way for the Regal cinema), were rebuilt at Priory Garth, a house on Ralphs Ride, but all three were demolished in 1960 to make way for the Harmanswater estate.

Built in the early 1700s, Old Bracknell House stands at the junction of Crowthorne Road and Old Bracknell Lane.[12] It has been claimed this was originally a hunting lodge, housing the mistress of one of the King Georges, and on losing favour and being evicted, she put a curse that no more than one generation of any family would ever live in the place.[13] This seems to have been true for all the families who lived there when it was a private house with grounds of around 20 acres (including Bill Hill). It was requisitioned during the Second World War, and subsequently used as the local office for various government ministries, but now accommodates Bramley Wood Day Nursery.

Examples of workers' cottages, built with oak frames and with thatched roofs, can be seen at Frog Cottage in Frog Lane,[14] in Bay Road, opposite the Bullbrook shops[15] (both of which date from the sixteenth century), Rest Harrow in Frog Lane[16], the thatched cottage on the corner of Broad Lane and Larges Bridge Drive (seventeenth century),[17] and Cottrells in Sandy Lane (c.1700).[18] Littlecourt,[19] standing behind a tall brick wall beside the busy Warfield Road, dates from the same period.

Goddard's Croft stood in grounds of 26 acres on the southern side of London Road, opposite Longhill Road. The name was later changed to the better-known Martin's Heron (or Martin's Herne). Built around 1750, it was the home of minor nobility for much of its life (including General Gordon), and much visited by George III. In 1844, it was described as 'a late Georgian house of moderate size and pleasing appearance'. It was demolished in the early 1980s to make way for Forest Ride and the housing estate of the same name.

A trio of houses from after 1800 are also worth recording. Coppid (or Copped) Hall,[20] opposite The Elms recreation ground on Warfield Road, was built in about

The Crown Inn was the first documented inn in Bracknell, opening in 1644. The single-storey building on the side was the lock-up, where prisoners were held. Both were demolished in 1932 to make way for the post office. (Photo courtesy of Vin Miles)

1840 for Charles Cave, the local solicitor. It has a distinctive Italianate tower, which has helped it gain Listed Building status. The grounds originally extended to 15 acres, and adjoined the old Bracknell cricket field to the north of the High Street. The offices for solicitors Wilson and Berry for many years, it was converted into flats in 2020, preserving many original features.

Wick Hill House,[21] 'a handsome late Georgian manor', was built in 1835. The first owner was Francis Theodore Dudley Sewell, a lieutenant in the Royal Navy. After his death, it was purchased by Clement St George Royds Littledale, a 'gentleman' and Victorian explorer. The house is now divided into flats.

Old Malt House[22] in Cedar Drive also dates from the early nineteenth century with later alterations.

High Elms was another Georgian house that stood at the junction of Warfield Road and Clay Lane (now Park Road). An auction listing of 1857 describes a building with 'lofty drawing and dining rooms, kitchen, pantry, scullery, excellent cellarage, larders, six bed rooms, stabling for seven horses, coach-house, granary, green-houses with good garden … well stocked for winter, and orchard and meadow adjoining'. The building was still in use until the 1930s, after which it stood empty and derelict for twenty years before being demolished. The Elms recreation ground now occupies its former site.

In March 1720, the *London Gazette* contained a report of fourteen men on horseback armed with guns, along with two men on foot with a greyhound, all with blackened faces or other disguises, who had coursed deer in Bigshot Walk, threatened a keeper, and killed four deer. This was the first record of the actions of a group that came to be known as the Wokingham Blacks. They were protesting about the hardship of the ordinary forest dwellers, whose limited rights were being eroded by the expansion of estates and increased fees to collect peat and wood, and to kill game other than deer. One writer describes the Blacks as: 'social bandits who … used direct action as a means to resist the extensive changes that were taking place in Windsor Forest at that time'.[23] The Black Act was passed by Parliament in 1723, 'the most draconian pieces of legislation ever passed by Parliament in respect of the number of offences for which the punishment was the death sentence'.[24] Even pulling down a fence or blacking your face was punishable by death. Later the same year, a troop of mounted Grenadier Guards staged a pitched battle at Caesar's Camp with the Wokingham Blacks. Thirty men were caught, with four tried in Reading, condemned, and hung in chains.

Three annual fairs were held in Bracknell on Priestwood Common; these were first mentioned in 1737, and continued until 1888. The first, held around 25 April, was for the trading of cows and sheep, while horses were bought and sold in late summer, around 22 August. Cows were again available at the beginning of October, which was also a hiring fair when labourers 'auctioned' themselves for twelve months' work in return for board and lodgings. Fairs developed into large events with stalls and sideshows, but attracted poor reputations for drunkenness and immorality. Cases of assault and pickpocketing at the Bracknell Fairs would be mostly heard at the Wokingham Magistrates' Court. In his book *The Crowthorne Chronicles*, Roger Lord states the Bracknell Fair was 'beset by the gypsies of Edgebarrow Woods, a mix of Irish labourers employed in the building of Broadmoor Hospital, and locals from Wildmoor Common'.

By now, Bracknell was developing into a thriving little community, but its position beside the lawless heathlands of Ascot and Bagshot limited its potential. Houses and shops lined a cart track (now the High Street), usable in the summer, but often muddy, icy or flooded during the winter months. This was not a problem limited to Bracknell – the road system across the country was limited and poor, with routes maintained by local parishes.

Improvement of the roads occurred piecemeal across England in the eighteenth century, but made the movement of goods and passengers easier and faster. Regulated through Acts of Parliament, local trustees were allowed to levy tolls on a specified stretch of road, with the income used to improve and maintain it. Most English trunk roads were maintained in this manner until the 1870s.

The Windsor Turnpike Act was passed in 1759, and the road from Reading and Wokingham was extended across the open land of Priestwood Common and through Bracknell to Ascot and Virginia Water, a distance of 17 miles. The two toll gates in the Bracknell area were on the London Road near the main entrance to Lily Hill, and at Coppid Beech Lane (close to Beehive Lane). The tollgate at the former location was demolished in 2012, but a small cul-de-sac has been named Old Tollgate Close to mark its location. The nearby Allsmoor Lane was used by drovers, taking animals to Bracknell Fair, as an alternative route into Bracknell without paying a toll. Similarly, and if road conditions allowed, coaches would often use the back road to Wokingham (via Peacock Lane and Waterloo Road) to avoid the long hill up to the Coppid Beech (where the A329 crosses over the Wokingham Road). From a figure of £487 (£33,000 in today's money) in 1820, monies received for use of the road doubled within twenty years before falling, especially after the arrival of the railway in 1856. Tolls continued to be collected until 1868. Although still part of Windsor Forest at this time, the turnpike now enabled coaches to stop at Bracknell on their way to the west at The Red Lion, ending Bracknell's isolation. It was probably the arrival of the road that also encouraged William Watts to build the first mansion at South Hill Park.

Typical tolls in the early days of the turnpikes: passenger vehicles were charged 1s, while flocks of sheep or droves of farm animals were charged by the score, at 5d for twenty. The average taking at the Loddon tollgate during the first ten years on the Windsor Turnpike was £3, less at the two Bracknell ones.

Before the advent of a national postal service, a named recipient would deal with mail to and from the community. The system was initiated in major cities at the beginning of the eighteenth century, with a seven-fold increase in the amount of mail handled seen within fifty years. A receiver for letters for Wokingham was appointed in 1786, and one in Bracknell nine years later (although Charles Talmage was working at the village's post office two years earlier). Mail coaches now stopped at The Red Lion. The post of Receiver of Letters continued until 1814, when a postmistress in the High Street took over the role. An official post office was opened in the High Street in 1863, moving to Church Road thirty years later, when the lease on the original building expired.

Not everyone was happy to pay the turnpike tolls. Around midnight on 16 May 1797, two men knocked on the door of the toll gate house at Coppid Beech Lane. On opening his door, the gatekeeper Edward Bunce was shot through the head 'by person or persons unknown'. Two men of medium stature, dark complexion and 'suspicious appearance' had been seen in the area just prior to the incident, and a reward of £100 was offered for information leading to their capture and conviction.[25] However, no reports of any arrest or trial have been found.

The first local newspaper was the *Reading Mercury*, which started publishing weekly in 1723, and continued until 1987. The majority of its material was generated in Reading in early issues, with other local news creeping in as communications improved. With no 'roving reporters', newspapers were reliant on correspondents sending in material for items of interest outside the town. The *Windsor and Eton Express* (1812), *and Berkshire Chronicle* (1825), were two other early newspapers that included topics from Bracknell, along with the *Reading Observer* (1873). Wokingham's first newspaper appeared in 1903, but it took until 1956 for the *Bracknell Times* to appear, soon followed by the *Bracknell News*.

The *Reading Mercury* newspaper mentions Bracknell a few times towards the end of the eighteenth century, mainly for the sale of land, when it is being described as 'being convenient for the Ascot races'. One of these was Puddle Dock:

> consisting of a substantial-built brick dwelling house, with convenient outhouses, a garden, orchard, and a piece of very rich meadow ground adjoining thereto, containing in the whole, by elimination, one acre and a half, very pleasantly situated at the end of New Bracknell, in the parish of Easthampstead, and has an unlimited right of common of pasture and turbary ... The estate is capable of great improvement, and might be made a genteel residence at an easy expense.

This occupied the land south of the High Street, between The Ring and Market Street. Various properties were also available to let, including Easthampstead Park ('for a term of years'), and Down Mill Farm (opposite The Bridge pub), with 100 acres of dairy pasture land.

By 1774, a coach was running through Bracknell to London on Thursday and Saturday mornings, the return journey taking place on Mondays and Wednesdays.

It stopped at The Hind's Head at the top of the High Street, and The Mutton (The Shoulder of Mutton, which stood at the top of Beehive Road, Binfield). The cost was 4s (nearly £10 in today's money), with luggage being charged at a further 1s 6d per hundredweight. By the following year, The Bull had been added to the stops, which was also the venue for sales and auctions in the town.

In 1785, the *Reading Mercury* described how parties of soldiers were employed at an extra 1s per day to cut the royal rides through Swinley Forest. Rides had existed since at least the middle of the seventeenth century, but more were built during the time of Queen Anne (reigned 1702–14) and a more extensive network laid out during the reign of George III (reigned 1760–1820). Nine Mile Ride was probably built during this period, and Ralphs Ride in Harrmans Water probably dates from this period as well.

A new name appears on a map of 1790 in the Bracknell area: Ramslade. This was a hamlet just to the south-east of the High Street and covered the top end of Broad Lane. The Parks estate now covers the land belonging to Ramslade House, the site of the house itself now occupied by the houses of Ramslade Terrace. Earlier, in 1753, the vicar of Winkfield described it as: 'the property of Mr William Ford, dissenting preacher ... in possession of Royal Highness William, Duke of Cumberland. It is a small square-built house, three windows in front converted to be repaired, but was rather rebuilt at the change of the unfortunate tenant I. H. Esquire.' Ramslade House, 'very pleasantly situated in the Middle of the Stag Hunt, Windsor Forest', was available to buy or rent in 1775:

> consisting of four rooms to a floor, with two cellars, a wine vault, a good kitchen, a brew house, wash house, pantries, dairy, and all conveniences for a gentle family, a double coach house, and stall stabling for nine horses, a good garden well planted with wall espalier fruit trees, three fish ponds ... with carp and tench, and near forty acres of good meadow land.

It also had 'a right to a large extent to common land to feed cattle and cut fuel for the house'. Its proximity to the turnpike and post office were also mentioned in the advert.

In the book *A History of Windsor Forest, Sunninghill and the Great Park* by George Martin Hughes, there is a chapter on 'the military encampments in the forest from the days of the Stuarts'.[26] Military exercises took place over the course of three weeks in the summer of 1792. Caesar's Camp at that time had a commanding view over the miles of heathland to the south (neither the Royal Military Academy nor Camberley existed at this time) where the exercises took place, culminating in a display for the king and Prime Minister William Pitt. Army regulations had been issued earlier in the year, making a set of eighteen 'movements', or manoeuvres, mandatory practice for British infantry regiments. They had been devised 'with the aim of regularizing the Army's drill training and expurgating doctrines established during operations against irregular forces in North America which were unsuited to combat with European regular armies':

> Seven redoubts have been identified, built in an arc on the southwestern edge of the Bagshot Plain with an eighth on the nearby Butter Hill, just to the south. Each redoubt is roughly square with widths ranging from about 150 feet to 175 feet. They consisted of an outer ditch between six and ten feet wide, and about three feet deep, a bank rising about three to four feet above ground level and a hollow in the centre running at about the external ground level. Construction was by simply digging the ditch and piling up the spoil to form the bank. The banks may have been given additional height by positioning sandbags or soil filled barrels on the top. The most westerly Redoubt, which is on Wagbullock Hill, had some additional banks and ditches arranged on the edge of the hill probably at the time of the Boer War. These eight Redoubts are the only surviving example of a full battlefield disposition from the period although two of the seven redoubts have been seriously damaged in recent years. The one situated on Wagbullock Hill is now almost completely obliterated, probably by forestry work since World War One, although the Schedule Listing describes some parts of both the Redoubt and the later ditches as being still visible.[27] An exploded mine, used during the exercises, was found here in the later nineteenth century. Further damage was caused during fire-fighting of the Great Forest Fire in May 2010. There is now no sign of the Redoubt. The second most easterly of the other six in the Forest has been seriously damaged in recent years by unofficial digging by cyclists to create a BMX type track and obstacles. The remaining five are still in good condition although a couple are heavily overgrown with young trees.

I am indebted to Richard Brignall for the description of the redoubts, the descriptions being quoted from his excellent website on Swinley Forest.[28]

The exercises, involving around 7,000 troops, commenced on 23 July and finished on 8 August, when the important guests were in attendance. The event was described in the *Journal of the Berkshire Local History Association* published in 1997: 'In the event, the manoeuvres did not go entirely as planned. During the first period at Wickham Bushes ... the King and Prince of Wales rode over daily from Windsor.'[29] An artillery train had left Woolwich a week earlier, en route for the camp, while the infantry troops arrived during the two days before the exercises began. 'Their arrival was witnessed by the King, the Prince of Wales, the Duke of York, and the Duke of Gloucester. The King throughout showed great interest in the manoeuvres; he was present almost every day, and occasionally took part in the fighting.'

The second day:

> was devoted to a review and a sham fight, at which Mr Pitt was present ... part of the heath ... caught fire, and burned with great fury, though it excited considerable alarm, and was with difficulty put out ... It had been a dry season and the heather was continually catching fire; on one occasion seriously endangering the safety of the camp ... though workmen had been busily engaged in sinking wells in various parts of the heath, the soldiers began to suffer from want of water.

Several of these holes were still in evidence a century later.

'The whole camp turned out to repel an imaginary attack' on the third day. 'This morning three alarm guns were fired at 2:30.' The first troops were ready within five minutes (some not entirely kitted out in their uniforms) with the whole army ready within a quarter of an hour.

Disaster struck in the form of a heavy rainstorm when the troops made the night march to Hartford Bridge, near Hartley Wintney. The new campsite was a swamp (it rained for four days) and 'officers and men were laid low by colds and "fluxes" caused by contaminated drinking water. The proposed march to Beacon Hill, above Farnham, was abandoned and the troops returned to Wickham Bushes to prepare for the Royal Review.'

On the penultimate day:

> people were already beginning to arrive ... There was a dense fog, which very much interfered with the manoeuvres, as also did a mad bull ... who did not at all approve of the scarlet coats and the rest of the pomp of war. Such was the demand for carriages from London that it became almost impossible to get any form of conveyance. A large number of the ordinary hackney coaches ran down from town drawn by four horses. The price of a seat in one of these was two guineas [about £350 in today's money]. The Heath was now covered with vehicles of all descriptions and many people spent the night in their carriages. By 6am on the final day already over 100,000 persons were upon the ground and some reports double this number later in the day.

The *Lady's Magazine* describes:

> A pavilion was prepared for the reception of the royal party, commanding a view of the whole line from right to left. Their majesties were saluted on their appearance upon the heath ... at eight o'clock ... At nine o'clock the whole of the forces passed in companies and troops before the pavilion which the royal party occupied ... perhaps the only part of the review which was seen

by many of the populace ... Ten batteries or redoubts ... had been erected and taken possession of by the artillery, who on a signal being given, all began to cannonade from one end to the other ... After some time, they were attacked by the infantry and silenced.

There was then a break as everyone, including the soldiers, took 'refreshments'. A report in the *Reading Mercury* a century later describes the chaos:

The supply of food was not nearly sufficient for the large number of people who required it, and a free fight for provisions ensued. Water was very scarce, and the unfortunate horses suffered terribly. Many of them lay down in the woods exhausted, and absolutely unable to move. A bucket of water was purchased for as much as five shillings [more than £40], and a bottle of beer was considered cheap as the same price.

The *Lady's Magazine* continues: the display recommenced at 2 o'clock when the military performed 'several manoeuvres and evolutions, with the grand and tremendous conclusion of springing mines and blowing up the forts'. The report concludes: 'We understand this was carried into execution, but not with the expected result.' A postscript concludes that most of those watching would not have seen much as the exercises were spread over a wide area with 'evolutions so rapid and dextrous ... that four-fifths of the visitors might as well have been in London as on Bagshot Heath'. One spectator got a little too close to the action one day and 'was nearly killed by a cavalry charge but had the presence of mind to throw himself flat down in the road, and the ... squadron passed over him', while an aide-de-camp was 'rather badly hurt being thrown during a charge down the steepest part of White's Hill'.

Due to a lack of adequate transport, 'a great number had to spend the night on the Heath ... The remnants of the good folks ... returned *the following day* in some thousand buggies drawn by as many lame horses which had returned to Bagshot for these unfortunate people.'

The publication mentioned above concluded:

The Review and the final exercises went well but they were marred by the large number of spectators that came by coach, foot, and horseback. One estimate said that 50,000 came in various vehicles. The exercises finished by the soldiers being persued [sic] for miles across the open heath by coaches containing 'well-dressed sprightly females.'

The whole event was 'all the rage', with special coaches running from London on a daily basis to bring spectators. Scenes from the camp were staged at Astley's and Sadler's Wells Theatres as 'songs, dances, scenes both comic and serious, and military spectacles of all kinds filled the programmes'. A coach left London just before midday every Monday for Bagshot, 'returning from the camp at 5 the same afternoon, with a guard and lamps'. Local inn-keepers did a roaring trade. One 'enterprising host had sign-posts erected all over the Heath to direct visitors to his establishment ... fitted up in a commodious manner for the reception of the Genteel Company'. A play and a burlesque in London the following year included scenes based on the military exercises.

Meanwhile, local matters concerned the local populace. Complaints were made to the Lord of the Manor at Easthampstead:

> that many persons claiming to cut turf on the heath and wastes for their own uses, and others, having no right so to do, have of late cut great quantities for sale, and to be carried out of the manor, contrary to the ancient custom and usage in that respect, and much to the prejudice of those entitled to cut turf within the manor for their own uses.

A statement appeared in the *Reading Mercury* in April 1795 to the effect 'that any such offenders in future, will be prosecuted to the utmost of the law for such offences'.[30] Incidents such as this were soon to have repercussions that would change Bracknell and the surrounding area.

3

Before the Railway

Not being an old village, Bracknell had no church before 1800, with a visitor commenting on 'the general depravity' of the inhabitants of the place. Prayer meetings were held in the house of William Foster, a newcomer to the village, with occasional visits from Thomas Burgwin, a Baptist minister. In 1801, Burgwin licensed a house as a place of worship, and in 1808 a building was adapted as a meeting house and licensed for worship. The church was officially formed in 1813. By 1820 the building was in a dangerous condition, and a chapel and schoolroom were built. These were demolished in 1858 and a new chapel and schoolroom built, opening in February the following year. From 1865, the former Sunday School was used as a private day school providing 'middle class education'. Mr Crockford, the schoolmaster, and his wife, also accepted boarders at their own house. The school prospectus guaranteed 'no corporal punishment'.

The church closed in 1967, having been compulsory purchased by Bracknell Development Corporation for the redevelopment of the town centre, and meetings were held at Harmanswater Community Centre until a new church building (St Paul's United Reformed Church) opened in 1970. Bodies from the burial ground around the old church were exhumed and moved to the cemetery in Larges Lane. This sensitive operation was conducted behind sheeting, with many a youngster expecting to see ghosts rising from behind it!

1809

George III's Golden Jubilee was 'a spontaneous effusion of love' according to one of its chroniclers. There was a national day of celebration on 25 October when 'town and village folk feasted on roast ox, plum puddings and strong beer. Sermons were preached, "God Save the King" sung heartily and food and alms distributed to the poor.'[1]

The Congregational Church was opened in 1859. It was demolished in 1968 due to the town centre redevelopment. The NatWest Bank now stands on the site. (Photo courtesy of Stewart Willis)

1810

William Ware and his 13-year-old son, also called William, were returning to their home in Frimley from the October Bracknell Fair when 'they were stopped by a gang of men armed with bludgeons, who robbed them of the goods they had been purchasing, their watches and cash'.[2] Young William tried to defend his father and was bludgeoned to death, according to the newspaper reports; other sources state the boy was taken to The Horse and Groom pub, where he expired. The perpetrators were thought to be Irish labourers working on the building of the Royal Military Academy at Sandhurst, six of them 'having absented themselves on the morning after the murder'. Some were traced to London while another was apprehended on board a ship at Northfleet, Essex, trying to flee the country.

Roads southwards from Bracknell were still in a very poor condition, as remarked upon by the *Berkshire Chronicle* in 1829: 'A quantity of loose round gravel has been carelessly thrown upon them, eminently well calculated to make travelling all but an impossibility.'[3]

1812

Two hunts in the areas were advertised in the *Windsor and Eton Express* from this year, one starting from The Golden Ball (which stood on the Wokingham Road at the top of Jocks Lane); the other at Barrow or Burrow Hill (The Horse and Groom). While the latter still exists, The Golden Ball has long since disappeared. It first appears as The Golden Acorn in the 1750s, with the name appearing on maps as late as 1856, and still in use in 1888 (when the Golden Acorn estate is being used to describe land). The local Garth Hunt is named after Thomas Colleton Garth of Broad Hinton near Twyford, who was master of his own hounds from 1852 until 1902. The dog kennels moved to Kennel Lane, Priestwood in 1908.

1813

An inquiry commission was set up in 1805 to examine and report on the ancient Windsor Forest laws. The final report concluded that 'crown land claimed a number of rights to which it as not entitled ... 500 acres had been enclosed without authority, 340 encroachments had been made on His Majesty's soil.' The various lodges were in a poor state of repair or even uninhabitable, and the whole area was run down. Such papers as could be found at Windsor Castle were inconclusive, and many had been destroyed or simply disappeared. It was finally decided that 'the whole muddle was best left alone and to define Windsor Forest by a new Act of Enclosure'.

This changed the landscape as former heathland was planted with pine trees, ancient trees (many in poor conditions) were felled, common land was enclosed, and old earthworks levelled. Landowners took the opportunity to annexe land for their estates, while the poorest found areas they had used for generations had now become off limits. Henry Dormer Vincent was able to purchase Lily Hill the following year for the princely sum of £5 (just over £300 in today's money) 'for the purpose of building a stable, coach house, etc'.[4]

A meeting was held at Upper Ship Inn, Duke Street, Reading, on 9 February 1829, to form the Society of the Protection of Public Roads from Encroachments. The Marquis of Easthampstead was accused of 'one of the grossest cases of the infringement of public rights ... and a total disregard of ... public rights'.[5] Although the stopping of some roads had been prevented, the lack of complaints by any parishioners when others had come before the magistrates had weakened their case. The closure of two roads had been appealed in 1825, but the Closure Orders confirmed. By July, it was being reported:

> For some time past The Marquis of Downshire's right to the possession of several roads and footpaths ... has been disputed. The wastelands within the parish have been recently enclosed, and the roads in question were, very much to the inconvenience of the neighbourhood, stopped up, and the soil thereof allotted to his lordship by the authority (it is alleged) of the Enclosure Act. On

behalf of the public, it is contended that the right of way has never been legally extinguished, and in order to prevent unnecessary expense and irritation, an offer was made to try the right by admissions in the most amicable manner. His lordship not having returned any answer to that proposition ... the roads were once more thrown open to the public by a gentleman who resides in the vicinity, having employed a party of workmen to break down and remove the hedges, banks, and palings, by which they were enclosed.

The marquis countered a month later, contending 'the game and the fish ... having, for some years past, been much destroyed by unqualified persons, poachers, and others, who have trespassed thereon contrary to law'. Trespassers would be prosecuted, while 'all gentlemen who are qualified will desist from sporting thereon. All stray dogs found hunting will be shot by the gamekeepers.' Although complaints about closed roads and footpaths continued for several years, the last statement on the matter came in 1930 when ERDC discovered a road at Amen Corner under their jurisdiction that they had failed to maintain for 113 years!

Adverts started appearing in the Reading newspapers from 1813 for the Bracknell Fairs, where horses, cows and sheep were available for purchase. The fairs would have seen people travel from miles around, some upright citizens, others not so upstanding, with reports of pickpockets or assaults appearing in the local press. In August 1827, the *Reading Mercury* recorded 'there was a short and indifferent supply of horses, cattle and sheep. The demand was uncommonly dull.'

Towards the end of July, the English Romantic poet Percy Bysshe Shelley came to live in Bracknell for a few months. He had recently embraced vegetarianism and resided in the home of Mrs Harriet de Boinville at High Elms, 'a country house in the then rural Bracknell', which stood at the junction of Warfield Road and Park Road. Here she had established a vegan commune with several other like-minded people, known as The Bracknell Circle. Shelley published two poems the following year under the title 'At Bracknell'. There is a blue plaque to him on Reeds Hill farmhouse, although no evidence has been found to support him living there.

1814

The year started with bitterly cold weather and heavy snow. Several reports of trapped people and horses appeared in the *Windsor and Eton Express* in January, and it was still lying at the end of March. Mail to Reading was 'greatly retarded'.

Mr Maslin had plans 'available to view' at Martin's Heron House for those 'desirous to contract to making a new gravel road through Windsor Great Park'.

A reward of one guinea was offered after 10-year-old Stephen Hale (also known as Stephen Woodison) went missing. He was described as having 'a fresh coloured complexion, light eyes and lightish hair', and was last seen at Loddon Bridge, heading towards Reading. He was with two women, 'very shabbily dressed', and two boys, 'supposed to be trampers'. Stephen was wearing 'a man's pair of velveteen breeches, which reached to his ancles [sic], a man's brown coat with the skirts cut off, and a man's hat'. There was no record of whether he was ever traced.

1816

This was the year without a summer, although a brief respite in August allowed crops to be gathered. The eruption of Mount Tambora in the East Indies (present-day Indonesia) the previous year was the most powerful in recorded human history, and caused disruption to the global weather for three years.

1818

On 1 January:

> an excellent dinner consisting of old English fare of roast beef, plum pudding, etc. was provided at The Red Lion Inn, Bracknell, for about sixty boys and girls, who are educated and the most needy of them clothed through the philanthropic benevolence of Richard Parry, Esq., Mrs Vincent (of Lily Hill House), and a few ladies and gentlemen of the parish of Warfield.[6]

Later in the year, it was reported the venue had been 'upgraded with new sleeping rooms, new stabling, a new brick and tiled lock-up coach-house, and additional post-horses'. There were reports of a similar event two years later.

1820

Jonathan Gwynn set up a carrier business, ferrying goods between Bracknell and Reading.[7] The Red Lion was the hub of Bracknell's transport, and within ten years he was running his service three times a week, while William Wootten ran a weekly service to and from London. Another carrier in Binfield also stopped at The Red Lion on his way to London on Tuesday afternoons, and to Reading on Saturday mornings. By 1840, Gwynn's business was running from his home in the High Street, although many several other carriers in Reading were also covering the route to Bracknell and using The Red Lion. His son Edmund took over the business in 1851 but sold it four years later, just before the coming of the railway.

1821

George IV had come to the throne the previous year, and was determined to have a lavish coronation ceremony. Organised in just six weeks, this took place in London on 19 July. In line with much of the country, Bracknell celebrated with roast beef, plum pudding, and beer.

1825

Old Bracknell House was being offered for sale, described as being:

> in the best part of Berkshire. A residence planned for the entire accommodation of a respectable family, with corresponding offices of every description, large garden, greenhouse ... environed by fifty acres of park-like grounds, beautifully timbered, and approximating to two compact farms, with a fine lake, abundantly stored with fish. The estate altogether about 220 acres.

Its proximity to Windsor and Ascot is highlighted, a 'fine lake ... not at all dissimilar to Virginia Water ... The neighbourhood is proverbial for being social and respectable, and the parks of Lords Limerick and Downshire surround this delightful property.'[8]

Martin's Heron house also came up for sale at the same time:

> a desirable and compact estate ... comprising a commodious cottage villa, or Sporting Box, containing 7 sleeping-rooms, and 2 dressing rooms, dining, drawing, and breakfast rooms, a good kitchen, and convenient domestic offices, coach-house, stabling, a productive garden, lawn, and about 46 acres of pasture and arable land ... a dry, healthy country, with good shooting, and near the stag and fox hounds.[9]

1828

A blacksmith's shop opposite The Red Lion came up for auction, along with three adjacent cottages. It was noted that 'as the situation is on the high London Road, and the neighbourhood is good ... no persons except of respectable character, and who can give satisfactory references need apply'.[10]

1829

Bullbrook Farm came up for auction, including all the household furniture and farming stock. The latter included 'waggons [sic], carts, harnesses, ploughs, three useful draught horses, pigs, implements, etc.' The contents were for sale again in 1843. Eastern Road now occupies the position of the farm.

Ramslade House was also available to rent (for a period of fourteen or twenty-one years). It possessed 'every accommodation for a genteel family, with pleasure grounds, garden, orchard, stable, and large coach-house', plus up to 100 acres of land if required. 'The salubrity of the air and attractions of the premises are undeniable,' trumpeted the *Berkshire Chronicle*.

A reward of £22 12s (over £1,700 in today's money) was offered just before Christmas for information on two men accused of swindling. At the beginning of the month, the pair had taken premises in Bracknell for the supposed purpose of carrying on the corn trade. They purchased corn from farmers in the vicinity of Maidenhead, Wokingham and Reading but failed to pay for any of it. They were then seen leaving Bracknell on 13 December, travelling towards Reading, accompanied by a young woman and two small children, in a large, two-horse cart.[11] Twelve months earlier, a man 'calling himself Stone' rented a house in Wokingham and obtained goods both there and in Bracknell before disappearing. It was reported in the *Reading Mercury* he had perpetrated the same crime in Essex, but using a different name.

1830

There were continuing complaints at a February meeting of the Society of the Protection of Public Roads from Encroachments about the Marquis of Downshire making 'improper stoppage of roads in Easthampstead'.[12] In one instance, this necessitated a detour of 1¾ miles. Correspondence from Bracknell attorney William Makepiece to the Marquis of Downshire had received no response, so he had reopened them. However, a section now required repairs, but the late Surveyor of Highways had neglected to do so despite a ruling from a judge at Maidenhead, being himself a tenant of Lord Downshire. The matter of who was responsible for the repairs was subject to a court case in Abingdon the following year. The Crown brought the case against the parish of Easthampstead, but they argued that as the highway was previously built as a ride for George III, it was the Crown's responsibility, producing a 77-year-old resident to confirm this. The court found the parish not guilty.

1831

Harmans Water was advertised for sale: 'an allotment of freehold land, containing 74 acres ... The premises are well suited for building on ... There is a fine sheet of water on the premises.' The lake was quite extensive at this time, and may well have extended to the opposite side of the Bagshot Road.

The coronation of William IV took place on Thursday, 8 September, with all communities celebrating the event. 'The residents of Bracknell were not behind their neighbours – a fat sheep was roasted whole for the poor, and a large company sat down to an excellent dinner at ... The Red Lion. In the evening a general illumination and a grand display of fireworks took place.' The festivities took place four days after the ceremony in London.[13]

1832

The argument over Bond's Lane (the section of Binfield Road across Priestwood Common) came up in court again in March. Lord Downshire contended that as the road had been built by the Crown, it was not a public highway and he therefore had the right to fence it off. Anyone using it was trespassing on his land. The defence contended the local populace had also been using the road since it was constructed, making it a public highway. After a long deliberation, the jury found in favour of Lord Downshire.[14]

Efforts were made to move the 'polling place' for elections from Wokingham to Bracknell, but these were unsuccessful. There was no universal suffrage at this time, and only male landowners were eligible to vote. The nominations for the candidates for a general election later in the year was held in Market Place in Reading in June, and a 'cavalcade from Bracknell accompanied with flags, banners and music' attended the event. In October, it was noted that the agent for two candidates in the forthcoming election was in Bracknell, attempting to persuade the opponents of his candidates to change sides.

1833

John Saunders, the proprietor of The Red Lion, was declared insolvent, and James Ruddock took over the running of the establishment, describing it as 'an inn and posting house'. In a notice to 'the Nobility, Gentry, and Public in General', he hoped 'by strict attention, to gain that share of public patronage, it will be *my* constant endeavour to merit, by having good horses and careful drivers, well-aired beds, genuine wines, spirits, etc. with moderate charges'. But just two years later, Ruddock was in the Debtors Prison for London and Middlesex, with three London addresses subsequent to The Red Lion, and John Barrow had taken over the running of it.[15] Meanwhile, the venue continued to be a centre for activities, including pigeon-shooting matches.

1834

In March, the Marquis of Downshire was prosecuted by William Makepiece. Prior to its enclosure in 1827, several trackways crossed Easthampstead Heath (Priestwood Common), leading to roads on its perimeter, and 'going to the different villages lying in all directions around it'. The roads all had directions posts and, it was claimed, were all civic rights of way. Makepiece spoke for two hours and called several witnesses; the case for the defence was equally protracted, and the jury's decision was not reached until 9 p.m. They found that although all the roads were ancient highways, they were under the direction of His Lordship, and he was therefore not guilty. But the case soon came back before the Reading Spring Assizes. Although the parish had been included under the 1813 Windsor Enclosure Act, the open lands, 'consisting principally of Easthampstead Heath were inclosed under an Act in 1821'. Nine tracks or roads ran up to and across the heath prior to the enclosure, although several of them were legally 'extinguished' by the Act's commissioners six years later. The argument centred around Bond's Lane, which ran across the common but had now become a cul-de-sac – had it been a 'public highway' previously or an 'occupation highway'? The judge found in favour of the former, and ordered the road should be reinstated. The Marquis of Downshire appealed the decision in the Court of King's Bench, the most senior criminal court in the country, but the appeal was rejected. Suitably chastened, the marquis subsequently supplied alternative routes when stopping up footpaths on his land.

Two months later, Priestwood Cottage, 'situate close to the turnpike road, within a quarter of a mile of Bracknell', was being offered for sale. It came with an option of 2 acres of meadow and 4 acres of arable land. 'No one will be allowed to convert it into a house of business.' This was later called Priestwood House and stood on land now occupied by Portman Close – for 'cottage' read 'comfortable villa'. The house was briefly owned in the 1880s by Dr Charles Caldecott, who did much work on dealing with patients with mental health issues.

1835

Poor law unions were created in 1834 for the administration of poor relief. Prior to these, supporting the poor was the responsibility of individual parishes (both Binfield and Winkfield had their own small workhouses). Governed by a board of guardians, the unions were responsible for the administration of poor relief in their area. Easthampstead Poor Law Union was formed on 27 July 1835, overseen by a ten-member elected board of guardians, representing its five constituent parishes – Binfield, Easthampstead, Sandhurst, Warfield, and Winkfield with Ascot. The parish of Crowthorne was added in 1890.[16]

The workhouse buildings incorporated a group of almshouses almost opposite Easthampstead parish church, built about ten years earlier. A new infirmary was added in 1869 (to cater for infectious diseases), while tenders were being sought in 1871 for 'the erection of receiving-wards, bath-room, and for certain alterations to the Union House'. Proposals for an isolation hospital on the site ten years later were abandoned, but tenders were being invited for 'the erection of new casual wards, and for carrying out certain alterations in the men's wards' in 1883. A new board-room block was built in 1901 (early meetings had been held at The Red Lion). Berkshire County Council took over the running in 1930, when it became a Public Assistance institution. After the formation of the National Health Service in 1948, the infirmary was used as a hospital for males with learning difficulties. After the closure of the hospital, most of the buildings were demolished and the Church Hill estate built, although the oldest buildings remain and are used as offices for the Bracknell Community Mental Health Team.

A report from the Poor Law Inspector in 1868 recorded:

Easthampstead Workhouse opened in 1835 and covered Bracknell as well as the other local parishes. Part of the complex still remains, housing mental health services in Bracknell

I am most happy to congratulate the Guardians on the very clean and cheerful condition of the wards. I heard no complaint, and the inmates appear to be very kindly treated. I suggest to the Guardians that before next winter they should make provision for setting the able-bodied men to work in wet weather, as I understand that they occupy the aged men's wards, which are too comfortable for them. I should like to see basins provided for the boys to wash in, instead of the troughs.[17]

Reports of treats for the children in the workhouse appeared in the press from time to time – an outing to Caesar's Camp, visits to the school fetes at Easthampstead or Bullbrook schools, or games, tea and cake in the grounds of Coppid Hall at Wick Hill or the rectory at Easthampstead.

By 1867, the average number of inhabitants was around fifty, and the number of children as low as six. With only five parishes supporting the establishment, there were calls in some quarters for it to be combined with Windsor or Wokingham to reduce the cost to ratepayers; in 1874 this amounted to just over £1,000 (£83,000 in today's money). While many inmates were only in the workhouse for a short period, others were there for a longer time, including some with illnesses such as epilepsy, paralysis, or cancer. In 1861, long-term residents of at least five years included a cripple, an illegitimate child, a woman of 'weak intellect', a labourer with 'brain fever', and two suffering from 'old age and infirmity'. Twenty years later, the workhouse held a total of eighty-eight inmates, including six 'idiots', 'three imbeciles', and a single woman who was 'deaf and dumb'. Not all those with mental incapacity were housed in the workhouse; the Easthampstead Union were paying for ten persons at Broadmoor in 1875, along with three 'residing with relatives, and one in licensed house'. Some residents would finish up in the workhouse through no fault of their own. Josiah 'Sandy' Johnson appears there in the 1911 census – he was a drover at Bracknell market and had been bitten by a pig!

1836

The Stagecoach Directory published in this year lists two coaches running from London to Reading, via Bracknell. The New Post Coach ran from The Black Lion in Water Lane (near the Tower of London), departing at 3 p.m. on a daily basis. The journey took five hours and the coach could transport up to fifteen passengers. Another coach left The Saracen's Head, Friday Street (near Mansion House tube station) at 10 a.m. on Tuesdays, Thursdays and Saturdays. It took an hour longer, and carried three fewer passengers.

1838

The Great Western Railway had opened their line from Paddington as far as Maidenhead, with Reading having to wait another two years for its arrival. Firms running coaches reminded their patrons they were still operating in the meantime, offering the only connection between Bracknell and the capital. It would be another twenty-eight years before trains called at Bracknell. The cost of sending letters was reduced, with those going to Windsor now being just 4*d* (£12 in today's money). But those from London came via Reading, and any delay to the train resulted in them arriving up to three hours late.

In September, a brief announcement in the newspaper promised: 'On Tuesday next ... the conquering match between six gentlemen from Bray, and six gentlemen from Bracknell, each party having been victorious, some good play is expected. Also a match of cricket between two players from Bracknell and two from Bray.'[18] A conquering match was a deciding game between two winning teams, but how do you play two-a-side cricket?

By the time of Queen Victoria's coronation, the Reading and Windsor newspapers were crammed with details from their respective town's celebrations. Some of the other larger settlements in Berkshire received brief write-ups, but little Bracknell did not warrant a report. We have to assume the events mirrored those of previous coronations, with plentiful food and drinks, perhaps some music and dancing, and fireworks rounding off the day.

1839

'A respectable young man, of Bracknell, has undertaken, for a wager of £2 [nearly £150 in today's money], to walk one mile and a half in fifteen minutes ... from the Four Horse Shoes, Warfield, to the Hind's Head, Bracknell ... bets are 5 to 4 on time.'[19] It was later reported that 'the young man ... won his wager by performing the distance one minute and thirty seconds within the given time'. This competitive pedestrianism was the forerunner of the modern-day sport of race walking.

In August, an announcement appeared that 'the partnership between James Baxendale and Richard Sparks Young, common brewers at Old Bracknell, has been terminated by mutual consent, with the former taking over the running'.[20] This enterprise took place at the Brewers Arms (which changed its name to the Downshire Arms in 1909).

1840

'On Thursday night [15 February] a supper was given at the Crown Inn, Bracknell, by Lieutenant Sewell, R.N., of Wick-hill house, near Bracknell, to the tradesmen and mechanics employed in re-building his mansion ... The party, after enjoying the feast, were amused by some popular songs, and closed the evening with a ball.'[21]

1841

The Reading registrar of deaths produced figures to compare the number of deaths per head of population in the town with those in the Easthampstead district. Although the figure for Easthampstead had improved from 1 in 53 in 1839, to 1 in 62 by 1841, deaths caused by insanitary conditions caused large fluctuations from year to year in both areas. Life expectancy in Easthampstead was also five years higher.

A large storm hit the Bracknell area on 27 May, causing damage to Easthampstead Park, Wick Hill House, and the houses of attorney William Makepiece and grocer John Fouch 'were injured to an unparalleled extent. The havoc amongst the standing crops was also immense – fields of wheat, peas, beans, and other grain being levelled and beaten out; the garden grounds also suffered in an equal degree.'[22] Detailed weather records only began to be kept in 1850, but this storm was still being referred to some twenty-five years later.

At the end of the year, William Wilcocks, a saddler and harness maker who lived and worked in the High Street, was declared insolvent, but he was trading successfully again by the end of the following year. One has to wonder whether repairs from the storm a few months earlier might have been the cause.

1842

In July, the Berkshire Temperance Association held 'one of the largest meetings yet witnessed in this county' at Bracknell. The temperance movement originated in Scotland in 1829 with various non-conformist church groups heavily involved, and became a mass movement later in the century. They concentrated their reforming efforts on working-class men who were seen as the principal consumers of beer to excess. With numerous pubs and long opening hours, alcohol was freely available in Victorian England.

Bareknuckle fighting, or pugilism, was illegal but authorities often turned a blind eye due to its popularity with the gentry. The *Windsor and Eton Express* reported on an event held locally:

> A fight took place at Ramslade ... between Johnny Walker and Ned Adams, both celebrated pugilists, and which ended after an hour and twenty minutes hard fighting in favour of the former. This match caused more than ordinary interest in the vicinity in consequence of Walker ... being backed by some of the sporting gentry of the neighbourhood. The headquarters on the morning of the fight was Virginia Water, and a ring was first formed near that place, but the 'beaks' disturbed the combatants. The Waste, a field near Swinley, was next pitched upon for the sport, but on inspection that spot did not appear to satisfy the 'managers' and a second move was ordered to take place. The parties now proceeded to Ramslade, where the fight came off without any interruption and was witnessed by a large number of the 'fancy generally, and admirers of the art' in this vicinity, including a good sprinkling of the aristocracy of the neighbourhood.[23]

Walker was acknowledged as the British Champion after this fight, having beaten all three other contenders for the title.

1843

A Benefit Society held their meeting at The Hind's Head in May. Before the Welfare State, these voluntary associations provided mutual aid and benefits, including financial security against unforeseen emergencies such as unemployment and sickness.

In a letter to the editor of the *Reading Mercury* newspaper in September, reference was made to the Primitive Methodists in Bracknell who had just opened their new chapel, which accommodated up to sixty persons. It was situated in Downshire Way, behind the row of houses there named Priestwood Terrace; the chapel's burial ground still exists behind a tall wooden fence at the corner of Downshire Way and Binfield Road. Among those buried there was Edmund Gwynn, the carrier. After holding a service, the congregation proceeded to a meadow off the High Street, where two booths containing tables had been prepared for a meal. 'At six o'clock a public meeting was held *after which* a collection was made to aid in defraying the expense of the building of the new Chapel.'[24] The Primitive Methodists merged with the Methodists in 1933.

Barekunckle fighting was illegal, but authorities often turned a blind eye due to its popularity with the gentry. This fight took place at Ramslade (now The Parks) in 1842.

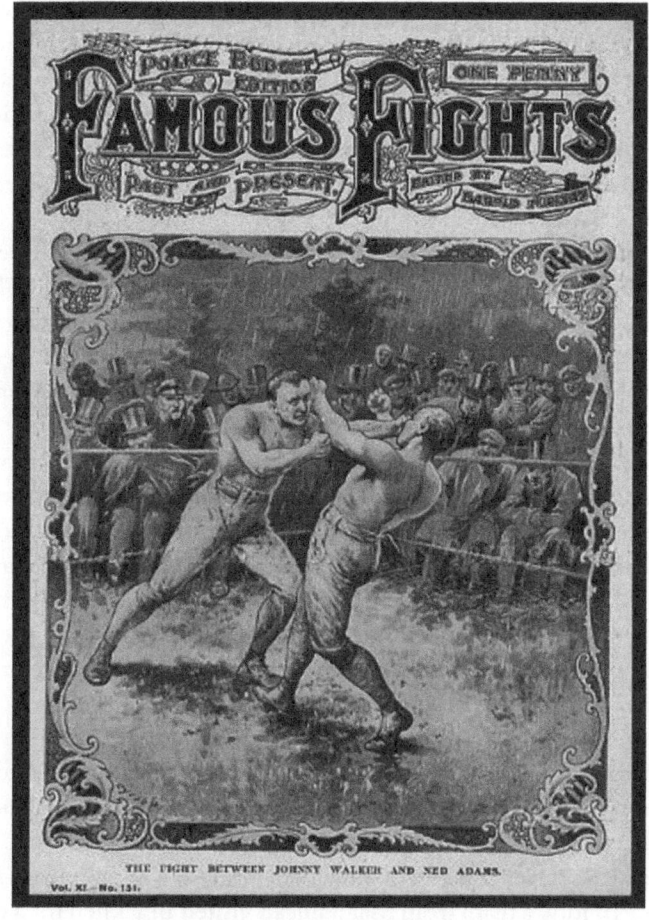

1844

Pigot's Directory published in this year describes Bracknell as:

> a little thoroughfare hamlet ... adorned with many genteel residences and delightful villas, occupied by fashionable families ... Letters from London and parts East and South arrive every morning at half-past six, and are despatched thereto every evening at half-past seven. Letters from Bath, Bristol, and parts West arrive (from Reading) every evening at half-past seven, and are despatched thereto every morning at half-past six.

The postmistress, Esther Maslin, lived adjacent to The Red Lion, a part of the town known as West End; West End Post Office was still operating well into the twentieth century. She had taken over from a Mrs Parker, who was dismissed 'for being in arrears with the accounts and irregularity' in 1836. Joseph Ure ran a National School for boys, William Dicker Stroud operated a boarding school in Clay Lane (now named Park Road), while young ladies might attend a day school run by octogenarian Ann Davies. Charles Cave featured importantly in local affairs, being attorney, superintendent registrar, clerk to the guardians of the Easthampstead Union, and agent for the English and Scottish Fire, Life and Loan Society, while James Freeman and Thomas Croft dealt with the health of the populace. There were four public houses – The Bull, The Crown, The Hind's Head, and The Red Lion – along with Ann Boswell, who sold beer at an address on Priestwood Common. Shopkeepers and trades included no fewer than seven bakers, a butcher, four grocers (most were also tea dealers), five boot and shoe makers, three drapers and tailors, two dressmakers, a straw hat maker, a stationer, a smith and farrier, two wheelwrights, two saddlers, a corn dealer, a gardener and seedsman, and several men offering building services such as bricklaying, carpentering, plumbing, painting, paperhanging, and glazing, while one builder had a side line as undertaker! Three years later, *Kelly's Directory* calls Bracknell a village that 'consists of a long narrow street, inhabited principally by small shop keepers'. It also adds it is 'situated on the main road to the west of England, and being in a woodland country, the scenery is rendered very beautiful; the roads are also remarkable good'.

'Several parcels of meadow and arable land, situate at the west end of Bracknell, fronting the Forest turnpike and Binfield roads calculated for building in continuation of the village of Bracknell, with a house, stable and shed thereon, and a beer-shop doing a good business' were advertised for sale. The houses built here started the expansion of Bracknell along the Wokingham Road.

In July, a team from Maidenhead visited Bracknell for a cricket match and were severely trounced, scoring fewer runs in their two innings than the home team had managed in one. Two months later, the Bracknell club is mentioned again, defeating the club at Bagshot in a return match (the first game had been played a week earlier) by two runs. 'An excellent repast was provided by Mr Roberts, of The Red Lion' (which had undergone yet another change of owner). The Royal Oak in Bullbrook was also hosting dinners if The Red Lion was fully booked.

1845

Due to its expansion, Bracknell was now being referred to as 'a little post town' rather than as a village. It also saw the first recorded visit to Bracknell by a reigning monarch. The occasion received a full write-up in the *Illustrated London News* edition dated 25 January of that year:

The Queen's Visit to Strathfieldsaye

On Monday afternoon, about half-past two o'clock, the Queen and Prince Albert left Windsor Castle, to pay their promised visit to the Duke of Wellington, at Strathfieldsaye. Her Majesty was attended by the Marchioness of Douro, the Hon. Amelia Murray, the Earl of Jersey, and Lord Charles Wellesley. His Royal Highness Prince Albert was attended by Mr. G. E. Anson and Colonel Bouverie. The Royal party proceeded across Ascot-heath towards Bracknell, up to which place there were no preparations for welcoming her Majesty, deserving of particular detail. Opposite the Crispin [lately the Loch Fyne restaurant], the escort was relieved by another party of the 17th Lancers, under the command of Captain Hayworth.

At Bracknell, though the place is small, the inhabitants had done the utmost in the short notice rendered possible, to welcome their Sovereign. In this respect they presented an example of what must have struck those who have witnessed her Majesty's various progresses through the country – the extraordinary rapidity with which those preparations which have been so often described, and which are so similar in different places, are got up. No sooner is it known – and very often this is not till nearly the eleventh hour – that her Majesty is to pass along a particular route, however remote or rural, than a new life seems infused among the inhabitants, and all is bustle and excitement. Triumphal arches spring up in a night, in places where such things were scarcely heard of before. Flags and banners waved from the houses, processions are formed, addresses concocted (where the places visited are of sufficient importance), and such inroads are made upon the evergreens, for the formation of the various devices, and the decoration of the streets, that the visit of a swarm of locusts could not more effectually denude the trees and underwood. At Bracknell, the good folks did their utmost to make the village gay and handsome on the occasion of the visit the Queen.

There were no less than four triumphal arches of evergreens, one at the entrance, two at different points in the road through the place, and one at the other end, opposite the Red Lion Inn. The first arch was inscribed 'Welcome', with 'V' on one side, and 'A' on the other. It was hung with flags. The second arch bore the inscription 'Loyalty to the Queen,' and was also hung with flags. The third was in some degree similar; and the fourth, that opposite the Red Lion Inn, was inscribed, 'May happiness attend you,' and also 'For God, the Queen, and the People.' It was also hung with flags, and the front of the inn was very handsomely decorated with evergreens. Almost every house in the village was in some way adorned, in honour of her Majesty's visit. A considerable crowd had assembled, who cheered loudly as the Royal cortege drove up, a band playing the national anthem. Upwards of 300 charity children also were assembled, who were afterwards regaled at the expense of the inhabitants.

Here the Royal party changed horses, and the escort was also replaced by another party of the 17th Lancers, under the command of Captain Crawshaw. While the change of horses was taking place, the Queen was presented with a bouquet of beautiful flowers by Mrs. Croft. Her Majesty received it very graciously, and was most loudly cheered as she passed. At Coppice Beech-lane-gate, a short distance further on, a handsome arch was thrown across the road.

More excitement would have been in the air in August when a new railway line was being proposed that would pass though Bracknell:

The Direct London and Exeter Company intend to form their terminus in the most central part of London which can be obtained. It will be in the immediate vicinity of Sloane-street and Knightsbridge … From the London terminus the line will branch off to or near Hammersmith, Turnham Green, Brentford, Isleworth, Hounslow, Staines, Egham, Ascot, Bagshot, Bracknell, Binfield, Wokingham, Kingsclere, Andover and Salisbury; Shaftesbury, Sherborne, Yeovil, Crewkerne, Axminster, or from Salisbury to Cranbourne, Blandford, Dorchester, Bridport, Axminster, and Honiton, to Exeter.[25]

The London Illustrated News *carried a report of Queen Victoria's visit to Bracknell on her way to Strathfieldsaye. Flags, banners, and arches of evergreens decorated the High Street for the occasion. (Photo courtesy of Mary Evans Agency)*

William Delane of Bracknell was on the company's committee.

Meanwhile, the Great Western Railway also had plans for a line running southwest from Paddington, crossing the Thames at Staines, and running slightly to the south of the current line. It is not clear whether a station was planned for Bracknell, but it would probably have been near The Horse and Groom if one had been built.

The Reading and Reigate Atmospheric Railway also proposed a line from Reading running north of Wokingham, through Easthampstead, Farnborough, Dorking, Reigate and on to Redhill.[26] The following month, the Reading and Reigate Railway also proposed a line through Bracknell. 'This line will commence at the Reading Station of the Great Western Railway, and proceed by Wokingham, Bracknell, Sunninghill between Ascot and Bagshot, and by Chobham ...' A revised route, heading south from Wokingham rather than east, was approved the following year and opened in 1849.

Later, in November 1846, the Windsor, Staines and South-Western Railway also announced plans to apply for an Act of Parliament to build a line from Richmond to Windsor, 'with a loop line through Brentford and Hounslow'.[27] From this line, they planned another from Staines, with further branch lines running off of it, to link Egham, Thorpe, Windlesham, Chertsey, Chobham, Bisley, Pirbright, Sunninghill, Old Windsor, Winkfield, Easthampstead, Warfield, Binfield, and Wokingham. With railway mania gripping the country, many lines were proposed but never got off the drawing board, or failed to generate enough capital from backers to be built. It would be more than ten years before Bracknell saw a train.

Bracknell Railway Society has a wealth of information on other railway schemes in the area that failed to see the light of day.[28]

1846

'New rooms' were added at The Hind's Head, and the Winkfield Agricultural Association (including the Marquis of Downshire) dined there; the Royal Forest Agricultural Association also held their future meetings at the new venue. In July:

> The Rev. W. Coombs, Independent Minister of Bracknell has (much to the regret of the members and congregation) resigned his ministerial office in connection with the Chapel at that place, and a public farewell tea meeting took place at the new rooms adjoining the Hind's Head, Bracknell ... at which about 100 persons partook of that delightful beverage 'which cheers but not inebriates.'[29]

But the Lord's Day Society annual meeting in November continued to be held at The Red Lion, an organisation 'aimed at the protection of the Lord's Day'.

James Withers of Reading ran a coach service from Wokingham through Bracknell, Binfield, Warfield and Winkfield, to meet the 9.40 a.m. train at Slough for Paddington.

1847

At a public meeting held during April in Reading:

> of the clergy and laity in the Deanery of Reading, for the purpose of advocating the interests of the Diocesan Society, which as for its object the increase of church accommodation, and the number of parsonage houses within the diocese ... The Rev. W. Levett of Bray ... mentioned the want of church-accommodation in the parishes of Wokingham and Warfield. Bracknell was in Warfield parish, and was two or three miles distant from the church; the accommodation was insufficient for the people in the neighbourhood, and therefore the population of Bracknell was unprovided with church room. The circumstances of the parish were very peculiar: the living was miserably poor, and the incumbent unfortunately was insolvent. The excellent curate was exerting himself to the utmost to raise funds for building a new church at Bracknell, and the Archidiaconal Society had reserved a sum of £150 towards the object.[30]

'It would be difficulty to find a locality where the evils for want of a church are more apparent,' commented the Warfield vicar. 'It is therefore proposed to remedy such an inconvenience and evil by building a church.'

During the same month, the House of Commons Railway committee were hearing proposals from the South-Western Company to extend their Wandsworth and Richmond line (in the process of construction) to Staines, 'and from Staines, to pass a branch on to Windsor, to carry a through line by Egham and Bracknell to Wokingham, there to join the Reading, Guildford and Reigate line'. But it was the Staines, Wokingham and Woking Junction Company who finally built the line and stations, although the London and South Western ran the trains.

1849

Writing in January, a Warfield resident stated: 'The Hamlet of Bracknell ... It would be hard to find a spot in a rural neighbourhood where a Church is more required.' Plans for a parish church were now progressing. A committee for 'building a proposed church at Bracknell' advertised for 'plans and specifications, with the probable cost' from architects. 'The Church is to accommodate

300 (including children), to be of the pointed style of Architecture, the walls to be of brick, faced with stone, or with flint facings and stone copings.'[31] A committee of subscribers had been set up to raise money for the church with over £1,000 (almost £90,000 in today's money) raised in the first four weeks of the appeal, including £25 from the Marquis of Downshire, and £5 from both James Matheson, Esq. of South Hill Park, and the vicar of Easthampstead. Wokingham commented of 'knowing no place in our neighbourhood that has more needed one':

> Tuesday last [6 November 1849], being the day fixed for laying the first stone of the new district church at Bracknell, a very large assembly (amongst whom we observed several of the leading persons of the neighbourhood) was gathered on the ground. About four o'clock the Bishop of the diocese, with several of his clergy, in their robes, came to the site, and the service was at once commenced by his lordship addressing his crowded and attentive audience in his usual eloquent and impressive manner.

A sealed glass 'with its usual contents' and a scroll with details of the event was 'placed within one stone, another stone was lowered on it, the Bishop striking it with the mallet ... using the solemn words of the dedication.' Earlier in the proceedings, the bishop had made an appeal for funds towards the building of the church, which 'was liberally responded to, the collection at the conclusion amounting to £76 9s 3½d'.[32] In November 1850, the funds for building and endowing the church, which had by now been built, were in dire straits. On hearing of the problem, Prince Albert, the Queen's Consort, stepped in with 'a handsome donation of £50'. The consecration of the new church took place at midday on Wednesday, 25 February 1851, in 'most brilliant weather' by the Bishop of Oxford, with a second service at four in the afternoon, both events being ticketed. The ecclesiastical parish was not created until October.

1851

The census taken on 30 March gave 'the village of Bracknell' a population of 352, with a further 185 nearby at Bullbrook, Wick Hill, Clay Lane and Bull Lane, plus a single person living on Priestwood Common. The adjoining enumeration districts of Easthampstead and Winkfield added a further 110 residents in Bracknell and Bullbrook. The average age of everyone in the area was a mere 27. Just over half were born in the vicinity of Bracknell, demonstrating 'considerable personal mobility' even before the arrival of the railway. The population had risen to 2,508 by 1911, a seven-fold increase in just sixty years.

Henry Dormer Vincent had died at his house at Lily Hill on 22 May 1833. His son Henry William Vincent was by now building the property we see today, but on 19 January it was reported that 'a quantity of lead was stolen from the site for the second time in a short period'. A reward of £5 was offered on conviction of the offenders. This was not the only theft from Lily Hill. In June the following year, the gardener discovered that shrubs:

> consisting of a very valuable collection of American plants, cut, broken down, and carried away ... Boult, the constable, after some difficulty, succeeded in discovering where a truck had been brought on the grounds, and ultimately traced the stolen shrubs to The Crown Inn, where a Benefit Society meeting was being held. The club room was decorated with the evergreens, and from the information of the landlord, it appeared they were brought there by a person of the name of George, alias Jerry Banbury, who stated that he had leave to get them. The man was apprehended ... and fined £3 1s 6d [about £300 in today's money].

In December, Edward Spratley, the innkeeper at the original Royal Foresters, hanged himself from a fir tree behind the summerhouse at Lily Hill over a debt to the brewery; the remains of the pub can be seen in the grounds of Lily Hill near the lych gate on London Road. A verdict of temporary insanity was returned.

1852

Surveying for a railway line through Bracknell now began. In October it was reported that a Bill would be applied for in the next session of parliament for a line:

> which will constitute a junction between the Reading and Reigate line, and the South Western line, commencing at Wokingham and terminating at Staines ... the line ... will pass Egham, Englefield Green, Virginia Water, Sunninghill, Bagshot, Ascot-heath, Bracknell, Binfield and Warfield. These are populous and rich districts, thickly studded with gentleman's mansions ... The scheme is extensively patronised by the influential gentlemen of the neighbourhood.[33]

By May the following year, the Bill was before Parliament and being read for a second time. The route had been amended to pass through Egham and Sunningdale before passing along the side of Ascot racecourse, through Bracknell, and on to Wokingham. It was reported that 'the Commissioners of Woods and Forests, who possess extensive rights and property in the forest, have given their consent to the bill', and Prince Albert 'has also given his assent to the measure'. After 'strong opposition' at the committee stage, the Bill passed to the House of

Lords, where, 'to the surprise of both of the supporters and the opponents of the bill', it was rubber stamped and passed back to the House of Commons, where 'it will undoubtedly become law'. The bill was passed on 8 July 1853. It was hoped the line would be ready in twelve months, ready for Royal Ascot. The first sod (near Chobham Common) was cut on 4 October, after which the dignitaries 'adjourned to the Wells Inn, Sunninghill, and partook of a handsome dinner'.

1853

Samuelson's Patent Digging Machine was demonstrated on a farm in the Priestwood area. Pulled by six horses, it turned the soil with a forking action, replicating the work of forty to sixty men digging per day. Although put on show across the country for the benefit of forward-thinking farmers, it didn't catch on.

1854

Kelly's Directory had updated its description of Bracknell: 'The village itself consists of a fine open street.'

An establishment known as The Jim Crow came up for rent; this was the former name of the current Royal Foresters.

Built a few years earlier, Bullbrook School became a National School in 1858. It closed in 1981, its place taken over by Holly Spring School.

Progress reports on the railway line appeared in the press. By July, the line was 'in the course of construction'. In November, a labourer named Thomas Oliver was taken to Berkshire Hospital, having suffered a broken leg 'when a quantity of earth fell on him' while working on the line at Bracknell (in the cutting to the east of the station). The coming of the railway was a strong selling point for nearby properties and featured in the sale particulars for Newell Hall in Warfield, as well as for properties in Egham, Virginia Water and Ascot. Earlier in the year, the estate at Lily Hill was selling 1,400 Scotch Fir trees, to which they drew the attention of 'railway contractors and others'.

Bullbrook School was founded on 7 July and opened the following year for use as a Sunday School by the parish of Winkfield. By 1866, it had become a National School under the control of Holy Trinity Church, and is covered in the next chapter.

1855

By March 1855:

> works ... were progressing satisfactorily on the railway line. One half of the entire earthwork is completed, and one half of the permanent way materials on the ground. There would be no difficulty in completing the line for opening by August next ... The heavier portions of the cuttings [including at Bracknell] ...] are now completed.

The bridge over the Thames at Staines was still causing problems, as had been buying up land from some of the smaller landowners on the route. The last bus running east from Staines ceased at the end of the month, much to the dismay of local residents, who were of the opinion that the railway linking them to London had done nothing for the town. In May, the *Reading Mercury* reported the line 'is expected to be completed as far as Bracknell in the course of the autumn, but the whole line will not be finished in the present year'. But in June, another fall of earth in the cutting near Bracknell injured several men, one of whom, Thomas Woodason, was taken to the Royal Berks Hospital with a compound fracture of his leg, but 'being of debilitated constitution', he never recovered from the injury and died in hospital a few weeks later. Two other men died in separate incidents in the Egham area in the same year.

In July, a reader wrote to the editor of the *Windsor and Eton Express*, regarding progress on the line. Two gangs of navvies were at work in Wokingham, Binfield – 'nothing doing', Easthampstead – 'nearly completed in the rough ... Warfield (better known as Bracknell) – finished, Winkfield ... one gang of navvies, and one of bricklayers, getting on very rapidly.' Other parts of the line to the east were either 'trifling' or 'nearly completed'.

In December, another reader put pen to paper, having walked part of the route and described progress on it. The bridge over the Thames at Staines was still under construction. The line had been laid east of Egham station, and this section 'is in a more forward state than any other part of the line' but 'a deep cutting is yet to be done'. The section from Ascot is described:

> we enter the parish of Winkfield. It reaches the road near Lavander Farm [now Lavender Golf Course on Swinley Road], crosses the same under a bridge, crosses Whitmoor-bog [now the site of the Ascot sewage treatment works] on a slight embankment, and also the Warren ... crosses Broad-lane over a bridge. We now come to a deep cutting which continues throughout the remainder of this parish, and also that of Warfield (better known as Bracknell), and a short distance into Easthampstead. An embankment now begins ... crossing the road from Bracknell to Easthampstead on a bridge [now the Twin Bridges]. Entering into Binfield, it crosses two parish roads on a level ... The soil consists principally of heavy clay, and it will take a very considerable time to complete the line in this quarter.

Meanwhile, the section to Wokingham 'calls for few remarks'. Only three stations were named in the railway company's prospectus – Egham, 'in Windlesham' (Longcross), 'the third at Coopers-hill ... close to Bracknell', although land had been purchased in Ascot 'within three hundred yards of the Grand Stand'. The imminent arrival of the line also sparked an increase in land becoming available at auction for the building of new properties in and around Bracknell.

A steeplechase was held on land at Priestwood Common between John Sewell Esquire of Wick Hill House and James Kitcat, 'a gentleman well known with the Queen's hounds, residing in the neighbourhood'. The event, which was for a wager of £20, was won by Kitcat, but not before both men had fallen off during the 3-mile race.

An inquest was held into the death, from delirium tremens, of David Hayward, publican at The Bull. His wife continued to run it for several years after his death.

1856

A freak accident occurred in February 1856. A night watchman was employed every night to keep watch on the materials being used in the railway construction. Irishman Peter O'Brien, probably one of the labourers on the project, sat talking with him one night and failed to notice the leg of his trousers had been set alight by the fire they were sitting round, until he had received severe burns on his leg and thigh; the injury being treated at the Royal Berkshire Hospital in Reading. Two men transporting materials for the line from Windsor were convicted of selling it instead.

The Peace Treaty at the end of the Crimean War was signed in May. It was celebrated in Bracknell 'by a tea for more than three hundred local children, with a marching band and fireworks later in the evening'.

The railway line to Bracknell finally opened on 9 July 1856 (the section from Egham to Ascot had opened five weeks earlier, in time for Royal Ascot), although there were no reports in the local newspapers of the momentous occasion. An advert for the sale of fine draft horses a few days later noted that trains from London arrived at the newly completed station at 9.34 a.m. and 11.22 a.m., and those from Reading at 8.06 a.m. and 11.01 a.m. A timetable published in the *Berkshire Chronicle* in November shows four trains departing for London on weekdays, and two on Sundays, the journey time being approximately an hour and twenty minutes. A similar number ran to Reading, taking twenty-five minutes to reach their destination. By 1862, five trains were running from Waterloo to Bracknell. In 1900 there were ten trains per day running from Waterloo to Reading, by 1914 there were fourteen, and the number had risen to eighteen by 1922, although services tended to be 'irregular'. Early steam trains only had hand brakes on the locomotives and guard's van. The line was used for trials on a system of continuous brakes, operating on the locomotive and all the coaches; a system adopted in 1881.

Bracknell Railway Society's website states:

> the station at Bracknell had two short platforms, 160 feet in length, and a small goods yard on the Up side. It was sited 'conventionally', that is at the break from a cutting into the long bank toward Wokingham. This made construction of the station and its facilities as cheap as possible at the time with minimal earthmoving, but later expansion meant the extended goods yard being built on the embankment ... The main traffic at the time would have been agricultural goods.[34]

The station building was 'a low two-storey affair with a central booking hall, and the Station Master's accommodation above it', built from local brick. Passenger traffic expanded steadily from Bracknell after the 1870s, with the station being upgraded and enlarged, including lengthening the platforms; the goods sidings to the west of the station required the up platform to extend east, under the original brick bridge carrying the Bagshot Road. The original goods yard and sidings were greatly expanded in about 1880 to service the local cattle market and brick industry, and it was the biggest on the line between Feltham and Reading.

Before the Railway

It was closed by British Railways in 1969. The signal box, built in the mid 1870s, remained in use until 1974.

The opening of the railway offered exciting opportunities to local residents if they were able to afford to travel. In August, they were able to travel to Kew Gardens or Waterloo Bridge Station, and a day's outing by train was offered to Crystal Palace at the end of September, leaving Reading at 8.45 a.m. The price, which included admission costs, varied between 4s and 6s (£15 to £22 in today's money), according to the class of carriage occupied. A couple of weeks earlier, the line had opened to goods, terminating at Nine Elms (Vauxhall) station. By the following year, Bracknell was being described as an 'improving town' in sales literature. Many locals with vehicles for hire for Royal Ascot Week feared the worst, but the railway company suddenly raised their prices substantially, with a return ticket to the races from Reading costing 7s 6d (almost £30 in today's money). Racegoers boycotted the newer mode of transport and the horse-drawn vehicles did a roaring trade.

While the coming of the turnpike road made local travel easier, the railway afforded transport to anywhere in the country, not just for passengers, but for goods as well. This was to have a major impact on Bracknell in the coming years.

The first train arrived in Bracknell on 9 July 1856. Note the signal box controlling sidings (just out of shot on the left), which were used for coal and goods. The station was demolished in 1974 and replaced by the current one. (Photo courtesy of Bracknell Central Library)

4

Victorian Times

The arrival of the railway not only revolutionised the transport of goods and passengers, but also of information. Mail now travelled faster and more frequently, so articles and letters could be written for inclusion in the Reading newspapers and more Bracknell news items started to appear. Sidney Hobley (born 1903) remembers seeing an old mail cart, kept in a shed on Broad Lane after it came to the end of its working life. 'It was a lovely thing to look at when it was all polished up. It was like a huge box on four wheels, with the Royal Coat of Arms, and was painted red.'

1857

There was more leisure time for some, with a game of cricket played at the start of July: 'In the small and quiet village of Bracknell, where this most interesting scientific game has for years been neglected, a club has recently been established, which ... bids fair to become a strong and important one ... notwithstanding the incessant rain during the day.'[1] A team of married men beat a team of unmarried men by 24 runs. Two months later, the first cricket match between Binfield and Bracknell clubs was played adjacent to the Roe Buck Inn (now the Daruchini Restaurant), with the home side running out comfortable winners. A few days earlier, Bracknell had lost to Windlesham by ten runs. Matches started in the mornings, and four innings were played during the course of the day.

In September, Robert Rogers obtained an alcohol licence for the 'newly erected' Railway Hotel, Bracknell (soon renamed The Station Hotel), which became a venue for some of the auctions held in Bracknell, now being described as a 'fast improving town'. Rogers also placed adverts announcing the first cattle sale in Bracknell, to be held 'in the meadow adjoining the Railway Tavern ... on the 15th day of October', an event subsequently held on a monthly basis.

1858

Having been founded four years earlier and used by Winkfield Parish as a Sunday School, Bullbrook School now became a National School under the control of Holy Trinity Church. 'A grand morning and evening concert' of religious and popular music, featuring two performers from Bristol and another from the Chapel Royal at Windsor, was held there in August, the first of many events in the facility before Bracknell acquired a hall. The first Inspector's Reports show the girls' school in 1866 was 'a shade better than the boys in the lower part of it and in discipline, but is in a very unsatisfactory state. Mistress is young and without experience.' There were regular reports in the local newspapers for more than thirty years of parents being fined for not ensuring their children attended school.

During the summer, special excursion trains ran to Crystal Palace 'from ... Bracknell and other stations of the South Western Railway ... at a low rate of charge'. Similar trips to Portsmouth were also advertised, with fares ranging from 5*s* to 10*s* (about £20 to £40 in today's money). Meanwhile, George Reeves was still offering a carrier service from Reading to Wokingham, Binfield, Bracknell and Easthampstead three days a week.

1859

The year started with the news that 'a new chapel is to be forthwith commenced in the improving village of Bracknell, Berks. The chapel is to be built in a simple and unostentatious style ... to seat 200 persons'. This was the Congregational Church that stood on the site now occupied by the Natwest Bank. Although the architects were a Reading firm, the builder was William Lewis, a Bracknell man. The church was opened on 5 July, 'when two very eloquent and impressive discourses were delivered' in both the morning and evening by figures from London. 'The edifice was greatly admired, and pronounced ... one of the most chaste and elegant structures ... ever seen – a perfect gem, in suitable keeping with the natural and picturesque beauties of the surrounding scenery.'[2]

James Lane, who had run the Philosophical School in London for twenty years, opened a new establishment, College House on Bagshot Road (approximately where the Glebewood estate is now). Adverts announced: 'Education suited to commercial or professional life, including Book-keeping, Latin, French, Music, Drawing, Timber measuring, etc.' Later publicity added: 'Youths are also prepared for Engineers, Architects, Surveyors, Agricultural and Analytical Chemists.' The fees varied between 20 and 30 guineas per annum. No further adverts followed, and Lane moved to Wokingham.

At the end of the year, the formation of the 'Royal Foresters' Volunteer Rifle Corps, 'promoted by the magistracy, gentry and neighbourhood of Bracknell, Warfield, Winkfield, Easthampstead, etc.', was announced. The unit was later absorbed into the Royal Berkshire Regiment as their Territorial Battalion.

1860

Tenders were being sought in March for the enlargement of Holy Trinity.

Nurseryman John Saunders had run a business on Bagshot Road on the site of the Sports Centre. After his death earlier in the year, the entire stock from the nursery was auctioned in November, but within a couple of years his son Richard opened an American nursery, selling 'roses, conifers, ornamental and evergreen shrubs, fruit and forest trees'.[3] Henry Vincent's estate at Lily Hill featured many plants from the Americas, so this was probably the source for them. The business, known as Easthampstead Nursery, started in 1830 and closed fifty years later with the death of Richard. Confusingly, the same name was used by a new enterprise adjacent to The Horse and Groom, roughly where Elizabeth Close is. It opened about ten years later, and closed in 1918.

1861

The Bracknell Supply Stores opened on 11 May, better known as the Thomas Lawrence Stores, which would come to dominate commerce in the High Street. It started with 'a choice assortment of millinery, mantles, flowers, etc'.[4] By the following year, they were promising:

> the newest, largest, and cheapest stock of goods in the county, consisting of house and table linen, plain and fancy dresses in great variety, calicoes, hosiery, boots, shoes, and clothing, carpets, etc. The Showrooms are replete with every novelty for the season in cloaks, mantles, jackets, plain, fancy, and trimmed bonnets, millinery, flowers, feathers, shawls, parasols, etc. and are marked at such moderate prices as cannot fail to ensure a ready sale. Funerals completely furnished.[5]

By the following year, deliveries were being made to Warfield and Winkfield on Tuesdays, Binfield, Easthampstead and Waltham on Thursdays, and to Sunninghill and Ascot on Fridays. By 1900, around 130 people worked at the store, and the enterprise covered 3 acres of floorspace.

1862

At the end of April, some of the military officers from Sandhurst organised some horse racing at Wick Hill, the Staff College Steeple Chases, comprising five races 'which afforded excellent sport to a capital company, including many ladies'.[6]

The Bracknell Gas Company was formed in May, with the gas works constructed in Station Road the following year and leased to a Mr Crockford. Messrs Boulton and Nash took over the lease in 1865, which included meters as well as the plant.

The year also saw the formation of Highway Districts, which grouped civil parishes into units for the upkeep of local roads. Binfield, Warfield, Sandhurst and Easthampstead (which included Bracknell) were grouped together, responsible for 74 miles of road.

1863

The marriage of the Prince of Wales (the future King Edward VII) and Princess Alexandra of Denmark took place at St George's Chapel, Windsor, on 10 March. There was a report in the *Reading Mercury* of the celebrations held in Bracknell:

> The wedding morn was ushered in ... by the firing of cannon, etc. House tops were soon climbed, and trees that had been growing for years undisturbed were taken up and planted by the road-side to form triumphal arches. The victualling committee ... took the undertaking to dine 800 and give tea to as many more, in a spacious tent erected for the occasion ... 13 cwt of meat, 300 lbs of pudding, and seven barrels of ale, etc. soon vanished, after which a balloon race, a large bonfire, and fireworks, brought the day to a close.[7]

The following week, a letter was published with a description of a balloon flight over the area:

> The barren dreariness of numerous sandy roads over this district seemed well described in the name of the 'Devils Highway' ... This dreary view soon succeeded by one over the cultivated country beyond Windsor Forest, and passing over the long street of Bracknell and the town of Wokingham, we perceived the green meadows watered by The Loddon.

The Old Bracknell Brewery changed hands after the owner's wife died earlier in the year. The new owner immediately sold off the plant and obtained a new licence to run the premises as a pub, The Brewers Arms; the name changed to The Downshire Arms in 1909.

1864

Bracknell Literary Institution, a 'spacious building' adjacent to Coppid Hall, opened at the end of March, 'with a series of musical and dramatic performances ... The building comprises a spacious hall for lectures, class and committee rooms, with apartments for the hall-keeper ... chess, billiards, and other innocent games will be encouraged.'[8] 'Penny Readings', an entertaining mix of education and entertainment for which the entry fee was one penny, commenced two months later. By November, these were so popular 'that many were unable to gain admittance'.

Bracknell was not a healthy place to live, as evidenced by a letter to the editor of the *Reading Mercury* from an Easthampstead local calling for residents to 'be up and stirring in the drainage of your town. You have had several cases of fever – some fatal. Be warned in time, for the dreaded evil may be upon your devoted village when ye expect it not.' But the situation continued for another four years.[9]

1865

Henry William Vincent died at his home at Lily Hill in March.

A month later, the Prince of Wales was able to travel to Bracknell by train, 'where he was met by Prince Arthur, and the two of them then rode to The Golden Ball for the day's hunt'.[10] The prince had first ridden with the Garth Hunt at Wentworth the previous year.

Another school opened in the village in July. It was described as 'a new and commodious building ... a British School, where children of any denomination may receive a sound and liberal education', although only for those who could afford to pay for their children to attend. It was adjacent to the Congregational Church in the High Street, having previously been used as its Sunday School.

Two men were found lying on the benches at the railway station. They were wearing clothing from Broadmoor Lunatic Asylum, having escaped from there the previous day.[11]

1866

A new establishment appeared in Station Road, next to the gas works. Bracknell Brewery was first listed in the *Kelly's Directory* of 1864. Two years later, proprietor Frank Raxworthy placed an advert: 'Bracknell Brewery ... is now open to the public for the supply of first-rate ales, beers, etc., also good cheap beer for hay-making and harvest.'[12] The brewery had its own well dug in order to supply the water used in brewing.

Under the 1866 Sanitary Act, Bracknell was declared 'a Special Drainage District'. This Act compelled local areas to take responsibility for ensuring sewerage systems were in place, and to remove nuisances to public health. A perennial problem in the area was the clearance of streams, with some landowners failing to keep water flowing properly through their lands.

1867

'An amused Looker-on' from Bracknell wrote to the editor of the *Reading Mercury* in May (letter writers often retained their anonymity at this time):

> This is considered a very thriving place, and has some men of considerable enterprise and substance. We flatter ourselves we rather go in for progress, but somehow we do not altogether get on satisfactorily. For instance, there is the gas. Some years ago we were told we ought to have gas. That it was absolutely necessary. That we could not possibly do without it. That smaller places had gas and made it pay. That it would be shameful if such an important place should be without it. So a company was started, and the shops became brilliant, and we held our heads higher than ever. After a time, rumours were heard that the gas did not pay, and that we ought to have street lamps, that there was so much traffic to the station at night that it was positively dangerous for the roads to be left dark at night. Well, we did not all exactly see it, and some people said the only use of street lamps would be to help the drunken men to reel home from the public houses on Saturday nights, but of course this was all a mistake – as drunken men seeing double could not want any lamps at all, and the originators of this report were supposed to be men who had been disappointed in not getting shares ... A meeting was called and a rate made, which some of us did not like at all; and we have gone on paying rates, and stiffish ones too ever since. So now we have lamps, not only in our shops, but in our streets ... in our church, in our chapel, and in our institute. In fact, we have gas everywhere, only the worst of it is the gas won't always burn, and does smell most horribly. Sometimes the congregation is reduced to a very dim and religious light indeed; sometimes the reading room is suddenly plunged into total darkness, and ... the street lights burn on no fixed principle at all, but go out when they like.

The writer then goes on to describe how the smell is very bad around the gas works itself (and may be a health hazard): 'There is a brewery close by; surely it must injure the delicate hop flavour of the bitter ale.'[13] The following week, another correspondent added:

I can fully endorse the statement ... respecting the impurity of the gas supplied to the inhabitants of Bracknell. I use it in my shop and sitting room, and after a very few minutes after it is lighted the place is unbearable; we are obliged to open the window of the sitting room. As the impure vapour ascends, the bedrooms soon become full of the poison; the smell is very similar to a foul sewer ... 7s 6d per thousand feet is a stiffish price to pay for a bad article, and I for one shall certainly resort to oil or spirit lamp again, if we do not get a pure article for our money.

1868

In August, 'The Honorable Auberon Herbert, a Liberal candidate for Berkshire in the forthcoming General Election, addressed a meeting in the Reading Room at Bracknell.'[14] There was great interest in the meeting as many males had been enfranchised by the Reform Act the previous year. Although the Liberal Party were returned with a large majority, Herbert was not one of them.

Another improvement in the village was reported in October. Thomas Croft, the local surgeon, 'having for many years seen ... the ravages produced by the deleterious effects of bad water, has, at his own expense, constructed a conduit from a spring near the railway station to a reservoir about a quarter of a mile distant, and provided a pump with accessories for the use of the inhabitants.'[15] The pump stood in the High Street, opposite the end of Station Road; later three others were added, including one near the Crown and another outside The Hind's Head.

1869

The railway station 'was gaily decorated with flowers, hung in festoons, and a triumphal arch of evergreens and exotics' in the middle of August for the return from their honeymoon of Major Blacker and his Agnes (from Warfield Hall, her father being a county magistrate). 'On the arrival of the train, a numerous company greeted the young couple, and escorted them to the carriage which was waiting for them.'[16]

1870

John Marius Wilson's *Imperial Gazetteer of England and Wales*, published between 1870 and 1872, described Bracknell as:

a village, a chapelry, and a subdistrict, in the district of Easthampstead, Berks. The village stands adjacent to the Southwestern railway, 3 miles West of Ascot racecourse, and 4 East of Wokingham. It has a station on the railway, and a post office, of the name of Bracknell, Berkshire; and is a polling-place. Fairs are held at it on 25th April, 22nd August, and 1st October. It consists of one fine, long, open street; and there are several large mansions in its neighbourhood. The chapelry includes the village; is in the parishes of Warfield and Winkfield; and was constituted in 1851.

A weekly cattle and poultry market started in Bracknell, although an outbreak of foot and mouth disease in October temporarily limited sales. This was held on Thursdays at the top of the High Street, initially in front of The Hind's Head pub, with cows being driven to and from the station along Church Road. Later, the venue moved to the yard behind the pub.

Two years after inheriting at the age of twenty-four, the Marquis of Downshire was married in London before coming to Easthampstead Park for his honeymoon. 'At Bracknell, the most extensive and elaborate preparations were made to give *them* a very enthusiastic and hearty welcome ... many willing hands commenced the work of erecting triumphal arches and planting fir trees from the Hind's Head to the Railway Hotel at the end of the village.'[17]

The Bracknell Cattle Market started in 1870, and took place every Thursday. Its site, behind The Hind's Head pub, is now occupied by Bracknell and Wokingham College. It moved to Market Street in 1958, and finally closed in 1978. (Photo courtesy of Bracknell Central Library)

Decorations were also put up outside the post office, along with the office of Mr Cave (solicitor), the premises of Mr Gough (coach builder), Mr T. Lawrence, and Mr Pecover (tailor). There was another large arch at the Bracknell Brewery, plus one at the bridge over the railway, flags outside the station, while the Station Hotel 'presented a very gay appearance'. The Great Western Railway Band was engaged by the organising committee, who played a few pieces near the station before moving to The Hind's Head to meet the wedding party. Here there were speeches before the procession:

> continued its course through the village, and all along the line of the route the cheering was most enthusiastic ... Later the children of the schools were supplied with refreshments in the Fair Field ... In the evening dancing was commenced, and the Great Western Band played a selection of music till dusk.

1871

A new cricket club 'have taken a new piece of ground for the purpose of playing matches, etc.'.[18] This was its home for many years until the redevelopment of Bracknell's town centre. This club was only in existence for a short period, but another began in 1880, which is still playing today.

Plans were in the air for a railway connecting Windsor and Ascot, with two different routes being proposed, one of which would come through Bracknell. The route was still being discussed almost thirty years later, by which time ERDC had been formed and were taking an interest in the project, protesting against the possible drainage of Englemere Pond for its construction. Early plans were fiercely opposed by the South Western Railway Company, who saw it as competition to their line from Waterloo. Plans were resurrected in 1897, and again in 1900, before finally being abandoned in 1914.

1872

An inquest was held at the Station Hotel into the death of fireman John Stoneley, another railway fatality at Bracknell. Thomas Colwey said:

> I am an engine-driver on the S.W. Railway, and deceased was my stoker. We started on our up-journey from Bracknell yesterday at 12:05. I saw him almost directly after getting on the tender and open a box from which he took his food, and showed it to me. I had turned round, when I heard him say 'Oh.' I looked

back and saw him lying on his back on top of the tender. I shut off steam and went to his assistance. He never spoke. There was very little blood, and this was flowing from his head. I called the guard and brakesman, and together we took him off the tender, but he was dead ... After the deceased got on the tender we passed under a bridge, and his head must have come in contact with it.

Albert Fielder, a carpenter at Cooper's Hill:

Yesterday, when on a rick, I saw a train passing with deceased on the tender. Almost directly afterwards I heard a blow, and told the man who was working for me that the man must have hit himself against the bridge.

George Moore:

I am a goods guard, and in charge of this particular train. After passing under the second up-bridge from Bracknell station, I heard a whistle and put the brake on. As soon as I could, I went to deceased and found him lying on the coal ... Deceased was on his back with his head towards Bracknell. I only noticed one mark on his temple. We were going about six or seven miles an hour.

A verdict of 'Accidentally killed while going under a bridge on the South Western Railway' was returned.[19]

An announcement appeared in the *Reading Mercury* in August:

Notice is hereby given that Her Majesty's Postmaster General, having obtained the consent ... of the body having control of the roads between Earley, Bracknell (Forest Road) and Virginia Water, intends to place a telegraph over and along the said roads, and for that purpose to erect and maintain posts in and upon the said roads.

By 1852, more than 2,000 miles of electric wire had been installed in just fifteen years. Initially placed alongside railway lines, they were soon being placed in post offices to expand communications.

1873

Easthampstead Rural Sanitary Authority was formed in 1873. Among their responsibilities was the forced closure of any wells at houses in the area where the water was unfit for drinking. These organisations had been set up across the country to not only improve water supplies, but also to regulate new buildings.

1874

Life and death were integral parts of daily life in Victorian England. The Marquess of Downshire died at the end of March; he was just 30 years old. In contrast, 'one of the few remaining Waterloo veterans, Thomas Beckford, is now an inmate of the Easthampstead Union Workhouse ... Although ninety years of age, he is comparatively hale and hearty, and his wife ... is in the same establishment.'[20]

In November:

a serious accident occurred on Saturday evening to Mr Charles Lovell, of the Station Hotel, Bracknell. He was crossing the line at the railway station about 8 o'clock in the rear of a train which was stopping, and just as he got off the platform on to the line the train moved backwards a little, and some way or another his left ear was cut off entirely, and a serious flesh wound was inflicted from the front of the head to the back on the right side. Mr Croft, surgeon, dressed the wounds, and Mr Lovell is now progressing favourably.[21]

There was no footbridge between the two platforms at this time, the down platform being reached by boardwalk across the lines, with passengers clambering off and on the platforms. When the platforms were raised in 1880, this became even more difficult.

1875

Shoplifting was probably a new crime in Bracknell, but Thomas Lawrence was a victim. 'Eliza Scuffle ... was charged ... with fraudulently obtaining from the shop of Mr Thomas Lawrence ... on the 29th May, drapery goods to the value of four guineas'.[22]

1876

When the eight o'clock morning train on 4 March from Waterloo arrived at Earley station, Albert Ellis, the Congregational minister from Bracknell, was found dead in one of the carriages. An inquest determined he had died 'from natural causes, probably heart disease'.

By November, Henry Moore Vincent had taken over the Bracknell brewery, and applied for a licence to sell by retail beer, 'to be drunk or consumed off the premises'.

West End, the area at the bottom of Bracknell High Street with The Red Lion on the right. The water pump was the first attempt in providing a clean supply in Bracknell. It was superseded by a mains supply from Wokingham in 1896.

1877

Just before Christmas, the *Reading Mercury* reported:

> Rumour for a long time past has stated that it was intended to form a company to supply the town of Wokingham and neighbourhood with water, and various projects have been talked over and abandoned. However, now the scheme is fairly launched … It is proposed to sink an artesian well just beyond the brook on the Finchampstead Road, near the South-Eastern Railway, and there construct the necessary pumping engines, etc … The water … would flow to Wokingham and every part of Bracknell.[23]

Shares in the new company were being offered six months later.

1878

In February, The Golden Ball was being sold by auction, the owner and his wife having both died a few years earlier. Also advertised were 'ten acres of eligible building land on the Golden Acorn estate'. However, a map of 1881 only records

'Golden Ball (site of)', so it appears the new owner may have immediately demolished it.

In June, the Wokingham Fire Brigade visited Bracknell 'and went through several experiments with their engine. The engine was run from the top of the street to the pond at the bottom, the hose laid, and everything put in working order in a very short space of time.'[24] Bracknell did not get its own fire engine for another fifty years.

Two months later, it was reported that:

The sanitary authority have conveyed the water from the premises of the South Western Railway Station by means of a pipe drain to the lower end of the village, and also erected an ornamental pump, with gas lamp over, in the centre of the road leading out of Bracknell Street to the station, and another pump some two hundred yards higher up the street. An excellent supply of pure water will now be available.[25]

1879

'A public meeting was held of the ratepayers of Bracknell ... to take into consideration the means of paying for certain work done by the Easthampstead Union Sanitary Authority to give a supply of water to Bracknell. The meeting was very numerously attended.'[26]

1880

Boring was taking place for the proposed Wokingham waterworks 'with good results ... when a good source of water was found'. This was sufficient to supply not only Wokingham, but also Binfield, Bracknell and Sandhurst as well. 'Barkham was soon added to settlements to be catered for ... in addition there was sufficient water to supply Wellington College, the Royal Military and Staff Colleges at Sandhurst, and Broadmoor Lunatic Asylum.' It was estimated that 13,000 patrons would be supplied in total. Perhaps the very wet year led to ambitious targets as to how much water could be supplied.

In April, voting took place in the Bullbrook schoolroom for the general election that saw William Gladstone become prime minister for the second time. Unlike modern elections, this took place over a period of four weeks, with different parts of the country voting on different days. The whole of Berkshire voted on this date, with eligible men from the parishes of Binfield,

Sunninghill, Winkfield, Easthampstead and Warfield coming to Bracknell to make their choice.

The stationmaster's 14-year-old son:

> saved an old lady from certain death. Despite warnings, she attempted to cross the line in order to catch a train, just as a horse-box at the rear of it was being reversed into a siding. The height of the platform above the line was too great for her to climb up, but the young lad, with the assistance of another passenger who rushed to his aid, managed to haul her up in the nick of time.[27]

1881

In February, it was reported that 'the Bracknell District Burial Board are desirous of receiving tenders for the following works at the new cemetery at Bracknell ... including the erection of a mortuary chapel and lodge';[28] this is the current Larges Lane cemetery with Thomas Lawrence bricks being used for it. By October, an advert appeared for 'a steady and industrious man ... to perform the office of sexton at the new cemetery at Bracknell'.

In June, the *Reading Mercury* reported: 'Pipes for the new water supply have been laid to Binfield and Bracknell, and the enterprise was officially declared "open" in Wokingham by the local MP.' Over the years, the area supplied was gradually increased as pipes were laid under other roads, although the decision was always based on measuring the cost against the number of houses to be served.

Another railway worker was injured in August:

> As a platelayer named Charles Noakes ... was at work on the railway between Bracknell and Wokingham, the 4:55pm train from Reading, came up unperceived, and knocked him down, inflicting some severe scalp wounds. The unfortunate man was carried to Bracknell station, and was brought to Reading by the next train, and taken to the hospital.[29]

1882

This seems to have been a pretty uneventful year, with only one major item of Bracknell news reaching the papers. Tenders were placed to enlarge the gas works to include a new retort house, purifying house, meter and governor house. But by the end of January the following year, it was reported that 'Ascot District Gas

Company have completed laying a gas main from Bracknell ... having obtained permission to connect to the Bracknell Company's supply.' The Ascot Company would become a major local supplier, with customers in Berkshire and Surrey. By October, the Bracknell Gas Company was wound up, and the Ascot District Gas Company took over the local supply of gas; the Bracknell Gas Works had disappeared from the map by 1900.

1883

Bracknell Brewery was now advertising as being 'Under Royal and Distinguished Patronage' but no crest or coat of arms accompanied the statement. However, an undated price list records 'as supplied to H.R.H. Prince of Wales' against one of their beers.

Easthampstead Rural Sanitary Authority expressed their intention of applying for a Compulsory Purchase Order to purchase land for a sewage farm; this was to be at Down Mill Farm (opposite The Bridge pub) but the CPO was not issued for another ten years (along with another piece of land on Bay Road for a pumping station). In the meantime, Compulsory Purchases of land in Binfield and Warfield 'for construction of straining tanks or other apparatus, and for disposing of the effluent sewage by irrigation' were issued in 1886. Manor Farm on Binfield Road was also considered as a site for the sewage farm, but discounted.

1884

The year started with a storm in late January. Part of the roof of The Red Lion Inn was blown off, many other houses lost tiles, slates or chimney pots, and several trees were blown down.

1885

The 1885 United Kingdom general election was held from 24 November to 18 December. Voting was again held in the schoolroom at Bullbrook, on 3 December. Due to the increased number eligible to vote, two stations were opened, and both recorded a steady stream all day. The result was declared the following day at The Rose in Wokingham, when the Conservative candidate was declared the winner, taking around 60 per cent of the votes cast.

1886

Colonel Bagot Lane, the new owner of Lily Hill, died there 'suddenly' on 2 March. A few months later, it was announced that one of his daughters would marry one of the Earl of Lichfield's sons at the Primitive Methodist Chapel in Bracknell, a tin tabernacle in Green Lane (now the section of Downshire Way near Binfield Road), but the ceremony was actually held in Belgravia, London.

Bracknell shopkeepers agreed to close their shops during the spring and summer months on Wednesdays at 3 p.m., 'thus affording their assistants the privilege of one afternoon off during the week'. During the other working days, the shops closed at 8 or 9 p.m., and not until 10 p.m. on Saturdays.

The first mention of a football match in Bracknell was the one played between Bracknell Wanderers and a team from East Reading 'in very unfavourable weather' in mid-November, with the visitors winning by the only goal of the game. The report added: 'the "Wanderers" is a club of this season's formation, while their opponents are well known at the game'. By the end of the year, the local team had recorded a draw and a second victory, and in February the following year they trounced Winkfield by fourteen goals to nil!

At the beginning of December, a public meeting was held in the Reading Room 'to consider the subject of raising a memorial in celebration of the Queen's Jubilee'. A proposal for a 'large public hall ... the cost, estimated at £2000 [£180,000 in today's money] ... was carried unanimously'.

1887

A public meeting in June approved the plans for the proposed public hall, and a tender for £1,100 from Messrs Green Bros, of Colnbrook, was accepted unanimously. 'The foundation stone was arranged to be laid on the 20th (Coronation Day).' The celebrations of the day itself were reported in full:

> The proceedings commenced with Divine Service at Holy Trinity Church, when the form of thanksgiving and prayer specially arranged by the Archbishop of Canterbury was used ... At three o'clock a short service for children was held at the same church, and about 800 were present; after which a procession was formed and proceeded to the cricket field, headed by a band. A tea was then given to all children under the age of 15, and to adults above 50. Commemorative medals were distributed by the ladies at their respective tables ... Some capital sports were given, and after a distribution of buns to the children, followed a splendid display of fireworks. The whole of the day's

proceedings were in every way a success, and were thoroughly enjoyed by the large number of people present. The village had been very prettily decorated with bunting, flags, etc.[30]

The new Victoria Hall was opened on 8 December by Prince Christian (a son-in-law of Queen Victoria):

A guard of honour, furnished by 'L' Company of the 1st Volunteer Battalion, Royal Berkshire Regiment, numbering about fifty ... was mounted at the principal entrance to the hall, and received his Royal Highness with a Royal Salute. The Reading Town Band was in attendance ... The hall was very tastefully decorated with flags, and an excellent collection of plants supplied by Mr Sinclair, gardener to the Marchioness of Downshire, Easthampstead Park ... The hall ... will seat about four hundred persons. There is also a reading room, some retiring rooms, lavatories, etc.[31]

The Victoria Hall stood in Church Road. It opened in 1887 for Queen Victoria's Golden Jubilee and quickly became the venue for all entertainments in the town, including the first silent movies. (Photo courtesy of Albert Brant)

After the introductory speeches, 'His Royal Highness then declared the hall open to prolonged applause'. There were more speeches and 'the Opening Ceremony was then brought to a conclusion by the band playing the National Anthem as His Royal Highness proceeded to the reading room, where tea was served in good style'. The new hall quickly became heavily used for various meetings, dinners, bazaars, concerts and entertainments (including some from the Reading Excelsior Dramatic Company, who caused a complaint from one member of the audience of 'introducing questionable songs' into their programme). Professor Blumenfeld gave two of his 'celebrated legerdemain, etc. performances before large audiences', while his 6-year-old son 'performed some wonderful acrobatic feats'. The Quadrille Party also used the new premises. A touring group, the Queen's Minstrels, gave a concert (Victorians took a delight in the foreign and exotic, and singers with blackened faces were popular).

The following month, a 'public meeting was held in the Reading Room ... for the purpose of forming a football club in Bracknell. There was a large attendance and it was decided that the club should be named "The Bracknell Football Club," colours black and white.' The team attracted the nickname 'The Noble Army' due to their 'invincibility'.

Victoria Hall was not the only new building, with a Baptist Church (in Rochdale Road), Methodist Chapel (in London Road, adjacent to a hall opened twenty years earlier), and First Church of Christ the Scientist all opening their doors for the first time.

1888

'A choral society, long felt to be wanted, has been started in Bracknell, mainly through the efforts of Mr F. W. Drake [corn and coal merchant of Station Road] ... The first practise took place in Mr Hunton's Hall,' with their first concert taking place three months later in the Victoria Hall, 'which rendered great credit on the members and their able conductor'.

Priestwood, still part of Easthampstead parish, saw a new church opened. Erected at a cost of £781 (just over £70,000 in today's money) and dedicated to St Andrew, 'it is an edifice of red brick, with an apse; it will seat 150, and is served by the rector and curate'. The site on which it stood is now occupied by Boyd Court.

County Councils came into being with the Local Government Act of 1888. Thomas Lawrence was a candidate for a position as a councillor in Berkshire, along with Dr Henry Armstrong of 'Gilnochie' (the house, renamed Lynwood Chase, was demolished in about 1970, and an estate of the same name now occupies the site), and Sir Arthur Hayter of South Hill Park.

1889

Sir Arthur Hayter held a hustings at the Victoria Hall to a 'crowded and enthusiastic' meeting. One of the issues he raised was that 'in Bracknell, as in Warfield, it was clear that too many public houses existed, and some measure to limit their numbers must be taken'. This was met with 'loud cheers'. He also talked at length about the duties the new County Council would have to deal with. Of Thomas Lawrence: 'He advocated inefficiency coupled with extravagance … He described himself as the poor man's friend, in contradistinction, presumably, to his imagined foes, the poor man's enemy.' He also attacked Lawrence's ambivalent thoughts on other matters. Dr Armstrong also held a hustings at a crowded Victoria Hall on the same day, and attacked fellow candidate Sir Arthur Hayter, who had cast aspersions on his lack of political experience, but who had rarely been involved in local affairs, being a mere 'visitor' to the area. Lawrence based his campaign on what he had already done in the town, not just in terms of employment, but also the committees he served on. Later in the month, Hayter withdrew from the contest, throwing his weight behind Dr Armstrong.

The Victoria Hall was used as the polling station:

> A considerable amount of personal feeling was introduced into the election, and several circulars and handbills were circulated amongst the electors … Both Dr Armstrong and Mr Lawrence have held meetings in the district and they have been well attended, but Mr Lawrence being a large employer of labour, and also being very popular in Bracknell, he was considered the strongest candidate … Considerable excitement prevailed just before the close of the poll, when a number of working men recorded their votes, but during the day proceedings were very quiet … It was decided to count the votes at half-past eight o'clock, half an hour after the close of the poll, and owing to the comparatively small constituency, the result was soon declared. Both sides seemed confident of victory, but when the result was known there were expressions of surprise.[32]

The result was announced some forty-five minutes later, with Lawrence gaining 176 votes, against 119 for his opponent.

The proximity to Windsor meant that members of the royal family would visit from time to time. In July, a Bracknell vs Ascot cricket match was played on the Bracknell ground, with Prince Albert playing for the visitors. A team from the West Indies took part in the cricket week the following month.

An application was submitted to Berkshire County Council (BCC) by the South of England Telephone Company to erect posts along the Bracknell to Ascot Road. 'The company proposes to pay a rent of 1s per pole.'[33] The telephone connection was reported as being completed within two months,

Bracknell Cricket Club was formed in 1880, their ground being on the north side of the High Street. They staged an annual athletics meeting from 1891 onwards, which was attracting Olympic runners by 1912. The club relocated to Larges Lane in 1955 when the town centre was redeveloped. (Photo courtesy of Vin Miles)

although 'some considerable dissatisfaction is being felt by some of the inhabitants of High Street, owing to the ungainly looking black poles being erected outside of their premises'. A groom at The Hind's Head suffered concussion after falling from a horse and hitting his head on one of the poles, 'but recovered fully'. By 1895, Bracknell was connected to Wokingham by telephone, although the authorities had not granted permission for this link.

1890

Plans were announced for the enlargement of Bullbrook School to accommodate an additional 106 children. The *Reading Mercury* commented: 'The increase in the numbers attending the schools during the past few years has been considerable. In 1885 the average attendance was 155, while in 1889 the average reached 245.' The school summer holiday was extended by two weeks 'to enable the buildings, which are now somewhat advanced … to be completed within the fortnight'.

1891

Unemployment went from 1.4 per cent of the workforce in 1890 to more than 10 per cent two years later. Agricultural workers were particularly affected, and a soup kitchen opened for 'Easthampstead parishoners', distributing soup three times a week.

In August:

The first annual athletics sports, promoted by the Bracknell Cricket Club, were held ... on the cricket ground, for the benefit of F. Jennings, the popular ground man and professional. A capital program was arranged and ably carried out in the presence of over one thousand spectators ... Unfortunately, heavy showers fell during the day making the track very heavy for competitors and also very unpleasant for visitors.[34]

As well as running events, there was a wheelbarrow race, a sack race, and a bicycle handicap race (pneumatic tyres were excluded). There were also a couple of short races for boys, plus a hopping race. The event attracted a crowd of 6,000, twice the population of the town at that time. In later years, a small fair was set up in an adjacent paddock for the entertainment of children. The Athletic Sports became a major summer event and a very profitable one for the hosts.

1892

An influenza pandemic had been raging since 1889, but now it claimed its most prominent victim, Prince Albert, the eldest son of the future Edward VII, and second in line to the throne. As a mark of respect, the tradesmen at Bracknell suspended business at midday on 20 January (the day of his funeral). Shops were closed and shutters put up, while in most of the private houses, blinds were drawn. 'The influenza epidemic is still raging with great vigour, numbers of fresh cases being reported daily ... Mr Thomas Lawrence is still very ill from bronchitis, following an attack of influenza.'[35] The *Reading Mercury* listed Bracknell, Maidenhead, Mortimer, Wallingford and Swindon as the worst affected areas.

Under the heading 'Yet another religious body', it was reported the Baptists, Wesleyans, Brethren and Primitive Methodist had formed the Bracknell Gospel United Band, 'whose object is to hold open-air preaching on two evenings during the week', on Sundays and Wednesdays.

In August, more than 1,000 people turned out to watch the second annual athletic sports at the cricket ground, which was favoured by 'beautiful weather'. As well as the sports, 'there were the usual coca nut [sic] shies, rifle galleries, etc.' and the Wokingham Town Band 'played a good selection of music'. There was a mix of open and handicap races, ensuring all competitors had a reasonable chance of carrying off a prize.

In September, the Duke and Duchess of Teck, along with Princess May (later the wife of George V), arrived on the 4.45 p.m. train from Waterloo to visit the Hon. Arthur Walsh at Warfield Park, where they stayed for a few days.

'The station and platform were gaily decorated with evergreens, flowers, and bunting', while a 'Welcome to Bracknell' sign had been mounted over the exit gate. Crowds turned out to cheer them, and they received a similar reception two days later on their return from an outing to Reading to visit the Huntley and Palmer biscuit factory. The station had also been decorated three days earlier when the Marquis of Downshire returned from Ireland, where he had celebrated his coming of age. Prime Minister William Gladstone was similarly received the following year when staying at South Hill Park.

The Victoria Hall was the venue for an art exhibition in aid of the London and Southwestern Railway Widows' and Orphans' Benefit Institution in October. Over three days, it staged almost 700 pictures and other works of art from local residents, including 'painters and decorators, carpenters, labourers, chimney sweeps, etc.'. The event was 'well patronised by all classes of persons in the neighbourhood', with contributions from Bracknell, Binfield, Warfield, Easthampstead, Crowthorne, Wellington College and Wokingham – 'paintings in oil and water colours, sculpture, modelling in wax and clay, art needlework, art carving, fretwork, brass and iron work, china, pottery, and tile painting, amateur photography, pyrography, studies in black and white, charcoal, pencil, crayon, pastel, designs, etc.'. With so much on display, 'all the contributions could not be seen to best advantage, as with the limited space available … there was no alternative but to crowd them both on the walls and on the floor of the hall'. The exhibition had been well publicised in advance, and with the railway company also selling discounted tickets, visitors from 'Reading, Windsor, and other stations' visited as well. The 'prime mover' for the exhibition, opened by the Marchioness of Downshire, was stationmaster Edmund Taylor (the son of the previous stationmaster), who hoped to turn it into an annual event. However, after expenses had been taken into account, only a small sum had been raised, and it was decided to stage the event every two years.

Bracknell Wednesday Football Club played a bad-tempered match against Victoria FC in which they were accused of 'rough play', although as no reporter from the *Reading Observer* was at the match, they were unable to ascertain the full story. The club played their home games on a field in Vicarage Lane (now named Larges Lane), but not on the same site as the current football ground. Another club, Easthampstead Rovers, played on the same pitch.

1893

At the beginning of February, the *Berkshire Chronicle* reported:

An outbreak of fire occurred at the Bracknell Post Office shortly after 9pm on a Friday evening. Flames were seen issuing from the back part of the building, and an alarm was at once raised. Fortunately a number of persons were soon on the spot, and with pails of water soon succeeded in extinguishing the fire. It was found that the fire had originated in the postmaster's office, a match-boarded erection at the back of the counter, the supposed cause being the explosion of a small paraffin lamp. The sides and roof of the office were badly burnt, and the postmasters account books destroyed, besides a large number of papers belonging to the postal authorities. The Wokingham Fire Brigade had been called to deal with the blaze, but a messenger intercepted them before they arrived to tell them it had been taken care of, and their assistance was not required.

As a result of the blaze, the post office moved from the High Street to Church Road, only returning with the construction of new premises in 1934.

In June, it was announced that a tender had been accepted for a scheme for the sewerage and sewage disposal, with an estimated cost of £7,736 (almost £700,000 in today's money). 'Pipe sewers will be laid in the main streets, and part of the sewage will be pumped by steam pumps at the disposal site.' Three years later, the work was almost complete:

> The pumping machinery appears to be thoroughly satisfactory ... the sewage pumps are not very likely to get out of order ... The leakage into the sewer in High Street has been reduced to less than one half ... It is impossible to make all stoneware pipes absolutely watertight ... The amount of leakage is this scheme is very trivial ... The flushing arrangements at the top of High Street have answered admirably ... *and* every length of sewer should be flushed by this arrangement at least twice a week.[36]

The contractor had also offered to make good some of the damage to roads caused by his works, and the project was duly signed off shortly afterwards. Discussions about installing duplicate pumping machines (in case of breakdowns) dragged on for months – were they needed, should they be driven by oil or gas (the latter was cheaper, but running costs were higher)? Not all houses were connected to the sewers at first but this gradually changed, in some cases (such as at The Bull public house) only through enforcement orders from ERDC.

The marriage of the Duke of York (the future George V) and Princess Mary of Teck took place on 6 July:

> and right royally did the residents of Bracknell lay themselves open to celebrate ... The day was observed as a general holiday, with all places of business being closed. Beautiful weather prevailed throughout the day. Most of the houses in the High Street were decorated with flags, bannerets, bunting, and Japanese lanterns, etc, which had a pretty effect in the evening when lit up.

About 3pm, the children of the various elementary and Sunday Schools, headed by the Wokingham Band, marched to the Cricket Field, where a monster tea was provided under canvas ... Somewhat over 600 children were provided with teas, while in an adjoining tent about 70 persons of 60 years and upwards were also provided with tea ... After the tea, a program of sports was carried out ... *consisting* of flat races, obstacle races, egg and spoon races, donkey races, sack races, and provided great amusement both for competitors and spectators. During the tea, the band gave a selection of loyal and patriotic music, followed by an evening's program of dance music, of which numbers of the younger people availed themselves. A small cannon was mounted in the field area and a salute fired.[37]

The annual Sports Day attracted about 1,500 spectators, with the Wokingham Band again providing the music. Bicycle races and races over hurdles were also included for the first time.

September saw the Thomas Lawrence Stores in the High Street 'have three of their departments ... illuminated by electric light. In all there are 65 burners. The current is produced at the saw mills.'[38]

In October, the *Reading Observer* was able to report:[39]

A pillar box has been placed in the High Street, and this, together with the boxes in the London Road, Station Road corner, and at the railway station, are cleared a short time before each despatch, about 9am, 12 noon, 3pm, 7pm, and 9pm, also a collection which will be greatly appreciated, is made on Sunday evenings from each of these boxes about 6:30. There is also an additional delivery at 2:45pm, thus making four town deliveries.

1894

The Local Government Act saw the formation of Easthampstead Rural District Council (ERDC), with elected councillors meeting fortnightly in the board room at Easthampstead Workhouse. ERDC was replaced by Bracknell District Council in 1974.

Work started in July to build a footbridge over the railway lines built at Bracknell station 'to cater for the increased passenger traffic'. It was sited beside the road bridge and was of a standard design of the time, having a wooden lattice structure and a rounded, corrugated-iron roof, open at the sides. 'This will put a stop to the dangerous practise [sic] of passengers having to cross the metals from one platform to the other.'[40] The bridge was in a poor state by 1952 and was replaced by a concrete one, albeit without a roof.

The Cricket Club Sports was going from strength to strength. There were many more entries than in previous years, 'but a great improvement was noticeable in the class of athletes, quite a host of well-known performers' names finding a place on the programme'.

The second Art Exhibition was staged in October, to great acclaim from the *Reading Mercury*, 'with about five hundred works (nearly all meritorious) in oil and water colours, and nearly two hundred beautiful exhibits of art carving and other miscellaneous art works, the number of exhibitors extending to 170'.

A small convent school, St Joseph's Middle Class School for Young Ladies, opened in November in the High Street next door to The Bull, staffed by nuns from Ireland and France. The curriculum included 'the usual English Subjects, French, Music, Drawing and Needlework'. The school left Bracknell at the end of 1901, moving to Castle Hill in Reading, and subsequently to Upper Redlands Road, where it is now called St Joseph's College.

1895

By May, work had begun on the new sewage works. 'The work is being carried forward ... in a very satisfactory manner. Already the farm drainage is complete ... the excavation for the pumping station on the farm is finished, and a huge mass of concrete has been put in for a foundation.'[41] Landowners and occupiers through whose land the sewers were carried received compensation. The construction work was causing obvious disruption: 'going through Bracknell where ... they are just working on a new drainage scheme. You can guess how much I sympathised with the people there.'[42] The District Council decided that work would be suspended between the week before Royal Ascot, and the Thursday after it finished. By the beginning of October:

> the drainage works ... are about two thirds completed ... The trenches have varied in depth from four to fourteen feet, the latter depth being reached along Mount Pleasant ... The length of the sewers already laid is about five miles ... Both the storage tanks (one in Longshot Lane ... the other in Jig's Lane, Bullbrook) are finished, and the engine houses are now being pushed forward ... The contractors have employed sixty men on an average since the commencement of the work on March 11th last, and with one or two exceptions, they are local men.[43]

Cleveland Photographic Studio was also operating on London Road, run by two young unmarried women. Among their clients were the Duke and Duchess of Teck and their daughter Mary, the future wife of George V (the photos were probably taken on one of their visits to Warfield Park). These were not the first photographers in the town. Henry George was operating from London Road in the 1870s, while Charles Stephenson is listed in the 1891 census at an address in Station Road. Norton and Verel had premises in the High Street for a few years, as did Alan Etchells in 1911.

1896

At the beginning of June, ERDC received a petition that:

> begged to bring to your notice the serious condition of the water supply obtainable from the Wokingham Water Company. We are unable to obtain sufficient for domestic purposes, and for hours together are without any supply at all. Moreover, we cannot proceed with the connections of our house drains with the sewage system as there is not a sufficient supply of water to flush the drains, and to those of us who have connected there arises a very great danger of infectious disease by reason of being unable to flush the W.C.s or to get rid of the house sewage in the drains.

As the company was legally obliged to provide a good water supply, the council supported the petition:

> Mr McNabb, on behalf of the Water Company, said the Directors had laid out a large amount of capital in sinking a new well, etc., and they hoped soon to have a sufficient supply of water to meet all demands. No doubt the present short supply was partly owing to the water being used for garden purposes.

The council agreed to send a copy of the petition to the water company directors, who acknowledged receipt, 'but made no remark on improving the water supply'. Subsequently, they entered an agreement with Wokingham District Council in 'procuring a bacteriological and chemical analysis of the water supplied' every three months, the cost being covered by the two authorities. They were also intermittent reports of the water supply drying up completely, with the water company 'doing what was possible to remedy the complaint', and promising the directors would discuss the issue. The quality of the water was tested on a regular basis, and was often found to be 'unsuitable for domestic purposes'; residents were advised to boil it before use.

With water now being supplied from Wokingham, the water pump at the bottom of the High Street was not needed, so it was recommend it be removed 'and the site should be enclosed with a rail fence', although it was still there five years later, when Bracknell Parish Council 'considered it a nuisance'.

The Art Exhibition was again held at the end of October, and 'proved a thorough success from a social, artistic, financial and meteorological point of view. H.R.H. the Duchess of Teck was so impressed with her visit on the opening day that she honoured the exhibition with a second visit.'[44] This year there were musical performances as well.

The Bracknell football club struggled to find enough players to make up a team. After losing to Tilehurst by ten goals to two, they could only muster six to face Twyford and 'the match was scratched greatly to the disappointment of the Twyfordians'[45]. A report on their game at Reading noted: 'Still another defeat, and it really is not to be wondered at, for Bracknell took the journey to Reading ... with only eight players, one of these being a boy of 12 years of age.'[46] The game against Wokingham Magpies the following week was played in 'wretched, rain' with all the players 'wet to the skin ... with the exception of the Bracknell goalkeeper, who was well covered with a mackintosh'.[47] A few weeks later, 'the Magpies again visited Bracknell, this time to play the Old Bracknell Wanderers, a newly-formed club in that district'.[48] Twelve months later, the two teams met again. 'The match was the best contested game on the Wanderer's [sic] ground,

Old Bracknell Wanderers Football Club started in 1896, playing on a field behind The Downshire Arms. They later moved to a ground in Larges Lane (the pitch had a notable slope for many years) and were subsequently renamed Bracknell Town Football Club.

both sides playing for all they were worth.'⁴⁹ The home side were three goals up at half time, the visitors scored two and pressed for a third after the restart, only for the Wanderers to score again just before the end of the game.

This new team continues to play football, now under the name of Bracknell Town Football Club. The club originally played on a field near the Downshire Arms, before moving to Station Field, a site later occupied by Ranelagh School. According to the now defunct website pyramidpassion.co.uk, they moved to Larges Lane in 1933 to a ground that featured a significant slope, with multiple references to 'up the slope', 'downhill', and 'sloping pitch' in match reports. No record has been found to indicate where they played their home games before moving to Larges Lane, although a ground on Binfield Road has been suggested. However, the author has a fixture list from the 1921/22 season, indicating a ground in Vicarage Lane, the former name for Larges Lane. There are also reports of a 'sloping' ground in 1910, suggesting the date may be wrong by about a quarter of a century!

1897

BCC wrote to all the District Councils to gauge the feeling for building isolation hospitals. ERDC did not respond, but it was noted they had 'recently expended a considerable sum on an infirmary, and … were not in favour'. This backfired on the local authority, as three years later they were complaining that cases of scarlet fever were being 'imported' into the area. The disease was not uncommon, with one or two outbreaks in the area covered by ERDC being reported each month, mainly in the surrounding villages. Bracknell was not immune, though, with baker Richard Dearlove in the High Street contracting it in 1899.

A public meeting was held in the Victoria Hall in March 'to consider what steps should be taken in Bracknell to celebrate the Diamond Jubilee of Her Majesty'.⁵⁰ The unanimous decision was 'a subscription to raise sufficient funds to clear off the debt (£150) on the Victoria Hall, to make various improvements to it (especially in the Reading Room), and to provide an entertainment for the old inhabitants and children of the district'. Winkfield hoped to build a cottage hospital for infectious diseases and approached both Bracknell and Warfield to form a joint venture, but neither was willing and the plan was scrapped. The Bracknell committee approached the cricket club 'with a request to use their ground for the event, which in the past had been used for similar celebrations, but were met with a firm rebuff (on the grounds of damage to the pitch) on this occasion', although they were later offered 'a portion of the ground, excluding match and practise [sic] pitches'. But by then the committee had decided that 'Warfield Park would be a more suitable venue in terms of size and location.'

The Queen's Jubilee:

> was duly and loyally commemorated in the busy little town of Bracknell. Since Monday last the place has presented quite a gay and holiday appearance, High Street and Church Road being gaily decorated with flags and bunting, and at night prettily illuminated at various points ... The thanksgiving service was held at Holy Trinity on Sunday ... On Tuesday, all persons of the age of sixty and upwards living in Bracknell were invited to dinner at the Victoria Hall ... At 2pm, about 500 children assembled at the hall and sang the National Anthem, after which a procession was formed, headed by the Ascot Drum and Fife Band, when the children carrying flags and their teachers marched to Warfield Park ... where each child under the age of 15 was presented with a Jubilee mug, and they and the old people (who had been taken to the park in vans) partook of tea. A capital program of sports for the children was carried out ... The afternoon was varied with Punch and Judy show, swings, games, etc. The debt on Victoria Hall was cleared, with a further £50 used to install further lighting and ventilation, and repaint the exterior of the building.[51]

The BCC Finance and General Purposes Committee agreed to purchase a house for a police station at Bracknell. Three months later, they were inviting tenders to convert it into a police station, and build a new cottage and two cells. This stood at the bottom of the High Street.

The Cricket Club Sports meeting again took place:

> with a large crowd of around two thousand ... Some very fast times were recorded, giving rise to a suspicion that the track might be short. A large contingent of men from Windsor took part, and succeeded in carrying off eight of the prizes, while the two-mile bicycle race was won by a member of the Oxonian Club.[52]

1898

Adverts appeared in the *Reading Mercury*, starting in April, for the Bracknell and Easthampstead Brass Band, who were 'prepared to accept engagements at Flower Shows, Athletic Sports Club Feasts, etc ... Managers of local societies will do well to apply for terms, before engaging any other band.' Their first performance in public had taken place at a fundraising concert the previous month at the Victoria Hall; 'their performances were highly creditable, judging from the hearty plaudits by the audience', reported the *Berkshire Chronicle*. 'The performance of Mr Bert Albert with banjo and bones was also deservedly applauded!'

The first police station opened in 1897 and stood at the bottom of the High Street. The foundation stone for its replacement was laid in 1963.

There was a record crowd of 3,000, 'with people coming from miles around' for the Bracknell Athletic Sports, with the Reading Professional Town Band again being employed to provide the music rather than the new local ensemble. Members of the Windsor Liberal Athletic and Cycling Club 'again attended and as usual carried away some of the best prizes'. A donkey derby with optional fancy dress was included.

The fourth Art Exhibition was staged at the end of October, opened by the Duchess of Connaught. Entries came 'from as far away as Reading, Maidenhead, and Chertsey'. It was also noted the exhibition included some 'trophies' from the recent Battle of Omdurman in Sudan, submitted by Colour Sergeant Denby of the Grenadier Guards.

There was a major fire at the post office towards the end of November:

Early on Monday morning, an alarming outbreak of fire occurred at the Bracknell Post Office, situated in Church Road. One of the clerks entered the sorting department at five o'clock to receive the mails, when he found the premises full of smoke. At first he thought it came from a chimney … but on looking into one of the adjoining compartments (one of the clerks' retiring rooms), he discovered it was full of flames. He immediately roused the post-master (Mr Bartlett), whose residence is attached to the office buildings, and prompt measures were taken to arrest the conflagration, which was assuming alarming proportions. A telegraphic message was despatched to summon the Wokingham Fire Brigade, and the news that a serious fire was raging in the hamlet soon attracted a crowd of helpers to the spot. The sorting office consisted of a single-storey wooden building, linking the Post Office with the postmaster's accommodation. Some time elapsed before the Wokingham Fire Brigade could possibly reach the scene (it was two hours after the fire was discovered before they arrived), but in the meantime everything possible was done to cope with the disaster that threatened the whole block of buildings. As the fire threatened to get out of hand, all the books, official papers, stamps, etc. were removed from the office, and all the furniture from the house.

Police Sergeant Holloway and two local constables were soon on the scene, along with a Mr Swann, who was staying in Bracknell, and was said to have experience in dealing with forest and prairie fires abroad. He climbed onto the roof of the sorting office, throwing buckets of water handed to him onto the flames, prevented it spreading, and began to bring it under control. The fire crew completed the task of extinguishing the blaze. Although the building suffered severe damage, not a single item of post or equipment was lost, and all the paperwork and stamps were accounted for. How the outbreak occurred is something of a mystery.[53]

Bracknell still had no fire brigade at the time, a lack of a water supply preventing one from being formed when the matter had last been considered, although the mains supply had been laid on from Wokingham since then. The post office business resumed temporarily in the Victoria Hall.

1899

Warfield Parish Council requested ERDC to 'take steps to alleviate the existing nuisance and obstruction to traffic now caused by large char-a-bancs and carriages standing outside Bracknell station on Hawthorn Hill race days. The nuisance caused by this large number of horses standing around may be better imagined than described, as there are no scavengers to clear away. The sanitary condition of the road is deplorable.'[54] ERDC in turn passed the request on to the chief constable of the Berkshire Police Force.

There were several scarlet fever cases in the area in July, with Binfield, Crowthorne and Sandhurst badly affected, and further cases in Winkfield. ERDC were advised to close all the local schools to avoid it spreading further. By September, only six mild cases were reported, but numbers were rising again two months later, and Warfield School closed early the following year. Both scarlet fever and diphtheria were notifiable diseases, and the ERDC sanitary inspector would ensure containment measures were in place to prevent the diseases spreading.

Things were not improving at the sewage farm. In December, a letter was received from solicitors in Reading, acting on behalf of the landlord at the 'Bridge House' (where improvements were being made), complaining about the 'stench' emanating from it, and demanding ERDC take action. There was also a dispute with the local government board over the size of new tanks to be installed there. There continued to be intermittent problems at the site for several years.

The effect of international events were felt in Bracknell, as reported in *Reading Mercury*: 'The inhabitants of Bracknell and the district have responded well to the call for relief for our fighting forces in South Africa, where the Boer War had started two months earlier.' Second Lieutenant Bertram Lethbridge, brother-in-law of the vicar at Holy Trinity, was an early casualty at Ladysmith. Colonel and Mrs Mackenzie, of Ramslade House, organised an afternoon concert for the local War Fund, inviting well-known London musicians, who gave their services gratuitously. The Victoria Hall 'was filled to excess', and almost £70 was raised.[55]

1900

News was travelling fast from the Boer War in South Africa to Bracknell:

> The excitement at the news of the relief of Ladysmith [a day earlier] was still greater than that occasioned by the surrender of Cronje [on 27 February]. Business for a time was suspended, and additional decorations were put out. During the evening, the local brass band paraded the town, followed by a large crowd, who sang 'Soldiers of the Queen' and the National Anthem. Sergeant Alfred Barker of Easthampstead and Private Frederick Webb from Bullbrook are under orders to leave for the front.[56]

On receipt of the news of the occupation of Bloemfontein (one of the two Boer capitals) in March by Lord Roberts, 'the houses and shops in the High Street were gaily dressed with flags and bunting. A dramatic entertainment entitled "Boer and Briton," was given in the Victoria Hall two days earlier by Mr Dobell and Co. and attracted a large audience.'[57]

In May, it was learned a few days in advance that the Queen would be passing through Bracknell on her way to Wellington College:

and great preparations had been made to accord her a loyal reception. Early on Saturday [17 May] came the news of the relief of Mafeking and further efforts were made to celebrate the auspicious events. No expense was spared, and Bracknell was en fete after midday, business then being practically suspended. The route taken by Her Majesty was through Winkfield, along Clay Lane [Park Road] to the top of the High Street, thence along Church Road, over the Station bridge into Crowthorne Road. The road was prettily decorated, every house making a gratifying display of either flags, bunting, or mottoes, whilst various devices in gay bunting spanned the road at intervals. Visitors began to arrive about 1pm from all the outlying districts, and took up their positions on the line of the route, and by four o'clock, the time Her Majesty was supposed to arrive at Bracknell, the crowd could be counted in its thousands ... About 4:30pm a roar of cheering, which was taken up along the line, announced Her Majesty's approach. On arriving near 'The Elms', the horses were changed (a relay having previously been sent on and stabled at the Hind's Head Hotel), and the journey resumed ... Besides the route taken by Her Majesty, the whole of the town, especially the High Street, was gaily decorated, and all business premises were closed for a period, to allow the assistants to take part in the reception accorded Her Majesty.[58]

The Queen recorded the day in her personal diary: 'Bracknell was beautifully decorated.'

Bracknell Athletic Sports continued to go from strength to strength with a crowd of around 4,000:

So well had the handicappers performed their work that very close finishes were of frequent occurrence. Not only were the entries far in excess of those received for any previous meeting, but a great improvement was noticeable in the class of athletes, quite a number of well-known performers' names appearing on the programme.[59]

Mr Samuel Raven of London applied for a provisional grant of a full licence in respect of premises in course of construction at the corner of the road leading from Bullbrook to Bracknell station (Church Road). Premises had already been purchased by the applicant, who proposed to make them into 'a first-rate residential hotel'. This was the Forest Hotel, which was never the success the owner had hoped, only being full for the racing during Ascot Week.

ERDC gave permission in October for Messrs Lawrence and Sons to lay a tramway across the road to their Swinley brickworks, subject to the work being carried out to the satisfaction of the highway surveyor. An offer from Ascot District Gas Company to light the district lamps at 4s 6d per 1,000ft of gas was accepted.

1901

Another local sporting venture appeared in the press:

> Not the least in the attractions in the neighbourhood will be the links of the newly-formed Golf Club which opened on Wednesday last. The weather was against a large attendance, but those present, including several visitors, expressed themselves highly pleased with the excellent course laid out ... already nearly fifty members have been enrolled.[60]

But it seems this attempt to form a club was unsuccessful, as in December:

> a public meeting was held at the Victoria Hall ... with the object of forming a golf club ... Mr S. W. Lawrence then reported that he had already taken about 26 acres of meadow land forming part of the Warfield Park estate, and that a nine-hole course had been prepared and was now ready for play.[61]

This was an area bounded by London Road to the north, Allsmoor Lane to the east, the railway line to the south, and Broad Lane and Martin's Lane to the west. Three years later, a golfing handbook described the course as 'a short one. The ground stands high and is situated in a picturesque spot, the soil is sandy, covered with good old-established turf, and very and firm even in the wettest weather.' The club continued until the First World War.

The newspapers published on 26 January 1901 contained columns edged in black, announcing the death of Queen Victoria at Osbourne House on the Isle of Wight four days earlier. In Bracknell:

> the sad news that Her Majesty had passed away was received late in the evening on Tuesday last, and has thrown the deepest gloom over the inhabitants. Only as recently as 'Mafeking' Day, Her Majesty visited Bracknell on a day the memory of which will live long in the mind of everyone, but never more distinctly than now. The flags on the Victoria Hall and elsewhere are drooping at half-mast, and other signs of mourning are apparent everywhere. The loyal 'Crown' Lodge of Oddfellows, who were assembled when the sad tidings were received, making final arrangements for their ball for the following night, at once postponed the affair indefinitely, and a resolution of condolence and sympathy with the King and Royal Family was passed in silence.[62]

'Larger congregations than usual attended Holy Trinity Church to mark their respect for the recent death of Queen Victoria' the following day. 'At the end of the service, the "Dead March" in Saul was played (a piece traditionally played at State funerals), while the congregation remained standing.'

The Queen's reign had seen Bracknell change, prosper and expand. The population more than doubled between 1861 and 1901, while the number of traders trebled. The arrival of the railway had prefaced its expansion and development, which would continue over the coming years. With a new century and a new monarch, the inhabitants must have looked forward with optimism.

5

Brickworks in Bracknell

Although bricks and flat tiles have been found at the Roman settlement at Wickham Bushes, it was not until the seventeenth century that bricks started to be used again for building in the area. The tower at Winkfield Church carries the date 1629, the lower parts of the one at Easthampstead Church date from 1664, while The Old Manor is of a similar age.

To make bricks, the clay was first milled (mixed into a plastic state) before being moulded and cut into standard sizes. It was then left to stand in drying sheds before being fired. Rubber bricks were made of finer clay, which had to be filtered and settled before being moulded. After drying they were fired, although at a lower temperature, and were still soft enough to be shaped or 'rubbed' before being left to harden. They were often shaped for arches, windows and other features, and were of a higher quality than ordinary bricks. In contrast, Oxford clay bricks were milled and moulded but did not require drying before firing. Organic matter in the clay also meant firing was reduced, leading to faster production and reduced costs. Bracknell bricks were more expensive but judged as high class and more often used in important or prestigious buildings.

The first down-draught kilns would have been simple structures with a tall chimney. The bricks would be put inside and the kiln sealed, which was then heated by a fire to bake the clay. After the firing was completed, both the kiln and its contents were left to cool down, and the bricks removed. The kiln was then cleaned before the next cycle began. Beehive kilns were circular in plan, with fireboxes arranged around the circumference, but otherwise operated in the same way. The Hoffmann kiln, invented in Germany in 1858, allowed for continuous use. The fire in this may burn continuously for years; at Binfield, the fires only went out three times between 1928 and 1963. Queenie Cotterell (born 1908) remembers beehive kilns at Lawrence's brickyard in Priory Lane, and some were added later at the Binfield brickworks at Amen Corner; other brickyards in the area used the Hoffmann kilns.

There were a few small brickyards scattered around Bracknell by the beginning of the nineteenth century. Most would only be open for a few years, closing when the clay was exhausted or when the buildings close to them were completed. In many cases, it is not possible to give dates for many of the early brickyards as the first Ordnance Survey map of the district dates from 1870, and earlier maps do not show sufficient detail to identify them. But in 1817 there is mention of Brick-kiln Lane, linking Gough's Lane and Priory Lane in Warfield.[1] In November the following year, The Red Lion was 'upgraded with new sleeping rooms, new stabling, a new brick and tiled lock-up coach-house'.[2] Material for these works could well have come from a site on the southern side of Skimped Hill Lane, which appears as a small, flooded area on the Easthampstead tithe map from 1849, roughly at today's junction with Market Street. Eileen Shorland wrote in the 1960s that 'older parishoners will remember the brick kilns opposite The Bull, edging the lane'.[3] In 1825, 'a capital brick kiln, with six acres of excellent brick earth, tile shed, and other appendages, situated on the Wokingham Road ... two miles from Bracknell. Earth is already dug sufficient for making upwards of 200,000 bricks; there is plenty of sand and water upon the premises' was available, which was probably one of the pits at Amen Corner.[4]

Not all the brickyards were large enough to provide an income to support an entire household. The 1851 census records Roland Fielder, licensee of The Royal Standard in Binfield, also listing his occupation as a brickmaker, employing two men, while William Butler, a farmer and brick burner near The Roebuck, employed eight men and two boys. But the bricks for larger buildings, such as Wellington College in Crowthorne and Bear Wood near Wokingham, were excavated and manufactured on site.

As mechanisation was incorporated into the manufacturing process, mass production of bricks at reasonable cost became possible, leading to their increased usage in buildings. This, coupled with the arrival of the railway at Bracknell at the same time, allowed an explosion of brick production in the area as plentiful supplies of coal to fire the kilns could be brought in. Many young men came to the town for dependable work, often with families, causing the population to grow by 50 per cent in just twenty-five years. Between 1852 and 1964, there were more than twenty-five different brickworks in operation at one time or another, and the yard hooters sounding across the area would become a familiar sound. Most bricks in the area were of London clay, but at Swinley (and a couple of small yards in Crowthorne), a mixture of clay and marl was used to make rubber bricks.

Thomas Lawrence, who owned the department store in the High Street, came to dominate the brickmaking trade as well. When Loughlin Webb, a brick manufacturer living on Priestwood Common, died in 1864, Lawrence bought the enterprise. By 1898, he was running brickworks at Swinley, Easthampstead, Warfield and Wick Hill, as well as establishments at Pinewood and Wokingham.

By 1893, 'Thomas Lawrence bricks had been used in 300 towns in England, besides several in Ireland and many foreign towns.'[5] At its peak, his yards were producing 12 million bricks per annum,[6] and in addition, his Warfield yard was turning out 10 million tiles per year. Not content with sending bricks to London, he then entered into a contract to fill the returning trucks with waste material, which was then buried in the worked-out brick pits, thus earning money on both the outward and return journeys. After his death in 1901, the brick side of the business was run by his son Herbert until shortly before his own death in 1950.

More than 3 million Thomas Lawrence bricks were used in the construction of Royal Holloway College at Egham, with a similar number in Holloway Sanatorium. His bricks were also used in the construction of Westminster Cathedral and Madame Tussaud's in London, as well as the London County Council Buildings on the Thames Embankment, the former Collins Barracks (now the National Museum of Ireland) in Dublin, the former Carnegie Library (now the Carnegie Heritage Centre) at Kingston-upon-Hull (it is likely other libraries commissioned by the benefactor Andrew Carnegie also used the same bricks), the former Technical School (now the Marlow Road Youth and Community Centre) at Maidenhead, Wokingham police station, the pillars for the racecourse gates as well as Lloyds and Barclays Banks in Ascot, the Brownlow Hall in Newell Green, South Hill Park, the Larges Lane Cemetery Chapel, the former post office in the High Street, and the original Royal British Legion building in Rochdale Road in Bracknell. They were also used in restoration work at 10 Downing Street, Eton and Harrow Colleges, Windsor Castle, and Hampton Court.

Bracknell railway station was handling 2 million bricks per annum by 1884, while in 1901 there were concerns about the amount of traffic (both carts and traction engines) transporting bricks to Ascot to build the new grandstand there, and its effect on London Road. But fluctuations in demand inevitably occurred, and things were particularly bad in the summer of 1905. At the end of August, the *Reading Mercury* reported: 'During the last two weeks, more than one hundred men have been turned away from the brickfields at Bracknell, and a great many others in the building trade are walking about.'

During the Second World War, brick production ceased, with the drying sheds used for storing food, timber, ammunition and spare parts for aircraft. By 1945, the *Berkshire Mercury* reported 'the brickyards are lying idle in Bracknell, Swinley and Wokingham. They formerly employed 250 men, making 10 million bricks per year.' The local brick industry never recovered after the conflict. Obsolescent methods and machinery made it impossible to compete with larger brickworks with cheaper raw materials and modern machinery. This, combined with the competition for labour by the expanding local industry of the New Town, brought an end to most of the brickmaking in the Bracknell area, although the works at Gough's Lane struggled on until the 1980s. Ralph White remembers working there very briefly:

I got a summer job there in the early '70s as a 16-year-old student. My tasks were to hose a bank of clay with water to soften it, dig out a wheelbarrow full, wheel it back to the brick making shed over rickety planks placed over a landscape of deep, rainwater-filled clay holes, spade it out into a churning machine that broke up any stones and spewed it out the other end, divide it up and spade it out to four surly brick makers on piece rates; repeat. Those buggers never once spoke to me. I think it was because I was a 'new towner' ... I stood it for just one week and felt bad at the time that I couldn't last longer than that. Hardest physical work I'd ever done.

Swinley

There is a reference to brickmaking at Blane's Farm near Ascot (now the Beaumont Forest timber merchants on Swinley Road) in 1862, with a homestead called Brickfield Cottage (the current cottage of that name dates to 1897). At its peak, there were fourteen cottages at the site, which employed about seventy moulders.

Thomas Lawrence was advertising 'first class, red building bricks, and very superior washed red rubber bricks' at his Swinley Yard (on the east side of Swinley Road) in 1873, and a year later he obtained the contract to supply the bricks for building Royal Holloway College. In 1878, a horse-powered rail track was built from the yard to Ascot West railway station (located where King's Ride crosses the railway line) in readiness for sending bricks to Egham a year later. A man with a red flag was stationed at the King's Ride crossing to signal to traffic when trucks were approaching. Platforms were added to the station in 1922 for racegoers to use during race meetings.

Drying sheds allowed work to continue in the winter, when men would walk from the Warfield works when production had ceased there. A foreman sold beer to the men, but the cost was deducted from their wages. Thomas Goodchild appeared in front of the Wokingham magistrates in 1879 for failing to fulfil his contract. The *Reading Mercury* reported on the case:

> John Butler, foreman to Mr Lawrence, said he remembered Goodchild coming to work on the Monday, and on Tuesday he put him on filling and emptying the kiln. He continued at that up till the Saturday night. The kiln held 57,000 bricks. Defendant left on Saturday, leaving a number of the bricks undrawn. They were paid 1s 3d for a thousand bricks. It was the custom to finish a job, and not to leave a kiln partially emptied ... Mr Wheeler said Mr Lawrence was in a very extensive way of business, being under a contract to supply Professor Holloway with millions of bricks for a large building and it was important to

him ... that the men he engaged should know that if they undertook a contract, they must not break it by leaving work unfinished.

Another court case was reported on 24 October 1888, involving a fracas between gamekeepers employed by the Royal estate and some of the brickyard workers. Two of the brickmakers were charged with attacking one of the Queen's men. Each side in the case called witnesses to back their side of the story – an unprovoked attack, or insults hurled at Lawrence's men to which they retaliated. Thomas Lawrence himself gave evidence, saying that the men were good workers and had never given him cause for complaint before. His evidence was crucial as the case was dismissed.

Walter Spencer was born in Chavey Down in 1894. Later in his life, he recorded his memories of the Swinley brickyard:

> I was born at Oak Cottages, North Road ... which were built by my father and his father in 1885. My father was employed there for 30 years, from 1880 to 1914, and it was a large concern, employing about 150 men.
>
> Father dug clay in winter and loaded it into small trucks which ran on a light railway to the moulding sheds. He was up to his knees in mud and received five old pence a cubic yard for this, the 'clay bay' being carefully measured out each day by the foreman, William Read, who also owned a 'beer-off' near the yard and lived there.
>
> In the summer father worked a 'PRESS', a machine for stamping and trimming bricks as they came from the 'moulder' (or brick maker). This press was mounted on four wheels and pushed along a stack of bricks about 100 yards long, 5 feet 6 inches high and 4 feet broad, all neatly stacked in rows, direct from the Moulder. Each brick was taken separately from the stack, placed in the press and stamped 'T L B', then replaced on the stack and left to dry out.
>
> This operation was done by pulling a lever causing a movement down when the brick went in and a return as it came out. For this operation father received 3 shillings and 3 pence per 1,000 bricks. These rows of bricks would stand and be 'weathered' for about a week, for them to be hard enough to go into the kiln to be 'fired'. In wet weather they would need 'covering' and 'boards' 6 feet long and 5 feet 6 inches high were used for the sides, and 'caps' consisting of straw, battened together by two strips of wood 6 feet 9 inches long and three feet wide placed on top of the row.
>
> In summer, father worked from 6am to 6pm except Saturday (pay day) when he finished at 1pm. Should it rain, ether Saturday afternoon or Sunday, he would have to go two miles to 'cover-up' his row of bricks. He received no extra pay for this, but if he neglected to do it was stopped three pence a thousand on his pressing.

After bricks had been 'kilned,' they were loaded on to railway trucks on a single track railway which ran from the yard to Ascot West Station, on the London to Reading branch a mile away. This line was on a gradient from the brickyard to the main line, so that three trucks loaded with bricks ran with no form of locomotion but three strong shire horses were driven down to Ascot West to pull three trucks back to the yard, loaded with coal for the kilns, and these trucks were unloaded and filled again with bricks the following day.

A brick maker received one penny a brick, and a brick maker (who shall be nameless) who rode a three wheeled tri-cycle to work, took two bricks home every day in his saddle bag of the tri-cycle, total twelve bricks a week, and laid them on Saturday afternoons. He built his own bungalow at Bullbrook by the time he retired from Swinley Brickyard!

I got a great deal of information by strolling around when I took father's midday meal, and was known personally to many of the employees. After my father loaded the clay on to small flat-bottomed trucks which ran to the 'Clay bay' on light metal tracks, it was pulled on an endless chain, suspended by a large hook, and gradually lifted to about 10ft from the ground. It moved along at about four miles an hour, and by a succession of wheels, fixed horizontally on a wooden structure, reached a moulder's mill, where a cylindrical iron tank, about six feet wide and ten feet deep was fixed. Inside the tank were two steel propeller blades which revolved, and as the clay contained in the truck arrived at this 'Pudlock Hole,' a man, known as a 'Hooker' who stood on a platform with a hooked pole, liberated the truck end and disgorged the clay into the Pudlock. It was made more soluble by the steel blade as it descended and finally dropped on to the 'Moulders table' which was circular. The whole of the Mill was roofed in with sheets of corrugated iron and there were usually four moulders in a Mill.

The moulder handled the clay with two boards, about one foot long and six inches wide, and placed it into a wooden mould, with a detachable board covering the bottom. He sliced the spare clay off the top with a wire cutter and passed the brick contained in the wood mould, on to the 'stacker' who loaded it on to a flat barrow and conveyed it to a 'stack' when the barrow was full. This stack started from the Mill and ran for about 100 yards down to the kiln. This was also running parallel with other stacks and each Mill had four stacks where the bricks were 'pressed' and 'weathered' until they were hard enough to be handled by the 'Kilner'.

Another brick yard was opened about half a mile from the old yard, on discovering that more 'Clay Bays' had been found with clay of a much more refined quality. The yard was called 'Klondyke' and the celebrated TLB RUBBER was produced here. These were slightly larger bricks and were more smoothed faced. They were very durable and consequently dearer in price. TLB bricks were famed in their day, and the 'Rubbers', a slightly bigger and better-quality brick, were used to build the forts outside Portsmouth Harbour, which have stood the test of time, weather, and salt water.

TLB actually stands for Thomas Lawrence Bracknell. He also owned another brickyard at Wokingham, where the 'Star' brick was produced. This was a much cheaper brick because of the quality of the clay, and did not sell very well.

The process of making rubber bricks was described in Michael Dumbleton's booklet, published in 1978:

> Special clay from Swinley was mixed with water in the wash mill, a cylindrical tank with radial rotating rakes. The slurry, free from any stones, then flowed down a wooden sluice, through screens to remove roots and other debris, and into settling ponds called 'rubber bays'. After some months the clay was dry enough for use. The rubber bricks were made like ordinary bricks, in steel-lined 9, 12, or 14 inch moulds, but had no frogs and were stamped T.L.B. with a hand stamp. After firing the bricks, gauge work, cut with a mechanical slit wheel, was made to order using card templates, and mouldings were rubbed using a wooden gauge box.[7]

It was probably the opening of this new yard that prompted Sir George Russell, MP for the Wokingham constituency (which also included Bracknell), to raise the issue of the Swinley works in Parliament on 2 June 1896:

> I beg to ask the First Lord of the Treasury, whether the attention of the Commissioners of Her Majesty's Woods and Forests has been called to the recent serious disfigurement of Swinley Woods in Windsor Forest, owing to the destruction of timber which is taking place in consequence of the fumes arising from the kilns of a local brickmaker; whether these kilns have been erected, and added to from time to time, under the sanction of the Department; whether the conversion of a large portion of this ancient Royal demesne to commercial uses is in accordance with the terms of the Act for the inclosure of Windsor Forest; whether he is aware that the destruction of the subsoil in the process of digging clay involves an interference with one of the principal roads in the district, namely, the highway leading from Ascot Heath to Bagshot Park; and whether the Commissioners propose to take any action in the matter?

The response, from the Chancellor of the Exchequer, was able to reassure him:

> The Commissioner of Woods, from a recent personal inspection, is satisfied that no material injury is being caused to the Crown woods at Swinley by the brick works, which are in other ways beneficial to the land revenues. They were

established on Crown land, let for the purpose about 35 years ago. Further land has since been let, the last increase in area being made in 1880; but about 18 months ago the area let was varied by the surrender of part not suitable for brick-making purposes and the letting of other land of equal area instead. The land now let for brickmaking was not acquired by the Crown under the Windsor Forest Enclosure Act (which, however, does not prevent lands enclosed thereunder being used for commercial purposes), but was purchased by the Commissioners of Woods. The interference with the highway consists of its being used by carts, barrows, etc., conveying clay to the works. The highway is not under the charge of the Commissioner of Woods, who considers further action on his part to be unnecessary.[8]

The 'interference' was 'a tramway ... at Tower Hill', authorised by ERDC earlier in the year, which connected to a clay pit on the opposite side of the road.

Brickyard worker Bill Mott met with an accident in April 1902, as reported in the *Reading Mercury*:

The man was riding on a railway truck, loaded with bricks, down the incline into Ascot West siding, when, in attempting to get off, he slipped and fell under the truck, the wheels of which passed over his legs. The unfortunate man was at once removed to the Cottage Hospital, where Dr Fielden of Bracknell found it necessary to amputate one leg and the other foot.

At its height, the Swinley works operated eight kilns, but this had reduced to two by 1939, when brick production stopped because of the war. It never resumed after 1945, and the lease on the site ran out six years later:

Each kiln had walls up to one metre thick and was fired from the bottom by coal. The process was to fill each kiln with 120,000 bricks, then bake for three days on a low fire followed by seven days on full fire ... The work was thirsty and back-breaking for the workers, some of whom lived on the site and were partly 'paid' with beer. Even the transporting of the coal to the works and the finished bricks to the Ascot West station was arduous. Ten tons of coal was loaded on a truck and pulled by horse on a single railway line that went up a slope from the station to the site. The transportation of the finished bricks was easier if not more hazardous. The loaded truck was allowed to freewheel down the slope controlled by one man using a hand brake.[9]

Twelve hundred RAF personnel were stationed in Ascot during the First World War. The main stores were situated on the west side of King's Ride, near Ascot West station, on a site that had previously been part of one of the Swinley brickworks. In 1918, the military authorities wanted to close Swinley Road as it went past the Aircraft Depot, but ERDC refused to give them permission. Brickmaking at the site resumed after the conflict had ended and continued until the Second World War. Ascot West station continued to be used during the conflict, with a prisoner-of-war camp established nearby.

London Road

There was a brickworks on the north side of the London Road in 1822, opposite the house at Martin's Heron, but gone by 1870 (the area is now occupied by Hawkins Close). The remains of a building in the grounds of Lily Hill Park, the original Royal Foresters pub, may have been built with bricks from this site.[10]

Gough's Lane

There were already extensive brickworks in use here by 1817, south of Brick-Kiln Lane. A new clay pit was opened to the north of the lane soon after 1900.

The brickworks in Gough's Lane were already established by 1817. This photograph shows them in about 1972. One of the flooded clay pits is now a newt reserve. (Photo courtesy of Stewart Willis)

In August 1863, '200,000 extra stock of good building bricks, in convenient lots and other effects' were being sold by auction at the site. By June 1865, 'a quantity of valuable prepared earth or clay for burning bricks, tiles, squares, pipes, etc. also for burning stock bricks, now lying in the Warfield brick yard, belonging to the estate of the late Mr L. Webb' was available. Thomas Lawrence bought the enterprise and was advertising for brickmakers just two weeks later. The new owner was soon advertising 'superior machine-made plain house tiles', adding that he 'could deliver by his own cart'. By the end of 1881, garden pottery, such as vases, was also being sold. Lawrence was not averse to using the law – when petty thefts from occurred the site, he took the perpetrator to court.

In May 1900, 15-year-old Alfred Watts slipped and fell onto the clay machine at the site. His arm was badly crushed, and the lad was taken home (to Broad Lane) where Drs Bradford and Fielden 'were soon in attendance, and decided to amputate his arm above the elbow'. Despite the physical handicap, his family needed him to earn money, and by 1911 he was working as a golf caddie at one of the local golf clubs. His neighbour, John Shute, suffered a similar fate early the following year.

Thomas Lawrence died in 1901 and one of his sons took over the running. By 1906 he was selling the:

> Trade Plant, Machinery, Fixtures, Utensils, Rolling Stock, Sheds, Kilns, Two old cottages, Barn, and Effects. The whole of the Trade Plant, Machinery, Sheds, Kilns, and Effects, comprising a 30 h.p. portable engine by Clayton and Shuttleworth, a 30 h.p. horizontal engine by Tasker and Co., two 15 h.p. Cornish boilers by Tasker and Co. [a horizontal boiler], an iron saw bench, a 8½ inch grindstone, a Sturtevant American blower [for removing fine dust], a steam pump, two large tanks, pug mills [machines for mixing and working clay], crushing rolls, clay grinding pan with two 18 inch runners, power windlass, tile machines, quantity of shafting, plummer blocks [supports for a rotating shaft], couplings, driving wheels, socket piping, standing weighing machine, crowding, navvy and off bearing barrows, brick trays, shelving, brick tables, tip waggons, four brick carts, two spring vans, pony cart, straw and wood caps, double and single back boards, a quantity of brick moulds and models, carpenters' benches, smith's bellows, anvils, tools, old iron, etc., a quantity of plain and ornamental ridge tiles, best handmade building and moulding bricks, etc., etc. Office desks and furniture, iron safe, the erections of 9 kilns, large drying sheds, 2 old cottages, barn, engine sheds and other buildings, quantity of hack bricks and drain pipes [bricks still drying], brick rubble, etc.[11]

Eric Cotterell's father was working here at this time:

making cricks and 'squares' by hand. The 'squares' were special bricks used in baking ovens. They were a foot square and three inches thick. My father was the only man in the yard who could make them – you had to be strong to do it. He had to pick up a hundredweight of clay [just over fifty kilos] and throw it into the mould ... He was paid 12/6d for 100 'squares' and the same for 1000 bricks ... Tiles were also made at the yard. They were machine-made in the Twenties and early Thirties. The engine rolled out a continuous layer of clay on a wooden platform and wires came down to cut out the tiles ... The pug-boys collected the clay from where it was dug out and brought it to the benches. They prepared the clay for brickmaking by mixing it with water ... The brickmakers would then take the prepared clay or pugs and throw it into the moulds. The top was smoothed with a wire cutter and the mould turned over on to a piece of wood. The bricks were laid on a flat wheelbarrow or 'hack' to dry out. They were laid or 'skintled' on their sides in a herring-bone pattern with gaps between, and were stacked in layers three feet high. They were left to dry in the open before firing.

The clay was dug from an enormous pit, thirty or forty feet deep, between Gough's Lane and Priory Lane. The pit was stepped in a series of terraces eight feet wide. The clay was dug by hand with a narrow spade and small horse-drawn trolleys brought it up from the bottom ... There were three or four beehive kilns at the brickyard. The kilns were circular, with an eight or nine foot wall, and had a domed roof. There were fire holes every few feet around the base of the kiln and there was a vent in the roof. The kilns were bricked-up when they were firing and a stoker manned them throughout the night. Men would work extra hours in the summer months to make up for 'lost' time in the winter when frosty weather prevented bricks from being made.[12]

Edie Muir[13] (born 1926) relates how two of her brothers worked here. 'They used to come home completely red with brick dust. To save my mother from washing their shirts, they both purchased a sixpenny shirt each Friday evening, which they destroyed after a week's hard work in the brick kilns.'

The tile-making process from around 1930 was described by someone working in Winkfield Row: 'The clay was extruded in a continuous strip by a machine, cut into individual tiles with wires, dried in stackable coved [sic] racks that gave the required curve, and fired on their sides in handfuls of five in niches formed between the green bricks in the kiln.'[14]

Things were not running smoothly in 1913, according to a report in the *Reading Mercury*: 'I took to drink to drown my sorrows,' was the explanation of Samuel Streak, a brick burner at Lawrence's brick kiln, Bracknell, at his appearance in Wokingham Magistrates' Court, having cut his throat with a razor. He had 'committed the offence' in the wash house behind his home in Gough's Lane at 6 a.m.

one morning. 'The kiln had been going wrong for some time, and I took to drink to drown my troubles.' The prisoner was sent for trial at the next Quarter Sessions. Streak lived in one of Kiln Cottages, a row of four dwellings built for his workers by Thomas Lawrence in 1890.

In 1920, 16-year-old Edward Lyford of Arborfield claimed compensation at Reading County Court for an accident that took place a few months earlier:

> From the evidence, it appeared that Lyford, a press boy on the brick-making machine, had his left hand seriously injured through putting it underneath a plate to remove a deposit of sand. He had been told by the foreman to use a bar for the purpose, but failed to do so. Judgment was reserved, but the newspaper contains no subsequent report on the decision made.[15]

Four scotch kilns were replaced by three circular tile kilns in 1920s, which in turn were replaced by a rectangular down-draught kiln in about 1950.

Gough's Lane Brick Works, further to the east, ran from 1926 to 1939, and was acquired by Lawrence's in about 1948. This had a Hoffman kiln, three scotch kilns and two beehive kilns. Bricks for bread ovens were produced in one corner of the site.

A fire at a shed on the premises in 1966 was quickly extinguished without much damage; this was one of several suspected arson attacks over several months in Bracknell. A 1967 plan to close the brickworks and build housing on the site was refused, went to appeal, and was turned down.

The kilns were converted to oil in 1970, which turned out to be a bad decision when the oil crisis hit in 1973, and they became uneconomic. The brickworks finally closed in 1985, and the last of the buildings were pulled down in the 1990s to make way for the housing development Lawrence Hill. A chimney, a memorial to the brickworks, was put in place in Goddard Way near the original site.

Folders Lane

An auction took place at The Red Lion in 1813 for 'a parcel of leasehold ground, called Wicks, containing two acres and a half, or thereabouts, of excellent brick earth, upon which are erected two neat and convenient cottages, brick and lime-kilns, brick and tile drying-houses, and other buildings, pleasantly and advantageously situate, at Wickhill, in the parish of Warfield, near Bracknell' to be sold.

There were brickworks on either side of Folders Lane, established after 1870. The large pond at Lakeside, and Jeans's Pond on the Braybrooke Recreation Ground (named after the local landowner), are the result of large-scale clay extractions. Lutterworth Close stands on the site of a further pit that was filled in.

Bracknell Pottery Brick and Tile Company were operating from here by 1881, with the newspapers in Berkshire and Surrey advertising 'Manufacturers of red bricks, plain, moulded, ornamental, roofing, and paving tiles. Drain pipes and chimney pots, etc.' The company was awarded silver medals at four Architectural and Building Trades Exhibitions in London in the 1880s (they finally achieved gold in 1889, albeit under a new owner). Despite these successes, the owner, William Fowle, was facing financial troubles. The *Reading Mercury* reported:

> The public examination of William Fowle, a bankrupt of Sunningdale, Bracknell, and Nine Elms, trading as the Bracknell Pottery Brick and Tile Company was held at the Court of Bankruptcy on 17th April 1885 ... Mr Moses Nash, of Bracknell, stated that shortly before the date of the receiving order, the bankrupt had executed a bill of sale for about £6000, which was thought to be invalid.

Fowle admitted 'he had engaged in betting transactions ... and lost between £2000 and £3000 altogether, of which £700 or £800 had been lost in 1884'. By July, his residence in Hampshire was being offered for sale by auction, and also the brickworks business, along with The Cedars ('a superior residence erected on the estate') and eleven other buildings. In March the following year, the *Hampshire Advertiser* recorded:

> Bankruptcy – Fowle, William (trading as the Bracknell Pottery Brick and Tile Company), formerly of Clatford Lodge, Andover, then the Steam Brewery, Bracknell, Berkshire, trading as Vincent and Co., now of Sunningdale and Bracknell, Berkshire, and Bourne Valley Wharf, Nine Elms, Vauxhall, formerly farmer and brick and tile manufacturer, then brewer, now brick and tile manufacturer – discharge suspended for twelve months.

The local auctioneer, F. W. Hunton, held the bankruptcy sale on the brickmaking business, which took place on 5 and 6 October 1886, where the following was available:

> a large quantity of machine, hand-made and moulded bricks of various descriptions and patterns, paving bricks and squares, fire bricks; the tiles comprise plain and ornamental roofing, double Roman, ridge (plain and ornamental), hip, valley, angle and mural tiles, agricultural pipes, glazed junction socket pipes, wheeling plates and planks, box, bearing-off and crowding barrows,

brick tables, plain tile trays, pipe and square shelving, brick boards; the valuable brick and tile moulds, potter's wheels, back caps, hurdles, canvas, elm boarding, 2 capital spring vans, 12 brick carts, Page's No 3 pipe machine with dyes, a Page's No 4 pipe machine with dyes, Hellier's double Roman tile machine, Hellier's patent brick-making machine with moulds, tile dressing machines, 2 Murray's brick presses, a Murray's brick and tile shaping machine, a steam chaff-cutting machine Tasker with Buggay apparatus, 3 sets of Clayton's crushing rollers, and numerous other items; 7 young active cart horses, sets of harness, blacksmith's tools, and office furniture.

The enterprise was taken over by a Mr Nichols, and the same advertising continued to appear in the local press.

Another less welcome article appeared in the same paper on 10 January 1891:

Samuel Springfield Kay, clerk to the Bracknell Pottery Brick and Tile Company, pleaded guilty to embezzling, on April 10th 1890, £3; on June 19th 1890, 12s 6d; and on October 13th 1890, £1 12s, the money of his employers [in total, almost £500 in today's money]. He also admitted a previous felony at Rochester Sessions in 1888. The prisoner was sentenced to four months' hard labour.

The sentence was served in Reading gaol.

The site was offered for sale again in 1898, and the National Telephone Company applied to ERDC to erect poles along Shepherd's Lane to it, but a map published in 1900 labels the site as 'disused'.

Bullbrook

The Bullbrook brickworks were in operation by 1891, when Thomas Crocker is listed as a farmer and brickmaker in the census, although there is a reference to Kiln Meadow at Bullbrook Farm as early as 1825. The brickworks extended from London Road westwards to Gipsy Lane; the site is now occupied by Eastern Road. The site is marked as 'disused' on the Ordnance Survey map of 1909, although Crocker's son continued to make bricks until 1915. Charles R. Collins Ltd were making tiles in the 1920s, with a new chimney and kiln in operation in the early 1930s, and continued until about 1960.

James Apsey, a labourer at the brickyard, was charged in 1907 with 'sleeping in an outhouse at Bracknell the previous day, not having any visible means of subsistence'. He was discharged on promising to go into the workhouse. He later found lodgings in New Road, working as a bricklayer after the brickworks closed.

The Bullbrook brickworks, pictured in 1931. Brickmaking on this site ran from 1891 to 1909, before reopening for the manufacture of tiles after the First World War. The circular 'tent' and surrounding buildings belong to Bullbrook Farm. The area is now occupied by Eastern Road. (Photo courtesy of Stewart Willis)

Mount Pleasant

A brick kiln existed for a few years at Mount Pleasant. In 1871, Edward Butler was a beer seller and brick burner, living at the Brickmaker's Arms, with his sons all in the same trade. The houses there were known as Kiln Cottages for many years. One of the residents, a bricklayer named Henry Ewins, attempted to hang himself in 1887. He had previously held a licence to sell beer in premises near Cooper's Hill, but the business had failed. The *Berkshire Mercury* reported: 'He sent a fellow workman for some beer, and in the meantime attempted to hang himself from a beam in a shed; but fortunately the other man returned in time to cut him down before he was dead.'

Skimped Hill Lane

We have already mentioned the small brick pit on the south side of Skimped Hill, which was back in use with kilns by 1870, but had disappeared by 1898. References to a pond 'at the bottom of the High Street' probably refer to the flooded workings that remained. At the west end, on the north side of the road, bricks were being made before 1870. This became the Thomas Lawrence Easthampstead Brick Works when it came up for auction in 1880. It had grown to cover almost the entire area bounded by Skimped Hill Lane, Wokingham Road and Easthampstead Road by 1898, with a siding connecting it to the railway.

There was an unfortunate accident at the site in July 1883. Twenty-seven-year-old Robert Palmer, 'a steady, hard-working man', went to a water hole in the brickyard to fill a can, but was found drowned there an hour later. An inquest was held in the Skimped Hill cottage of Joseph Smith, the yard foreman. Palmer was described as 'very steady ... a saving young man ... who always seemed very cheerful, and was engaged to be married'. Although in good health, he had recently complained of spells of giddiness, and it was concluded that one of these had caused him to fall into the water and drown.

The weather was extremely hot in September 1898, with the *Reading Mercury* reporting:

> During the past week the heat has been very trying, and many cases of collapse have been reported. Thursday's heat appears to have been the most trying, no less than 126 degrees being registered in the sun and 80 in the shade ... the majority of the men at the Easthampstead brickworks were compelled to leave at half time. Several cases of illness are described by the doctors as due to the weather.

Almost twenty years earlier, 15-year-old George Wilson came into the yard with a cart of brickbats (half bricks). An eyewitness related:

> The horse stopped and we tried to get him on. The deceased had hold of the horse's head, and I and another man were pushing. The horse went on, the deceased fell over some wood; before we could get to him, the wheel of the cart went over him ... he appeared to be killed instantly.[16]

In 1901, the Highways Committee of Easthampstead Rural District Council called attention to damage done to Broad Lane by carts drawing soil from a field opposite the Blue Lion to be taken to the Easthampstead brickfields. Although the council were prepared to make good the damage, the cost would be recovered from the offending firm if at all possible (the cost to the council was £68, over £5,800 in today's money). There was also 'increased traffic' on Bull Lane. Other roads in the area, especially Skimped Hill Lane, suffered from time to time from cartloads of bricks being transported over them. There were some delicate negotiations between ERDC and Arthur Lawrence, who had inherited his father's brickworks but was also a councillor.

All trace of the workings and the siding had disappeared by 1909, but Joseph Crisp made bricks here between 1928 and 1935.

Downmill

The Downmill Brick Works started up just before the turn of the century, commemorated by Kiln Lane, off Western Road. It too had its own siding off the railway line, operational in 1899 and in use until 1945. In July 1899:

> at the latest ERDC meeting, a report was made by the Clerk that the new Brick Company, who have purchased land, near the sewage farm, had placed a dam across the stream above the farm and were using the water for business purposes; consequently the bed of the stream, into which the effluent drained, was dry. He had also received a complaint from the lessee of Brook House, complaining the stream had been stopped. It was unanimously resolved that immediate notice be given the Company to remove the dam.[17]

The Downmill brickworks were situated on the north side of Wokingham Road, almost opposite The Bridge pub. This photo shows how clay was cut to leave large banks. A collapse at this site killed a worker in 1904.

In 1904, an inquest was held at the Bridge House into the death of Frederick James Fowler, 'who was accidentally killed through some soil falling upon him when working in a clay pit'. He had worked at the Downmill Brick Company for about four years. Three days earlier, a witness recalled:

> A man called out to me, and I turned round and saw the deceased running away from the bank, but some of the soil fell and knocked him down. It covered his body, and there was a little on his head ... We work in gangs of five, it is piecework. We are paid so much per 1000 bricks. I have worked in the same kiln for two and a half years, and have not known of an accident before. Deceased was picking at the bottom of the pit. It is very rare that we undermine. The bank was fairish straight and partly dry. I heard no warning. The bank was about seventeen or eighteen feet high.[18]

Another witness told how the fall had come from the top, not from further down as was usually the case, and there had been no warning signs. In the four years he had worked at the site, there had been a few slips, but no accidents. The foreman admitted he was not monitoring the men at the time of the accident, but had issued a general warning to them an hour or so earlier. A verdict of accidental death was recorded.

Less than three months later, William Webber died in similar circumstances. James Garwell, a director of the firm, was present and saw the incident:

> Deceased was engaged in getting down a fall of clay, and was undercutting it at the bottom. Some clay fell and struck him, throwing him on to the ground. Deceased fell head foremost. Not more than a barrowful of clay fell ... Since the last accident, all the precautions which were advised by the Home Office Inspector through the jury had been taken.[19]

The men were working on a bench 4ft off the bottom of the trench, with a vertical face of clay above them. Although the injuries did not appear too bad at first, Webber had fractured his skull in the fall, and died of sepsis.

In the early hours of Thursday morning in late November 1912, Bracknell was aroused by the continued sounding of a 'hooter', which proved to be at the Downmill Brickworks. One of the drying sheds was on fire and the call 'soon brought plenty of help and the fire was got under in a short space of time'.

The weather caused problems in the last week of 1914:

> In common with other parts of Berkshire, the low-lying parts of Bracknell and district were flooded out on Monday and Tuesday ... Water penetrated indoors at some of the houses in Wokingham Road. At the Downmill Company's yard,

the water swamped the fires in the kilns and spoilt a number of bricks, causing inconvenience to a firm busy with Army orders.[20]

The closure of the brickworks was announced in June 1915, but it was taken over by the Maidenhead Brick and Tile Company in 1920. A new tradition started whereby a flag was flown over the site when production topped 100,000 bricks in a week. Another accident occurred in 1925, resulting in a hospital visit for Edward Wharton where his hand was amputated.

A railway siding, just to the west of the current Twin Bridges, had been added by 1934. The site ceased operations in about 1950.

Amen Corner, Binfield

Two sites operated at Amen Corner, eventually trading under the name of The Binfield Brick and Tile Company. Binfield No. 1 was beside the railway line, east of Beehive Road and adjacent to the old Amen Corner railway crossing (this disappeared when Berkshire Way was built in the 1980s), while Binfield No. 2 was further north where the ice rink and ski slope were located.

There were two sites at Amen Corner, Binfield. This photo shows the one beside the railway line, started in the 1890s. Note the beehive kilns at the bottom of the picture, also the raised trackway connecting to the second site. (Photo courtesy of Albert Brant)

The first reference to Binfield No. 2, known as the Beehive Brickyard, was in 12 October 1864 when 'a sale by auction in the brick fields near Bee Hive Inn, Binfield, in lots varying from 5,000 to 10,000 each, about 200,000 superior Kiln Burnt red building bricks; also a quantity of splay, plinth, rubbing, and cutting bricks, club and paving bricks, plain and ornamental roofing tiles, scaffolding, and other effects' was advertised. George Fowler was offering 'a quantity of superior, red, kiln-burnt building bricks for sale' in 1867. Five children had gone to the yard one Friday afternoon the previous year 'to fish in a pond'. Five-year-old Arthur Charles Hibbins fell in and drowned.

The brickworks were bought by Robert Lawrence, the elder brother of Thomas Lawrence, who owned it until 1879 when he sold it due to ill health. The sale particulars noted: 'Although arrangements had been made to add sidings into the yard from the railway, these had not been implemented.' The siding was built two years later, not just for the brickworks, but also for public use (it closed in 1965); earlier requests for a siding in 1872 and 1877 had both been refused. Also refused was a goods shed, requested in 1882. George Hayden is listed as a brick manufacturer of Mutton Hill (close to the old Shoulder of Mutton pub, the site of which is now occupied by the Travelodge) in the 1891 census, having bought it three years earlier. He died in 1895, so the works were sold again: 'the property consists of 24 acres of land, containing good brick earth, ample water supply, railway siding (L & SWR), five kilns, sheds, etc. in good order and going condition'. An aerial cable was later added to move clay between the pits and kilns.

Workers at the brickyards were a mix of local men and others who moved to the area for work. George Long, a deaf brickyard worker and native of Binfield, appeared fairly frequently in front of the magistrates in the 1890s for being drunk. After the death of his parents, he appeared to be of no fixed abode, and was occasionally charged with sleeping in a shed in Bull Lane, or an outhouse belonging to corn merchants Drake and Mount in Station Road.

A fatality occurred in September 1896 when Amos Prouton, the foreman, was killed. His brother, John, gave evidence. Amos's job was to remove dry tiles from trays and put them into stacks. During this, the stack of tiles overbalanced and fell on him, burying him. Two witnesses saw the incident, while the owner of the yard said he had never known a similar accident before. A verdict of accidental death was returned.

Wokingham Fire Brigade was summoned at the end of January in 1897 when a fire was discovered on the premises one Sunday morning. 'The Brigade quickly assembled and were on the point of starting, when a second messenger arrived, informing that the fire which was of a slight nature, had been subdued.'[21]

Binfield No. 1 was in existence by 1898. An accident in April of that year was reported in the *Berkshire Mercury*:

Whilst Charles Horn, of Rose Street, Wokingham, was attending to a steam saw bench at the Binfield Brick and Tile Company's Works at Binfield ... a part of the gearing flew off and struck him in the face, causing a wound three inches long and rendering him unconscious. He was attended by Dr Swindale, and on recovering sufficiently, walked home. He is making satisfactory progress, although not yet able to resume his avocation.

Soon after, the site changed hands yet again, purchased by a Colonel Frederick Meyer Wardrop for £27,500 (£2.47 million in today's money). As he was resident in Vienna at that time, he had a local agent, but this was to later cause him problems. In April 1901, 'a new boiler being installed at the Binfield Brick and Tile Company fell on a man, fracturing his thigh'. In May, a fire broke out early on Saturday morning. The Wokingham Volunteer Fire Brigade received a call at 1 a.m. and were soon at the scene of the fire. 'It was found that the engine house and shed were well alight, but in a short time the flames were got under control. Considerable damage was done to the machinery, but this is covered by insurance. The cause of the fire is at present unknown.'[22] In November, the same newspaper reported 'judgment went against Wardrop over a case where £1500 had been drawn on a bank in Woking by his agent to cover the wages of men working at the brickyard'. Wardrop claimed the man was an employee so he should not be liable, but the Court decided he was a partner and ordered him to cover the cost. Presumably there were further problems, as Wardrop committed suicide four years after the acquisition, 'having suffered heavy financial losses'.

In 1904, Daniel Sharp of nearby Buckhouse Farm had taken over the day-to-day running of the firm, although Wardrop's widow still owned it. He was soon auctioning:

> a quantity of brick-maker's plant, comprising three Murray patent brick machines by Middleton, steam power pugmill, ditto clay mixer, deep well steam pump, about 200 dozen hake caps, 10,000 brickhays, brick tables, hake boards, navvy barrows, coke crusher, shafting, piping, crane, etc. Also three strong cart horses, four tip carts, harness, and numerous other items.[23]

But the company was now doing good business and were supplying bricks for new barracks at Windsor. Their products were described as having the appearance of old bricks, making them popular for those who wanted a new house not to look new! Binfield bricks were used to build the houses on the Roebuck estate in the village, the bricks being loaded into carts by hand and hauled to the building site by a steam engine, although only two trips per day were managed. Several houses in North View, Amen Corner, have ornamental brickwork, allegedly made for an order that was subsequently not paid for.

Two men were injured early in 1914, one of them seriously, when a large boiler of a traction engine holding some 700 gallons of water exploded due to a leaking tube:

> The engine was used for the purpose of hauling heavy loads of bricks from the yard. So great was the force of the explosion that the engine was hurled a considerable distance into a ditch, where it fell partly on its right side ... When the explosion occurred, Alfred Probert (23) was in the act of stoking up the furnace, and he was severely scalded over the greater part of his body, his face, arms and legs being the most seriously injured. Dr Fielden, of Bracknell, was immediately summoned and was soon in attendance, but the man's condition was so serious that ... it was considered necessary to convey him at once by motor car to the Royal Berkshire Hospital at Reading. Probert is likely to remain in hospital for some time. Albert Young, who was badly scalded on the face, was also taken to hospital, but was not detained as an in-patient.[24]

By 1920 the site was producing hand-made and machine-made roofing tiles. The Hoffman kiln was replaced by twelve beehive kilns, and an overhead cableway installed soon afterwards, connecting with No. 1 works. This had two brick-making plants, each with machines capable of producing 120,000 bricks per week. There were two Hoffman kilns, a down-draught kiln, and six beehive kilns. There may have been problems with one of the kilns in 1929, as tile rubble was being advertised early the following year, 'excellent for making up roads, paths or draining land'.

The workings beside the railway had expanded east as far as Longshot Lane by 1932, when a flooded pit formed a lake one fifth of a mile long. Remains of the railway siding were still in evidence until the early 1980s, long after the brickworks had closed.

Two more unfortunate incidents occurred during 1935. The first was a fire on 6 April:

> Damage estimated between £1000 and £2000 was caused by a fire which broke out at the works of the Binfield Brick and Tile Co Ltd ... The fire was discovered just as the men were going home and when the fire alarm was given, the hooter at the works was sounded as well. Both the Easthampstead and Bracknell and the Wokingham Fire Brigades were quickly on the spot and found they had to run some thirteen to fifteen hundred feet of hose over rough country to the clay pit from which water was pumped to the blazing tile drying sheds. Valuable machinery put in about five years ago was destroyed, together with the whole fabric of the building, which was mainly a timbered affair. The roof of the engine house caught fire, but this was put out and the steam was drawn

off the engine. A large kiln nearby was also saved. Many of the workmen, who number in all about two hundred, had been recalled by the works hooter and spent their half-holiday helping the firemen. The Bracknell Brigade spent over eight hours at the site, and four men remained at the works all night in case a fresh outbreak should occur.[25]

A few months later, Charles Clifford of Reading was killed when he was buried by a clay slippage. Although the weather had been wet previous to the accident, there were no cracks or warning signs prior to the collapse. The inquest was told there had been no similar accidents previously on the site, and a verdict of accidental death was returned.

In 1941, a verdict of 'Death by misadventure' was returned on Michael Harry William Cane, aged 10, the son of the railway crossing keeper at Amen Corner. The lad, along with another boy of similar age, had gone to a disused clay pit on the Binfield site that was partly filled with water. The boys took their clothes off and paddled in the water, before climbing onto the roof of a partly submerged hut. Cane jumped off the roof, surfaced once, but then disappeared completely. His body was later recovered by dragging in 12ft of water.

Before the Second World War, fifty to sixty men were employed by the Binfield Brick and Tile Company, producing about 200,000 bricks per week. This halved in 1963 when production was concentrated on one kiln, and ceased altogether in 1964.

The 80ft-tall chimney at the old Binfield brick and tile works at Amen Corner, which had stood for over sixty years, was demolished using explosives. The work was initially planned for January, but finally completed early one Sunday morning in April, with no trains running past the site until the topple had been done. Suggestions the site might be used for a refuse tip met with opposition from local residents, although this was later used, albeit with access from Longshot Lane. Would a petrol depot, another proposal for the site, have been any better? Five years later, the New Town Angling Club offered to rent the pit from ERDC for fishing, while Bracknell Gun Club wanted to use the area for duck shooting.

Bert Sarney remembers the disused brickworks from his childhood:

They were a group of ponds/lakes that were, I believe, gravel pits. I used to fish them as a young lad. Access to the first pond, Binnie 1, was via a path over the railway. Binnie 2 was the biggest and if you fell in you were immediately in deep water as I found out once. I also found out that swimming was difficult in a parka. There was also a Binnie 3 and 4, although 4 was very small and possibly not an official Binnie. They were called Binnies purely based on their location.[26]

Bert also recalls that Binnie 1 (beside the railway line) contained carp, pike and roach, while tench inhabited Binnie 3.

6

Before the War

A new century and a new monarch. Bracknell continued to develop, but there were gathering clouds, both socially and politically.

1901

Sydney Rowland of the Jenner Institute of Preventive Medicine submitted a report on a water sample supplied from the area on 7 January. 'The number of organisms present in the water was very high, so many liquefying forms being present that enumeration was not possible ... rendering it impossible to search for ... pollution ... It cannot be said the water ... is of a first rate supply.' The filter beds at the sewage works were still under construction, and the state of water in The Cut gave cause for concern. Three weeks later, ERDC considered a report from Messrs Charles Smith and Son of Reading that laid out the problems with the sewage farm, the lower tanks being slow to fill by gravity alone, and a suggested solution of installing a drain was adopted. By the end of the month, 'extensive additional works to meet the Conservators' requirements' were carried out at the sewage farm. 'These works it is anticipated will result in a great improvement in the character of the effluent.' Samples taken by the Thames Conservancy in December were reported to be 'satisfactory', although intermittent problems continued to plague the facility for several years.

Mr J. A. Hybert's Company appeared at the Victoria Hall in *Uncle Tom's Cabin* on two evenings in February. 'On both nights there was a crowded house. The play was well carried out by a company of English and American artistes. The negro songs and plantation glees were well sung.'[1]

ERDC decided that 'in the event of another heavy fall of snow that snow ploughs should be provided'. This had been prompted by the falls on 4 February, when 9in fell on Bracknell, and would also prove invaluable when it snowed heavily across the country later in the year in December 'with blocked roads and ... havoc for livestock. Many telegraph wires were brought down and the railways were brought to a standstill'. Meanwhile, by April many wells in the district were dry due to a lack of rain.

The Easthampstead Minstrels made their first appearance in Bracknell later the same month, raising funds for Easthampstead Cricket Club. The large audience was 'kept ... amused until a late hour', especially 'by the capital selection of music rendered by the orchestra'.

Earlier in the year, ERDC introduced a bylaw requiring the owner of land to supply 'a sufficient supply of wholesome water ... and sanitary accommodation' for anyone renting it. Frederick Hutt, the licensee at The Hind's Head, had rented a field to gypsies without providing either, and was now prosecuted. In his defence, he said that the gypsies had arrived on the land before the bylaw had been introduced, and that there was 'every convenience on the premises adjoining the field'. He was fined 5s (£20 in today's money). James Trendell of Bull Lane Farm received a similar fine for the same offence.

The annual meeting of the Bracknell Wanderers Football Club was held at the Social Club, 'the attendance of members being small'. The meeting then decided that owing to lack of support of playing members, there was no alternative than to disband and wind up the club.

Thomas Lawrence died on 14 October, having 'not been in the best of health for some years'. A lengthy obituary appeared in the newspapers, recording both his business and community achievements. The funeral took place three days later, all the shops in the town being closed as a mark of respect, with 'nearly all the inhabitants attending to pay their last tribute of respect to his memory'. He left an estate valued at just over £75,000 (about £9.3 million in today's money).

The Bracknell Brewery was also being offered for sale:

> A valuable freehold property ... with wine and spirits stores, stabling, and other usual buildings, a charming family residence, two paddocks, gardens, three cottages, and an eligible plot of building land. Situate close to Bracknell Station ... together with three fully-licensed freeholds, comprising The Station Hotel, Ascot, The George, Loddon Bridge, and The Hero of Inkerman, Bagshot, also the long leasehold premises, with off beer license, No 2 Mason Street, Reading.[2]

In response to a complaint from ERDC, BCC agreed to construct two new road drains, the existing ones 'being inefficient, and that the streets were sometimes flooded in consequence'. They also agreed to 'improving several paths in Bracknell', with ERDC and 'owners of adjacent properties' also contributing to the cost.

The Forest Hotel stood on the corner of High Street and Church Road, and opened in 1903. It was never a commercial success, and was purchased in 1914 by Dr Fielden as his home and surgery. It later had several uses, including as a Youth Hostel, before being demolished in 1958.

A sale of furniture was held over three days at Lily Hill House, the premises having been let on lease. 'Some high prices were obtained, there being keen competition for many of the lots.' Items included a Louis XV writing table plus a set of chairs in the same style, two Chippendale mirrors, a pair of Sevres vases, a French bracket clock, and 'a collection of fine old Sheffield plate'.

1902

The year began with the *Reading Mercury* speculating, 'Doubtless before long it will be found necessary to establish Cottage Hospitals in large increasing centres such as Bracknell, Wokingham, Hungerford, or in large growing villages like Hagbourne.'

Local builder John Charles Sargeant signed a leaflet circulating around Bracknell: 'For some years a need has been felt for a small hall for temperance and social work.' The hall, with a capacity 'numbering upwards of a hundred', opened in March in the Rochdale Road. There was an address from a visitor from Reading, and the Bracknell Band 'played selections of music at intervals with their usual ability'. Much of the labour had been 'voluntary and gratuitous', although appeals for funds to cover the cost of it continued into the following year. The building later housed the local branch of the St John's Ambulance.

The National Telephone Company applied for permission to erect a line of poles from Bracknell railway station to the Easthampstead Workhouse in the same month.

A smallpox epidemic broke out in London in 1901, with cases being reported across the country the following year (it is also possible that soldiers returning from the Boer War brought it back from South Africa, where it was rife). Seven cases of the disease at Sandhurst resulted in two deaths. There was also one case at Bracknell (an undertaker's man who assisted to bury one of the deceased at Sandhurst) which had ended fatally, and another at Brock Hill, Warfield (a man who attended the funeral). Schools were given instructions to refuse the admission of children who had not been vaccinated and whose parents would not have them vaccinated. A temporary isolation hospital at Whitmoor Bog was quickly set up, despite an initial refusal by the Commissioners of Woods and Forests (who administered the commercial functions of the Crown lands), jointly paid for by Windsor Rural District Council, but no further cases were reported in Bracknell. A few cases from Reading were also admitted until such time as their facilities were available. A report of the set-up was made to the Windsor authority:

> A temporary iron building had been erected for the accommodation of the nurses and servants. The tents were in good order, and in one of the marquees a heating apparatus had been arranged. A doctor had been engaged for sole attendance at the hospital, together with three nurses and a cook from Gloucester, an odd job man and a carter.[3]

Arrangements had also been made for the conveyance of food to and from the hospital, and telephonic communication established between the clerk of the rural District Council and the hospital. Water and drainage arrangements had been made. In return, Windsor agreed that Easthampstead 'be allowed to use their ambulance, provide it was properly disinfected the same day'. With the facility in place, ERDC designated chickenpox a contagious disease as well, with anyone contracting it required to go into the hospital, and diphtheria cases were also held there. By August, there were no smallpox cases at the hospital, but it was decided to keep the facility open for a few more months as the disease was still prevalent in the rest of the county. There are no more references to the Whitmoor Bog hospital being used after the end of the year; in any case, the Commissioners of Woods and Forests wanted the land back if no more cases were being treated there, but the Windsor and local council were still arguing about the costs more than two years later. It was pointed out that if Bracknell had had a cottage hospital, the outbreak could have been avoided.

The commissioners turned down a request for some land to use on a more permanent basis, although they later reversed their decision, only for ERDC to decide the site was unsuitable after all. Another possible site that was considered met with opposition from the Marquis of Downshire, being 'in proximity to his park gates, and he would only entertain any such proposal for a site on the furthest part of his boundary'. In case of future outbreaks of smallpox, ERDC decided (in October 1903) to look for 'an isolated cottage' that might be rented, possibly in conjunction with Wokingham (although this idea was later discounted), rather than go to the expense of building a permanent facility. A 1909 proposal for a new hospital, covering Easthampstead, Cookham and Windsor Rural Districts, as well as Wokingham, failed to gain support.

A large audience attended a public meeting at the Victoria Hall in April to consider how to celebrate the forthcoming Coronation of Edward VII. It was decided events would include 'giving a dinner to the aged poor', along with a tea to the schoolchildren. Originally scheduled for 26 June, the ceremony had to be postponed at very short notice after the King was taken ill and required immediate surgery. The effect of this in Bracknell was noted in the *Reading Mercury*:

> The news of the king's illness was received ... with feelings of consternation. Between one and two o'clock, vague rumours began to circulate that something had occurred to postpone the coronation ceremonies, and shortly afterwards several private messages were received to the effect that the Coronation would not take place, but the absence of any official news increased the feeling of uneasiness. It was not until the early evening papers arrived that the true state of things was known. During the evening, various alarming rumours were floating about, and it was not until Wednesday morning that the public were somewhat reassured when the papers announced that the King was progressing satisfactorily. In the absence of any official declaration, opinions varied with regard to the Coronation celebrations. The Bracknell Coronation Committee met and decided that all the arrangements should be postponed indefinitely, and the tradesmen also resolved to continue business as usual on Thursday and Friday.[4]

The uncertainty would have affected the Bracknell Brewery, which had sole rights to sell ale at the Reading Coronation Fete.

There was only a small audience at a meeting in the Victoria Hall to discuss the Education Bill going through Parliament. The Bill provided funding for religious instruction, primarily for Church of England and the Roman Catholic schools, and was opposed by many non-conformists.

William Coles of Warfield, who attended the Primitive Methodist chapel, 'proposed an attitude of "passive resistance"' in 1903, withholding some of his rates. Coles was one of four local residents who had refused to pay, including the minister at the Congregational Church. Although a similar case, already heard in West Ham, had gone to the King's Bench (but not yet been heard), the local magistrate decided to make a local decision, and ordered all four defendants to pay in full. A bicycle was seized from Coles in lieu of payment. A second batch of 'passive resisters' appeared before the bench at the next sitting, but the judgment was the same in all cases. There was some sympathy locally, with the auctioneer this time refusing to sell their items. Arguments continued via the letters page of the *Reading Mercury* for some time, and summonses for non-payment were still being reported two years later.

The Boer War had ended on 31 May, but the news of the declaration of peace was not generally known until two days later:

> when almost every inhabitant manifested his delight by displaying flags from every point of vantage. In the evening a thanksgiving service was held at Holy Trinity Church, which was very largely attended. During the evening, the Town Band paraded the streets, a large concourse of people assembling ... with displays of fireworks and other means, the people exhibited their pleasure the war had ended.[5]

'A good many London holiday children were sent down to parts of the district.'[6] The trips were organised by the Children's Country Holiday Fund to provide invalid or disadvantaged children with fresh country air for at least two weeks.[7] While the intentions were good, the organisation sometimes left something to be desired, with one case of thirteen children being accommodated in two small rooms coming to light in Bracknell. ERDC were soon on the case to prevent a repeat. After the First World War, the holidays resumed under canvas in various fields in Easthampstead.

Although Britain had a huge overseas empire, most local inhabitants would never have seen anyone from it. On Bank Holiday Monday, locals 'enjoyed a glimpse of a few of the Indian contingent now stationed at Hampton Court. Shortly after two o'clock the company, numbering about seventeen ... arrived at Bracknell Station, and were conveyed to Warfield Park ... where they were entertained in a marquee.'[8]

The rearranged Coronation took place on 9 August. By the morning, the town had been decorated with flags and bunting:

> Special services were held at midday at Holy Trinity Church and at the Congregational Church ... Afterwards at the Victoria Hall, dinner was provided for the older people, of whom a large number were present ... During the repast, music was provided outside the Hall by the Bracknell Band. After dinner, the school children assembled at the Hall, and after singing the National Anthem, marched in procession to a meadow in Clay Lane ... Here, sports, etc were carried out, and other amusements were provided for both old and young. After the company had partaken of tea, each child was presented with a commemorative

cup, and the prizes presented. The evening was devoted to dancing and other amusements, the programme concluding with an excellent display of fireworks.[9]

Later in the month, a touring theatrical group, Maggie Morton's Company, appeared at the Victoria Hall in the 'well-known play "Two Little Drummer Boys"'. Among those on stage was the 17-year-old brother of Charlie Chaplin. Earlier in the day, the employees of the Thomas Lawrence Stores were taken on their annual outing, with Ramsgate, Margate and Canterbury being the destinations this year. The firm closed their premises for the occasion.

A major fire occurred at the station early next month:

> Much consternation and considerable damage were caused by a conflagration in the goods yard at Bracknell station ... which, but for fortuitous circumstances, must have had very serious results. About 2:10pm, flames were seen to rise from the goods siding, where fifteen barrels of paraffin lamp oil were lying in store; and as the heat spread the barrels rapidly exploded, so that in less than a couple of minutes the flames shot up to a height from 50 to 70 feet, the brilliant light being overhung with a pall of dense black smoke. The oil ran in a broad shallow stream down the goods yard, flaming as it travelled, and fears were naturally entertained that the large goods shed would catch fire, but fortunately this risk was averted, partly by a breeze springing up in the opposite direction, and still more by the trend of the ground in the yard, which diverted the stream of oil to a surface drain, through which it poured blazing into a dry ditch, where it ultimately burnt itself out. Mr E. J. Taylor, the stationmaster, took prompt measures, with the help of Mr Tate [the railway clerk] and the goods staff generally, to avert possible disaster.
>
> Mr Taylor first telephoned to Ascot and Wokingham for the fire brigades [Bracknell still had no such facility itself], and then turned his attention to saving the contents of the goods warehouse, which at the time appeared in imminent danger, the invoices, books, and furniture being first removed, and afterwards directing the staff in the removal of goods from the warehouse stage, until it was found that there was no further cause for alarm ... In response to the telephonic messages, the Ascot Brigade arrived within half an hour ... and the Wokingham engine drove up shortly afterwards, but by the time of their arrival, the conflagration had exhausted itself, and there was consequently no need of their services.
>
> The damage done included the burning of the cattle pens in the goods yard, the scorching of several railway wagons, and the destruction of the fencing, and the entire burning out of Mr A. James' coal shed, a quantity of new sacks stored in which added to the fierceness of the fire. The adjoining coal office of Messrs Drake and Mount escaped with external scorching. A house between the station

yard and the Railway Inn was for a time endangered. The ground traversed by the fiery stream was like a heated oven, and surrounding trees and shrubs were scorched. Crowds of people were attracted from the village, and others came from Ascot and Wokingham.[10]

The *Berkshire Chronicle* noted that the Water Company had cut off supplies earlier that morning 'for some unexplained reason'.[11]

1903

Until now, any news from Bracknell appeared in the Reading newspapers, but January saw the launch of the *Wokingham and Bracknell Gazette and County Review*. Published from the basement of a shop in Denmark Street, Wokingham, the enterprise was a one-man business, the editor Francis Staniland also being the reporter, lead writer, typesetter, compositor and printer, as well as drumming up enough advertisers and business to pay for it. A year later the publication announced 'Mr J. W. Roe, of Surrey Cottages, London Road, Bracknell as our correspondent for the town.'

Lawrence's Stores Company was set up, offering forty thousand £1 shares; the directors included the three surviving sons of Thomas Lawrence. The prospectus noted there were:

> stores in Bracknell and Yorktown ... business has founded over 60 years, and comprises the following Departments: Drapery, Outfitting, Boots and Shoes, Grocery, Provisions, including beer, Wine, Spirits, Tobacco, etc., Builders' and

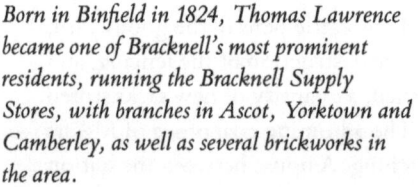

Born in Binfield in 1824, Thomas Lawrence became one of Bracknell's most prominent residents, running the Bracknell Supply Stores, with branches in Ascot, Yorktown and Camberley, as well as several brickworks in the area.

General Ironmongery, Furnishing, China, Glass, Stationery, Fancy Goods, Printing, Removals, Warehousing, etc. ... Delivery vans making regular weekly journals over a ten mile radius of Bracknell and Yorktown, including the well-known and populous districts of Bracknell, Ascot, Sunninghill, Sunningdale, Virginia Water, Windlesham, Bagshot, Camberley, Frimley, York Town, Sandhurst, Wellington College, Crowthorne, Wokingham, Binfield, Waltham, Hurst, Warfield, Holyport, and Winkfield.[12]

The stores were making a profit of £3,000 to £5,000 per annum.

The sewage farm was still not up to scratch. 'Although some alterations have been made, it has not yet been placed in a satisfactory condition, but improvement works are being carried out.'[13] Samples taken on 9 February were still not meeting the required standards. In May, it was reported there was 'a leak somewhere which was proving difficult to locate'. Two months later, it was noted that 'a ditch in Bullbrook, meant only for sewage outlet, was taking a lot of water from the brook itself (due to blockages), adding to the problems at the sewage farm'. Extra drains were also needed in the High Street, as a recent storm had led to the cellars of Lloyds Bank flooding to a depth of six inches. But by the end of the year, work was almost complete at the sewage farm, and the water samples taken by the Thames Water Inspector left him 'very satisfied'.

Overall, the year was one of the wettest on record in the area. Several residents offered to clear out the Bull brook but were waiting on Lord Ormathwaite at Warfield Hall to clear his section of the watercourse first. He refused to do so, claiming the council were partly responsible for it. A compromise was eventually reached whereby the council cleared the section, and billed him for half the cost.

ERDC ran an analysis on the water being supplied by the South West Suburban Water Company and wrote to them 'pointing out that their water needed more filtration'.

The Art Exhibition at the Victoria Hall in late October was opened by Lady Hayter of South Hill Park 'in the presence of a very large and distinguished company'. It was the first for five years 'owing to the long war in South Africa, to the death of the late Queen, and to the Coronation of the King, none of those sorts of periods being propitious for exhibitions of that sort'.[14]

1904

Led by two councillors and the town clerk of Wokingham Town Council, and involving residents both there and in Bracknell, a campaign began to press for a quicker and better service of trains between Waterloo, Bracknell, Wokingham and Reading.

In February, it was reported that 'owing to the lack of employment in the building trade and other local industries, there is considerable distress existing in Bracknell. To alleviate this suffering, particularly amongst the children, a number of gentlemen ... met together and discussed the advisability of opening a soup kitchen. This came with promises of support from local butchers.'[15] It eventually opened in 1908.

In March, Lieutenant-Colonel Mackenzie of Ramslade was appointed High Sheriff for Berkshire. He had had four previous nominations, although two came while he was fighting in the Boer War in South Africa.

Around 450 Cyclist Volunteers, representing London and suburban corps, took part in series of operations over Easter. The newspaper report, probably filed by an ex-military man, while going into great details about the men and tactics involved, skips over the actual action, only describing 'quite a number of interesting incidents'. The railway line at Bracknell became part of the exercise, with one of the 'forces' defending it on Easter Monday. After experiments by the military, bicycles were introduced to transport equipment. They were also able to cover longer distances than walking soldiers, and scouts and messengers used them during the Boer War. Later in the year, army corps manoeuvres took place over a wide area of eastern Berkshire, culminating in a 'battle' centred around Caesar's Camp. One side's artillery 'pushed up on some eminences by Bracknell ... although from the spectator's point of view, the operation was not interesting, as so little could be seen from any given point'.[16]

On 24 October, a meeting at the Victoria Hall voted to form a bowling club. Fifty pounds was quickly raised in subscriptions (£4,250 in today's money). The owner of the newly opened Forest Hotel offered to lease part of his meadow for seven years. The green was laid the following February, but cold weather inhibited germination of the grass seed, and the first planned match in May had to be cancelled, while practices took place on the tennis court at 'High Elms'.

Some local residents were at the forefront of 'modern' technology. Chemist shop owner William Sandwith jointly filed a patent for lubricants, while John Sergeant filed another for 'cycles, etc.'. Two years later, William Baker and Rupert Parker patented a modification to bakers' ovens, while Francis Sheppee of Holly Spring House patented a pumping engine in 1907.

1905

William Hunton, son of the town's auctioneer, offered an additional service via an advertisement:

> Persons desirous of emigrating to Canada should, before booking, consult me, as having lived in different parts of Manitoba ... Saskatchewan, and Alberta during

the last five years, being engaged in farming and ranching, I am in position to give every information as to employment, desirable districts for settlement, etc., Passengers booked through to any point in United States or Canada. Agents for Steamship Companies and Canadian Pacific Railway. Information and interview (by appointment) free of charge.[17]

Although the reign of Edward VII is sometimes seen as an untroubled 'Indian Summer', with an ever-growing middle class, living conditions for the urban and rural poor were often squalid. Canada offered opportunities for a new life and better prospects.[18] By 1911, adverts were also appearing in Reading for those wishing to emigrate to Australia (Fremantle, Adelaide, Melbourne, Sydney, Brisbane and Tasmania), New Zealand and Cape Town.

The position of sub-postmaster in the High Street had been vacant for some time. 'Can no-one be found in the Binfield and Wokingham Road district to undertake the duties of sub-postmaster for West End?' asked the writer of a letter to the *Reading Observer*. 'At present, and for the last month, residents in this part of the town have had to walk to the Bracknell head office in Church Road if they wished to purchase stamps, etc.,' complained a writer to the *Reading Mercury*. Thomas Mackey filled the post. A keen photographer, he offered a service selling postcards of local scenes, many of which are in the author's collection, showing the town and the surrounding area at the beginning of the twentieth century.

Representatives from Winkfield, Warfield and Easthamsptead parish councils met 'to consider the desirability of forming a civil parish of Bracknell'.

The Bracknell Athletic Sports at the cricket ground attracted around 4,000 spectators, but the organisation left a lot to be desired. The *Reading Mercury* reported:

> We missed some of the old faces from Reading among the officials, and a few of the new hands were scarcely so smart as required. The management of athletics sports is not child's play nowadays, and the mistakes made on Wednesday should not be repeated another year. The competitors in some of the cycle races were very dissatisfied with the state of things prevailing.

Despite warning notices, betting was taking place on some of the events, and 'several bookmakers came down from London to the village, and although the officials tried their best to stamp out the evil, their efforts did not meet with success. More police is probably the only remedy.'[19] The winner of the 100 yards, a soldier, was disqualified for having previously taken part in a professional event elsewhere. There were no criticisms of the following year's event.

The Art Exhibition two months later was met with critical acclaim: 'Some clever work was shown ... while the photography, carving, and needlework were excellent,' but was not so successful financially. As well as Bracknell and the surrounding villages, entries came from Twyford, Maidenhead, Windlesham, Sunningdale, Bagshot, Camberley, Earley, Blackwater, Waltham, Wargrave, Egham, Virginia Water, Chertsey, Sunnginghill, Ascot, Addlestone, Eversley, Shinfield, Barkham, Swallowfield, Arborfield, Sonning, Fifield, Shottesbrooke, Bray, Holyport, Wokingham and Reading.

A draft scheme submitted by the Board of Education for the establishment of a secondary school in connection with the Ranelagh Foundation (in Winkfield) was unanimously agreed by the local parish council in December. It was proposed to build the school near the Bracknell railway station, but within the parish of Winkfield. Berkshire Education Committee also supported the proposal, and promised an annual grant towards the facility.

1906

Voting in the 1906 general election took place nationwide over the period 12 January to 8 February. Party feelings ran high, with the windows of Bracknell's Conservative Committee rooms being smashed, along with those of the Liberals in Maidenhead. Locally, voting took place on 30 January, with the chief polling station being at the Victoria Hall, and another at the Bullbrook School:

> The scene outside the former place throughout the day was an animated one, especially towards evening, when a large crowd completely filled the roadway, every carriage and motor load of voters being loudly cheered by their respective sides as they drew up. The result of the election came as a great surprise to both parties. The Liberals had been working very hard and the district had been thoroughly canvassed. They have gained a very large number of supporters in the neighbourhood on account of the feeling against the Education Act.[20]

However, local voters bucked the national trend by not only re-electing their Conservative representative, but with an increased majority. Across the country, the Liberals won a landslide victory.

Later in the month, an enquiry was held at the Victoria Hall on the proposed provision by BCC of a new public elementary school for about 250 to 300 children at Priestwood. Winkfield opposed the move, stating they had enough school places to cover the children in their parish, while Binfield were also against the plan, preferring to build their own school. The decision to go ahead was made, however, with Binfield included later in the year. The school opened on 1 April 1908.

Children in the Priestwood area were taught in the old St Andrew's Church before a new school opened in 1908. It was already full and in need of extension just six years later. The building was demolished in 1999.

The Choral Society, after 'long winter practises', gave a performance of Handel's *Messiah* at the Victoria Hall at the beginning of May. 'The hall was well filled by an audience, amongst whom were several critics of music in general, and more especially of this well-known oratorio … the performance was the most excellent which has ever been the pleasure of a Bracknell audience to hear.'[21]

Founder of the local newspaper Francis Staniland was a staunch defender of keeping the sabbath holy, and railed against any event being held on a Sunday. No doubt his crusading was in part responsible for Harry Hambling, the Chairman of the Bracknell Hospital Sunday Parade Committee, to write to the papers:

We have reluctantly decided to give up any idea of holding a Sunday parade, at any rate until the autumn. The opposition which for years has been extended to the parade by the different religious bodies was so well organised last year and grew to such an extent that the results of the Sunday parade was a falling off of about £20 in our subscriptions to the Royal Berks Hospital, whilst the collection made in all the local chapels, etc. of the subscriptions of those who objected to the parade amounted … to about £5. Under the circumstances, my committee instruct me to give this public invitation to those conscientious objectors to organise a Saturday parade this year, and if it is a financial success we shall be perfectly willing to discontinue the Sunday collection, and allow the charity in the form of Hospital tickets to be distributed through the usual religious channels, which appears to be the wish of the opposition. Failing any attempt, however, to organise a Saturday collection, the committee will meet again in July and arrange for a Sunday parade to be held in the autumn, so that the Hospital at any rate, shall not suffer from opposition, which everywhere else but Bracknell is replaced by the hearty support of all religious bodies.[22]

The Parade eventually took place on 2 September, still a Sunday, and proved even more popular than in previous years. Thirty pounds was raised on the day, with the promise of another £20 to come (a total of £4,250 in today's money), with the money being split between the Royal Nursing Home at Ascot and the Royal Berks Hospital.

Thomas Croft, long-time doctor (and reputedly the oldest resident) in the town, died at the age of 84 after a short illness. He had spent practically all his life in Bracknell, qualifying in Edinburgh, before returning to work alongside, and eventually take over from, his father. 'He was for many years President of the Bracknell Cricket Club, and also greatly interested himself in all outdoor sports.'[23]

Another club was being formed in the town:

28th May will be a red letter day for the newly-formed Bracknell and District Rifle Club, for on the evening of that day Lord Roberts (who lived at 'Englemere' in Ascot) and Gen. Sir Charles Brownlow (of Warfield Hall) have consented to formally open the range at the Victoria Hall. The Club owes its inception largely to the efforts of Col. F. F. Mackenzie (of Ramslade House) ... Up to the present time, 63 members have been enrolled.[24]

1907

At the annual licensing meeting of the Forest Division of Berkshire in February, a sub-committee's report was considered:

We have carefully considered the question of the number of licensed houses in this division ... There are at present ... 164 licensed premises, made up as follows: 132 full licences, 13 beer houses, 10 beer off-licences, 9 wines and spirits. We are of opinion that there are many more houses licensed than are required by the population in the Division.[25]

This followed a government report in 1903 on 'the amount of drunkenness especially in country areas'. Bracknell had twenty-four licensed properties for a population of just over 4,000. The report went on to recommend the closure of some premises – for Bracknell these were The Brickmaker's Arms in Mount Pleasant, and The

Crown on the High Street. The case of The Crown was discussed a month later. It was stated as having 'five bedrooms for travellers, a three-stalls stable and two loose boxes, and a coach-house where three large or six small vehicles could be accommodated'. The High Street itself contained nine licensed premises at this time, with The Crown being 70yd from The New Inn, and 100yd from 'Mr Dearlove's licensed refreshment house ... On market day, a large number of farmers patronised the place ... The whole of the premises was in good order ... and was well conducted.' Mr Hunton, the local auctioneer, also put in a good word for it as being convenient for the market. Alfred Sweetman, the licensee, said that:

> business was increasing and the catering branch had improved greatly ... He opened at six o'clock every morning for the purpose of supplying tea and coffee to working men on their way to work ... About four commercial travellers put up at the house each week, and he supplied dinners on market days ... For the summer trade, he had laid out a tea garden ... and put forward a petition signed by 150 persons in favour of the licence being retained.

The managing director of Simonds Brewery, who owned the premises, also put in a good word for it, and the licence was renewed. The Bricklayer's Arms also continued to operate, finally closing in the 1960s.

The Twickenham Orchestra gave a concert at the Victoria Hall to raise funds for the Baptist Church. Cecil Clacey, who had worked for a time in Bracknell as a grocer's assistant, was the conductor.

Work started on a lych gate for Holy Trinity Church at the beginning of May. 'It is hoped that the work will be finished before Whitsun.'[26]

Later the same month, the Highways and Bridges Committee of BCC received a request from the Roads Improvement Association (a lobbying group created by the Cyclists' Touring Club in 1886),[27] who applied for permission to carry out 'certain experiments on the Ascot road ... between the Wells bridge [near Cheapside Road] and Bracknell, with tar-spreading machines with a view to the prevention of dust.' As the new road surface would involve extra expense, the committee agreed, provided the association paid £25 towards the cost. The *Windsor and Eton Express* carried an article about the test in its 1 June issue. The surfacing was part of a competition to find the best tar-spreading machine, and the best preparation of tar for road purposes. Tests were carried out at Twickenham and Staines, as well as Bracknell, and eight manufacturers entered their machines for a prize of 100 guineas (almost £9,000) and a gold cup, with a similar prize on offer for the nine brands of tar.

By July, the work on Ranelagh School was 'far on towards completion', while Priestwood School was also 'well on the way to completion by the end of the year'. Children in Priestwood were taught in the old St Andrew's Church prior to the school opening. But by 1914, the new school was proving to be too small, with insufficient room to house the juniors, and plans were drawn up to expand it.

A report on the Bracknell Athletics Sports in the *Windsor and Eton Observer* in 1907 observed that the ground was not flat, and this led to some cyclists coming off their machines during the racing (including all but the winner in the 2-mile race). 'A pleasant feature and due, no doubt, to the stringent measures of the new Act [the Street Betting Act of 1906 which made illegal off-course betting in public places], was the almost entire absence of betting.' A new innovation this year was a 2-mile steeplechase 'in which the competitors, after completing a circuit of the track, passed out into the natural country where a hilly course of about a mile had been flagged. This race was a pleasing variant and proved a decided success,' with the winner travelling from Kent to take part.

Military manoeuvres were again taking place in mid-September. 'A large body of troops passed through Bracknell at about 8 o'clock on Sunday morning on their way from Easthampstead Park (where they had camped) towards Maidenhead, a large number of inhabitants turning out to see them.'[28]

The Art Exhibition in October, now renamed the East Berks Art Exhibition, was opened by Princess Christian of Schleswig-Holstein (a daughter of Queen Victoria). However, 'a severe cold having robbed her of her voice, the formality was undertaken at her request by Lord Arthur Hill, M.P. (son of Lord Downshire, and Chairman of the organising committee). The Princess arrived 45 minutes late, due to a burst tyre on the car bringing her from her home in Cumberland Lodge.'[29]

1908

Old Bracknell Wanderers were cautioned as to the future conduct of their spectators after a referee's report, but the trouble continued and their ground was closed for the first two weeks of the following year.

A new Boys' Club Room was first used in March, when Colonel Browell (from Guildford) gave a lantern lecture on Church History. The magic lantern projected images on glass plates, and was the forerunner of the slide projector.

'The heaviest snowfall for 27 years'[30] fell in the last week of April. Although it was worst at the west end of Berkshire, Reading recorded a layer 12in deep, while the body of a man was found in a roadside ditch near Wokingham.

The town was proving popular with builders of new houses:

> Bracknell is remarkably well placed for building development. The freehold estate situated at Rounds Hill ... should command the attention of investors. The high position, the road frontages, the charm of scenery, the excellent railway facilities, its juxtaposition to Ascot and Reading, the ease with which

property here lets, all point to the fact that the development can extend in the direction of large or small residences.[31]

A public meeting 'to protest against the unjust proposals contained in the Licensing Bill', aimed at reducing the number of licensed premises across the country, was held in the Victoria Hall in early June.

Widespread drunkenness was an enduring concern, to which Victorian and Edwardian social reformers strove to find a solution. During the 1870s, an average of 40 gallons of beer per capita was consumed each year, with arrests for drunkenness more than doubling.[32] 'Bracknell made its voice heard,' reported the *Berkshire Chronicle* five days after the assembly. Nearly 800 people arrived at Waterloo from Bracknell and Wokingham for a mass protest in Hyde Park on 27 September, making up nearly 20 per cent of the protesters from the whole of Berkshire.

The Bracknell Athletics Sports was held 'in front of a crowd numbering several thousand', although the *Windsor and Eton Express* suggested that 'the judging in some of the flat events was not quite so satisfactory as usual'. Despite the best efforts of the authorities, some illegal betting still continued.

Ranelagh School opened on 21 September 1908. It could cater for up to 200 pupils, both boys and girls, 'although only 61 are at present on the roll'. Initially there were just four teachers, including headmaster Ernest Cleave.

In October it was reported that 'the new hunting establishment for the Garth Hounds, which is being erected at Bracknell, will be ready for occupation next May'. This was located in Kennel Lane, Priestwood. Thomas Colleton Garth had established the Hunt at Haines Hill near Twyford in 1851; it was named the Garth Hunt on his retirement in 1902. The new facility included 'huntsman's, whippers-in, and kennelman's houses, young hounds' quarters, bitch houses, slaughter houses, etc, and stabling for thirty horses.'[33] The slaughter house for 'farm animal casualties to feed the hounds' was well to the north of the other buildings, beside The Cut. Initially connected by a path, a tramway was later built to connect it to the rest of the kennel premises. Eddie and Peter Jaggard in their book on the Garth Hunt recorded:

> When puppies were born they were fostered out to local families for the first months of their lives, before being returned to the kennels to train with the pack. An annual puppy show was held in a field to the left of Quelm Lane, much to the delight of local children ... The first of these shows ... was held in the summer of 1910.

The Hunt amalgamated with the South Berks Hunt in 1962 and moved to Mortimer, due in part to expansion of Bracknell. Some of the old kennel buildings can still be seen in Kennel Lane.

The Garth Hunt started near Twyford in 1852. Kennels for the hounds were built in Kennel Lane in 1908, and the hunt moved their base there in 1919.

The circus came to town in November: Sir Robert Fossett's establishment (the title was adopted for commercial showmanship purposes but had no legitimacy). Fossett himself was billed as 'Champion Jockey of the World', performing tricks such as headstands and somersaults while riding bareback on a horse. 'At the afternoon performance, very few were present; in the evening however, there was a large company.'[34]

1909

The railway from Reading to Waterloo was by now a busy freight artery, and Bracknell 'had a large and important goods yard' with nine sidings at its peak, seven on the up (Bracknell) side, and two on the down side. Goods trains, mainly handling cattle, agricultural produce, bricks and coal, ran from London during morning hours, returning in the afternoons and evenings. There were also ten passenger trains between London Waterloo and Reading each day, running at two-hourly intervals. There were also a couple of runs between Ascot and Reading. A return ticket to London cost 5s for second-class travel (about £20 in today's money); first class cost 2s more. Shunting goods between Ascot West and Bracknell would hold up passenger services from time to time, as would the Amen Corner siding; there were clear instructions as to which trains had priority at various times of day.[35] The goods yard closed in 1969.

Warfield Parish Council set up a fire brigade in the town, with Winkfield and Easthampstead asked to help finance and support it. They were soon in action, attending two fires in May:

> It is considered that the recent fire at Priestwood works was maliciously caused, and Messrs Payne and Co. are offering a substantial reward for the apprehension and conviction of the offender or offenders. Considerable excitement was caused just over a week ago by another cry of fire, this time at the rear of the premises occupied by the Home and Colonial Stores in the High Street. A large crowd quickly assembled, and the fire brigade, with the hose cart, was soon in attendance, but fortunately their services were not required owing to the prompt efforts of those who discovered the outbreak.[36]

Mr Dyson's Gipsy Choir (a travelling vaudeville group) had captured the place by storm in May. 'Never has the Victoria Hall been so crowded for four nights running.' A playbill at another venue adds, 'This entertainment is not over praised, Mr Dyson having an abhorrence of Swagger and Bunkum!'

Old Bracknell Wanderers won their first trophy, the Ascot and District League Cup, although there was no newspaper report of the match.

The first instalment of Robert Baden-Powell's book *Scouting for Boys* was published, and soon led to the start of the Boy Scouts movement. The author had already made a name for himself with his exploits in the Boer War, and had held an experimental camp on Brownsea Island in Dorset the previous year (three brothers from Wellington College were among the boys taking part). A local Scout troop was one of many that sprung up across the country.

In August, many local youngsters were at a camp in the grounds of Easthampstead Park, which was visited by a reporter from the *Reading Observer*:

> A visit to the camp ... found the lads in good trim and looking very fit ... Fourteen tents, including canteen, guard tent, and two commissariat tents, sheltered two companies of the Bracknell and Wokingham Boy Scouts. The day appeared to be well filled, commencing at 6 a.m. and ending at 9 p.m., with the exception of one or two night alarms, wherein the lads have shown conspicuous alertness in response to the bugle.[37]

The week included a cricket match against the Wokingham Baptist Boys' team, ambulance skill tests, and an inspection from the Marquis of Downshire. A large number of visitors witnessed sports on Friday (including a fire lighting competition, a Victoria Cross race where competitors were required to jump hurdles while carrying dummy men filled with straw, and a potato race), after which there was 'some fifty friends and relatives of the lads sitting down to an excellent tea'. There was a church parade on Sunday afternoon, and the boys marched home the following day 'after a most enjoyable week'. Indoor meetings of the Easthampstead troop were held in Westwick Hall on Bagshot Road, 'the new parish room' (this stood on the position of the underpass beside KFC).

There was another military exercise in the district, as reported in the *Reading Examiner*:

> The town has worn quite a military air this week ... There has been a constant passing of troops through the streets, and on Thursday much excitement was caused by a supposed invading force on Winkfield Row. The scene of operations extended from Binfield to Ascot, bounded on the sides roughly by Bracknell and Cranbourne, with Winkfield as the centre. The novel sight was witnessed by almost all the inhabitants in the neighbourhood. Upwards of 15,000 troops were expected to encamp in Easthampstead Park before the end of the week.

There were disagreements between the Bowling Club and Mr Raven, the proprietor of the Forest Hotel, over the issue of women and children being allowed access to the bowling rink. Land was purchased for a new rink adjacent to the Bracknell Social Club, with Bowling Club members sharing their bar.

On Boxing Day:

> a match was played at Old Bracknell between Lawrence's Stores and Old Bracknell Wanderers, the game being arranged for the benefit of Mr Albert Lovegrove, the Hon. Sec. of Old Bracknell Wanderers, who met with a bad accident over twelve months ago, breaking his leg, and unhappily still being unable to work. A large number of tickets were sold, thus ensuring a large benefit to Mr Lovegrove.[38]

The unfortunate Albert Lovegrove later suffered another accident in a football match at Windlesham, which required treatment at the Middlesex Hospital in London, but his leg eventually had to be amputated.

The Boxing Day match became an annual event.

1910

Water supplied by the South West Suburban Water Company 'was found to be so impure as to be condemned as unsuitable for domestic purposes'. The situation was said to have been going on for several years, and the Windsor authorities 'are now writing to the Local Government Board to get things rectified ... If the bacillus coli communis can gain access, why not the bacillus typhosus which could cause a wide-spread and alarming epidemic of enteric fever?'[39] Residents were recommended to boil the water before use until the problems were rectified.

The railway company agreed to erect a footbridge, 'at their own expense', on the west side of the Bagshot Road bridge, but the war intervened and it was never constructed.

Edward VII died on 6 May, causing mourning across the country. The funeral was held two weeks later. While still the Prince of Wales, the future king had lunched at the stationmaster's house when visiting the neighbourhood:

> Mr Taylor (the stationmaster) very rightly interpreted the feeling of the inhabitants of the village in decorating the station with mourning, by covering the pillars supporting the verandahs on either side of the line with royal purple. Between the pillars were hung eight purple flags bearing white letters forming the pathetic word 'Farewell'; also several large and small evergreen wreaths (laurel, etc), with drooping flags within the larger wreaths.[40]

Following the lead of the cricket club, Old Bracknell Wanderers ran their own athletics meet. This took place on Whit Monday in mid-May this year, attracting 'nearly two thousand holiday makers'. Although the ground had been 'carefully prepared', it had an infamous slope, up which the competitors had to run.[41]

The new tennis club entertained Reading and Ascot in matches during June, but were well beaten on both occasions. 'The Bracknell Tennis Club (as far as good play is concerned) is quite in its infancy,' commented the *Reading Observer*.

The proprietor of the *Wokingham and Bracknell Gazette*, Francis Staniland, sent a petition to the London and South Western Railway Traffic Committee requesting a station halt at the Amen Corner crossing, but this was declined.

Over 4,000 attended the Bracknell Athletics Sports meeting in August, and 'a fine lot of athletes competed, the general standard being higher than last year', including runners from London, the army, and Cambridge University. Three new features appeared on the programme – the relay, donkey, and pig races. 'Great fun was created by the donkey race, laughter being loud when several of the riders were unseated. Another diverting event was the ladies' pig race. A young black pig was used for the latter event, and the ladies had a good run before the little animal was captured by Mrs Wigmore.'[42]

A few days later, the Easthampstead Boy Scouts held a camp for several days near Gormer Lake, just to the south of Nine Mile Ride. 'The vicinities of Camberley, Crowthorne, Finchampstead, and Wokingham were thoroughly explored' with 'bathing, boating, and fishing' taking place on Gormer Lake in the evenings. 'The various patrols in turn formed a guard around the camp during the night,' with the Bracknell Troop staging a planned raid just before midnight on the Friday. Multiple 'attacks' took place, but the defences stood firm and after two hours, Bracknell gave up 'and fraternised with the campers, who entertained them with refreshments'.[43] A similar camp the following year for several local Scout troops included a sports day, held on the lawns behind South Hill Park house. The camps continued annually until 1914; a district camp planned for August 1914 was cancelled after the outbreak of the First World War.

A hastily assembled team of local Post Office employees faced Easthampstead Cricket Club after the latter had their match postponed at short notice. The postal men appeared to be on their way to an easy victory, 'but owing to the call of duty five of the Post Office men had to leave',[44] but they still managed to hang on for an unlikely win with only half a team in the field.

There had been calls for women being allowed to vote since 1832, but these became more strident with the formation of the Women's Social and Political Union in 1903. Not all women were in favour of having the vote, with an Anti-Suffrage League set up in 1908. Lady Haversham from South Hill Park was a vociferous member, and chaired a meeting of the East Berks branch at the Victoria Hall (there had already been meetings in Wokingham, Windsor and Maidenhead).

Commission agent James Trodd lived in Church Road, the poshest area of Bracknell. He appeared before the magistrate in Wokingham, charged with 'keeping a betting house'. Acting on information, PC Legg went to the address on two occasions, and handed over a betting slip and 1s on horse races being held in Manchester. After obtaining a search warrant, the police entered the house and discovered 'a pile of betting slips and papers. Some new books showed the extensive business that was done.' Trodd was found guilty and fined £20 (£1,650 in today's money), his son £5 for assisting him, and several other men who had placed bets were bound over.

1911

A meeting of Easthampstead ratepayers took place in February in the Parish Room at Priestwood (this was located near the junction of Binfield Road and Downshire Way):

> Contrary to the general opinion, the expenditure of the District Council was not increasing … the only increase was found in the County Rate, owing mainly to the building and upkeep of schools, and taking over the roads … the present District Council offices were unsanitary, and not large enough owing to the increase in the work of the Council, necessitating the building of new premises in order to have all the offices under one roof (this was not a popular move due to the cost, although in reality it only contributed a farthing to the rates). The new premises were to be built in Stanley Road.

The system of dealing with children in the workhouse in Cottage Homes was also explained. The original Home was on Wokingham Road before a move to premises on Binfield Road in 1925; the new building later became the St Anthony's Boy's Home, and then housed the Bracknell Youth Offending Service.

Health and Safety is not a modern affliction. William Dee of Tilehurst appeared before the Wokingham County Bench, charged with 'giving a cinematic entertainment at the Victoria Hall, Bracknell, in contravention to the Cinematic Act ... on 28 January'. The show had taken place in front of an audience of 250 children and adults 'with no fireproof enclosure and no barrier to keep persons from coming into contact with the machine ... also there was no bucket of sand or water, or wet blanket, ready for use in case of fire'.[45]

Lady Haversham was due to chair another meeting of the Women's National Anti-Suffrage League in March, but was 'suffering from a slight chill' so her husband took her place. The *Maidenhead Advertiser* noted 'a resolution against giving women the vote was passed ... although a large number voted against it'.

The Berkshire Red Cross Society had been delegated to raise Voluntary Aid Detachments of Nurses, 'such as would be required in the course of mobilisation or in actual warfare'. Bracknell set up the second and third units in the county – sixteen women under Mrs Lilian Berwick of Gilnochie (later renamed Lynwood Chase; the house was later demolished and the housing estate still bears the name), and twenty-two men under Colonel Mackenzie of Ramslade House. 'These detachments are recognised by the War Office.'[46] An exercise was held on Easter Monday when both the men's and women's sections were involved. By 2 p.m., the nurses were setting up a hospital in the stables at 'Gilnochie', including an operating room, the cooks lit fires in trenches and prepared cakes, tea, coffee, barley water, beef tea and custard pudding. The men, along with Dr Fielden, arrived half an hour later, and went out to the 'casualties' (Bracknell and Easthampstead Boy Scouts) with stretchers and an ambulance cart. By 4 p.m., everyone was back at 'Gilnochie', having been 'treated' and fed.

The Bracknell Choral Society gave another 'excellent rendering' of the *Messiah* at the Victoria Hall. The two male soloists came from Eton College and St Paul's Cathedral. 'The audience was not large, but thoroughly enjoyed the musical treat.'[47]

Those attending the Old Bracknell Wanderers Sports Day on 5 June were subject to abuse from Henry Goddard, 'an aged inmate of Easthampstead Union'. Inspector Haddrell reported that the defendant had been arrested at 3.30 p.m., and was still intoxicated in the prison cells at 7 p.m. As he had a list of previous convictions dating back to 1885, Goddard was fined 14s plus costs.

A number of licence holders applied for various extensions 'on the occasion of the Coronation Festivities of George V on 21st and 22nd June'. After consideration, the chairman of the Wokingham bench announced that they could not see their way to grant extensions longer than twelve o'clock. The celebrations in Bracknell commenced with a short service in the church at noon. A dinner was given to the old people at one o'clock, 'at which their wants were amply provided for', accompanied by music played by the Ascot Brass Band. At 2 p.m., local children assembled at the Victoria Hall, each receiving a medal. After the singing of the National Anthem, they all marched down Church Road to a meadow at Cooper's Hill:

> There each child was presented with a Coronation mug, and prizes were given for the best fancy costumes ... Sports for boys and girls followed, and at 4pm the children sat down to tea. As there was plenty of tea, cake, bread and butter, and other provisions left, the visitors and parishioners present were also entertained with refreshments and tea. At 6 o'clock, an open-air concert was held on the field, to which the local talents contributed. The whole proceedings terminated with a grand display of fireworks and a bonfire, the latter, however, being somewhat marred by the rain.[48]

The following month, the Bracknell Voluntary Aid Detachments:

> gave a public display of Red Cross work on the Cricket Ground ... Fires were lit at which four cooks and two orderlies ... worked hard with excellent results. They provided 200 scones and teas for about 100 people. Fish (cooked in a paper), beef tea, barley water, soup and custard were all provided for the invalids ... At the same time, the nurses ... were preparing a hospital of nine beds in the cricket tent, and a receiving and operating room, with their interesting but rather gruesome paraphernalia. At 7pm a Boy Scout sent a bugle call across the ground to his wounded comrades to let them know that help was coming ... Immediately the stretcher bearers dashed off, and very soon the less seriously injured were being helped to walk to hospital. Then came frequent relays of stretchers bearing sufferers with closed eyes and apparently in great pain. These were put into the beds prepared for them on mattresses that had been stuffed with straw, and all eventually made a good recovery ... There were about one hundred lookers-on, who were admitted by batches of twelve to use the hospital, and the entrance charge of 3*d* covered expenses. The ambulance wagon, driven by Mr Anderson, was a new addition to the equipment and looked very smart, but unfortunately tender regard for the cricket ground prevented its being used.[49]

A long spell of hot and dry weather meant the growth around Bracknell was tinder dry. A heather blaze started by the side of the railway between Ascot, Bagshot and Bracknell in mid-July:

and spread with great rapidity. Before long, four fire engines, hundreds of men, and some ladies joined in the endeavour to beat out the flames ... The smoke could be seen for miles. By the time the fire-fighters had apparently got the upper hand, there were five miles of a devastated course.[50]

Fires were also reported at Chatham (which threatened an ammunitions store), Tunbridge Wells, Cannock Chase (where 500 acres were devastated), Coventry, Greenham Common near Newbury, and Aldershot, while six fires on commons were reported to the London Fire Brigade in a single day. At the end of the month, the *Windsor and Eton Express* carried a report on several fires in the Bracknell area:

> Starting on Friday last week, a series of heath fires have occurred in and near Ascot, the like of which have never been seen in the neighbourhood. The origin of the first outbreak appears to have been due to sparks from a railway engine, for soon after a goods train had passed through the Crown Land known as Whitmoor Bog, heather ... beside the line was noticed to be on fire. An alarm was given with all haste, but before many minutes had elapsed, the flames had covered a wide area and the situation had assumed a serious aspect. Devouring everything in its way – undergrowth, fir trees and fencing – the fire soon reached Swinley Road, catching in its progress, the Lavender Farm fence on the other side, and almost simultaneously entering the Stella Lodge [now Westwood House] and Brackens Estates [now Seymour Drive] which adjoin the Crown Land. By this time, the dense smoke and fierce heat coming from both sides, made traffic along Swinley Road almost impossible.

The Ascot Fire Brigade and several volunteers kept the blaze away from the Stella Lodge and Lavender Farm buildings (although some wooden buildings were burnt), and Ascot Road was also filled with thick smoke. Fortunately there was only a light breeze, and the fire was eventually brought under control without spreading towards 'the six or seven principal residences situated around Englemere' (including the home of Lord Roberts). At its height, it was estimated that hundreds of men and 'several well-known ladies' were involved in tackling the blaze. The Staines, Windsor and Ashford Fire Brigades afforded 'valuable assistance ... but the outbreak was not one on which the steam engines brought from these towns could be of much use'. Bracknell firemen also assisted, along with Crown workmen from Belvedere and Windsor Park. About noon the following day, 'fire broke out again in the vicinity of Swinley, this time nearer Tower Hill .... A slight breeze carried the flames towards the golf links between Sunninghill and Windlesham .... Another outbreak on the same day at Nine Mile Ride was got under control before damage to any extent was done. It was hoped that the heavy rain on Wednesday morning last would have prevented any further heath fires for some time, but on Thursday another outbreak cleared fifty or sixty acres in the vicinity of Swinley Woods.'[51] A couple of weeks later:

> a rather serious heath fire broke out in the early hours on Monday morning which at one time threatened danger to the residences of Mrs Lucena and Mrs Arkwright ['Westwick' and 'Firlands'] on the Bagshot Road. The fire broke out ... in Martins Lane and quickly spread to the woods at the rear of the houses. The fowls were moved from the outhouses, and some of the furniture was taken out of Mrs Arkwright's house, but thanks to the combined assistance of the Ascot, Wokingham, and Bracknell brigades, and the men employed by Easthampstead Rural District Council on the road near, the fire was kept at bay and subsequently got under control. Harmanswater lake was completely dry, owing to the prolonged hot and dry weather, so the firefighters had to beat out the flames.[52]

This was part of a prolonged heatwave across the country that lasted until 11 September. Temperatures peaked at 36.7°C, a record at the time and a figure that wasn't exceeded until 1990.

Amateur champions from Scotland, Wales and the army were among the competitors at the annual athletics meeting in August. The 'chase the pig' race had to be abandoned owing to a threat on the part of the police to make a test case on cruelty to the animal; this was replaced by a 100yd race for women. Five local Boy Scout groups competed in an 880yd relay for the 'Brownlow' Silver Challenge Cup (won by a team from Bracknell).

At the end of the month, The Forest Hotel was being offered for sale by auction. The new owner was Charles Murless, who had been running the Shakespeare public house in London's Buckingham Palace Road.

The Bowling Club's new green was officially opened by the local Member of Parliament, Ernest Gardner. 'The first game was immediately played against a team representing the firm of Sutton's from Reading, the visitors eventually winning by eight points.'[53] They had not long to wait before recording their first win on the ground, beating Desborough Bowling Club of Maidenhead a week later.

An enquiry was held in Reading to investigate whether a permanent isolation hospital was required and desired, to cover the eastern end of the county. ERDC were in favour, 'provided that the cost be not more than the ratepayers could reasonably bear, and the County Council contribute to the capital and initial expenditure'. Wokingham Urban and Rural Districts were opposed, while the two Windsor councils sat firmly on the fence, refusing to commit one way or the other. It would be more than twelve months before the inspector's report was produced and the relevant authorities responded. ERDC considered the cost 'excessive' and had already made arrangements to send any patients to the Maidenhead Isolation Hospital (which stood on the opposite side of the road to the current St Mark's Hospital).

The East Berks Art Exhibition, which took place in November and ran for four days, was opened by Princess Victoria, a granddaughter of Queen Victoria, who travelled to Bracknell by car in the morning to have lunch with a Mr George Littledale at Wick Hill House. Arriving outside the Victoria Hall at 3 p.m. with a mounted police escort, she was met by the 1st Bracknell Boy Scouts under patrol leader Albert Searle, and the Church Lads' Brigade from Binfield. A month later, the organising committee was requesting donations to pay off a debt of £21 (£1,730 in today's money) accrued from the two previous events.

1912

In February, electric lighting was being installed in Holy Trinity Church to replace 'the antiquated means of obtaining light'.

About sixty non-commissioned officers and men of the Berkshire Yeomanry Windsor Squadron were involved in exercises at Easthampstead Park in March, and were billeted for one night in various Bracknell hotels and inns. A few days later, a detachment of the Cameron Highlanders, with their bagpipes, paid a visit of two days' duration, making the Victoria Hall their headquarters.

The services at Holy Trinity on 20 April 'were of a very sorrowful nature ... and opened and closed by the "Dead March" on account of the terrible disaster of the "Titanic"', which had sunk five days earlier.

Old Bracknell Wanderers finished the 1911–12 season as champions of the Ascot and District League, and played their last game of the season at home against a side comprised of players from the rest of the league.

The Whitmor Bog site was being considered for a sewage works to serve Sunninghill and Sunningdale.

Two Olympic trials were held at Bracknell Cricket Club prior to the 1912 Olympics (which took place in Stockholm in May).

A fatal accident occurred at the railway goods yard in July. Albert Sermon and George Slyfield were lifting a tank of petroleum oil, weighing about 5 tons, from a truck:

> The tank was securely fixed to a crane, but the load proved more than the men could manage, and they were forced to let go the handle. As might be expected, it flew back with great force and struck Jack Sermon ... a violent blow on the head. He was conveyed to the Royal Berks Hospital, Reading, where he died shortly after admission.[54]

The Lily Hill estate changed hands, with Mr Jennings Scott McComb the new owner.

Among the competitors at the Bracknell Athletic Sports in August were the British National 220yd champion Willie Applegarth, 'making his first appearance since his return from the Stockholm Olympics where he had won a gold medal in the relay', as well as George Nicol, Richard Rice, David Jacobs, George Hutson and Italian Franco Giongo, who had all competed in Sweden as well.

On 19 November, 'strange rumblings they heard for about thirty minutes and the shaking of their windows and doors' were heard and felt in much of east Berkshire, including Bracknell. One eyewitness recounted, 'A deep, rolling noise seemed to come over the tree-tops from the south.' Failing any other explanation, 'the conviction gradually took root that the district had been visited by an earthquake ... although there was noise, there was no perceptible shock'.[55] The disturbance was never explained, although there had been a major earthquake in Mexico a few hours earlier.

1913

The organisers of the East Berks Art Exhibition decided they could no longer carry on running the event as they now had a deficit of £20 (£1,600 in today's money):

> Fortunately, however, this sum was successfully raised at a concert which was held with that object in the Victoria Hall, Bracknell ... We echo the hope expressed by Mr E. J. Taylor, the Hon. Secretary of the exhibition, that a revival ... may be witnessed within a very short space of time.[56]

The concert, it appears, was much better attended than the exhibition.

There was a major fire in mid-February at Bracknell College, a private boarding school in Church Road:

> Detecting a smell of burning wood, Mrs Hyson, wife of the principal, found that one of the classrooms was in flames. All the inmates escaped without injury. The Ascot and Bracknell fire brigades were quickly on the spot, but through inadequate pressure of water, were unable to save the building ... The cause of the outbreak is unknown, but the damage is covered by insurance. The building was practically gutted. Some part of the furniture was saved.[57]

The three-storey building was later rebuilt, but without the top floor.

A small boarding school for boys operated from this building in Church Road from 1897. A serious fire destroyed the top storey in 1913.

There was a crowd of around 5,000 for the Bracknell Athletic Sports, no doubt hoping to see Willie Applegarth, 'fresh from setting a world best time over 200 yards', but he was unable to attend, as was George Hutson, another top British runner. The 100m was won by an Australian, William Stewart. One source claims the 100yd and 800yd races were trials for the Olympic Games, due to be held in Berlin in 1916. 'Billy' Tucker, a cross-country international, 'made short work of his field ... on Boxing Day, and won the handicap from scratch'.[58]

1914

A crowded meeting, 'attended by many people from the surrounding district', was held in the Victoria Hall to protest against Home Rule for Ireland. The Chairman, Col. F. Mackenzie of Ramslade House, said the meeting 'had special reference to the Home Rule Bill which the Government proposed to pass – a measure ... of such magnitude and importance that it ought not to become law without the people of this country being first consulted'.[59] The Bill was still being debated in Parliament when war broke out in August.

Two new 25-horsepower engines were installed at the sewage farm. 'These engines are required as a result of the present ones being declared of insufficient power to deal with the increased volume now being received at the pumping stations.'[60]

The Forest Hotel was still failing to make much money and finally closed. Local auctioneers Messrs Hunton and Sons conducted a sale over three days in April, 'to dispose of the furniture, plate, linen, plate, pictures, glass, and general effects ... along with the stock of wines and spirits, cigars, etc.'. Doctor Fielden purchased the premises as his home and surgery.

At the end of May, 'The local members of the Voluntary Aid Detachment gave a display in the field adjoining "Hillside" [a house in Church Road] ... The Easthampstead Troop of Boy Scouts provided the "cases" ... There was a good number of interested spectators.'[61]

The children of the Baptist Church Sunday School held their annual treat on 5 August at the Victoria Hall, even though war had been declared the previous day. This was to be the last peacetime event in the town. The Bracknell Athletic Sports were planned for Wednesday, 12 August, but these were 'postponed'. A traffic census proposed for various roads in the area to assist in classifications of major and minor thoroughfares was due to be held in August was also postponed, as 'traffic now is not normal traffic'.

It would be a few years before life in Bracknell returned to normal.

7

The Effect of the First World War and its Aftermath

The settled life of Bracknell would be changed by the war, as it was across the country.

1914

The *Reading Chronicle* was published on Fridays, but there was a special edition on Wednesday, 5 August 1914, to report the outbreak of war. 'Grocery prices are already rising and people are "buying in" stocks of food.'

Any Bracknell news was still reported in the paper printed in Reading, but was dependent on someone sending it in. These reports were infrequent and patchy but the effects on the town can be gleaned from what was happening in Reading and elsewhere. All newspapers were subject to censorship (even reports of ERDC meetings disappeared from the press) so we must look for other sources to learn what was happening behind the official headlines. Snippets can be gleaned from the local parish magazines of the time, including news of casualties, the wounded, soldiers home on leave, or news from abroad sent home by those on the front line.

Just twenty-four hours after war was declared, Army Reservists and Territorials (men for Home Service) were 'in readiness', while Naval Reserves were on mobilisation notice. There was a feeling throughout the country that 'it would all be over by Christmas'. Within a few days:

> Inquiries at the Post Office show how keen the Reservists of the district answered the 'Call to Arms.' The office was kept open all night and a large

number of Reserve men who received the mobilisation papers late at night, presented their orders for payment during the night, ready to depart for their depots by the first morning train. By 10am, most of the men had left, all in excellent spirits.[1]

A call for volunteers was eagerly met with young men across the country signing up. Within a month, seventeen members of the Bracknell Working Men's Club had already enlisted; recruiting at Bracknell was said to be 'brisk'. There was no office for enlisting in Bracknell; men travelled to the town hall at Wokingham or the Royal Berkshire Regiment barracks in Reading. The local Boy Scouts troop held a rally: 'With their bugle band, they marched through the streets, followed by a large number of likely recruits.'[2]

Some forthcoming events were abandoned. The Bracknell Sports had been called off, although the annual general meeting of the Bracknell Old Wanderers Football Club went ahead as normal. Easthampstead and Bracknell sides played cricket on 15 August, while auctions and the Bracknell market continued 'where trade was brisk with good prices being paid'. Cinema lectures were held at the Victoria Hall, where:

> pictures depicted the mobilisation of our Army and some records of the German destruction of Louvain and Termonde, and their entry into Brussels ... In spite of the announcement that the whole of the nett proceeds would be given to the local branch of the Prince of Wales' National Relief Fund, it failed to attract large audiences.[3]

Two weeks after war was declared, ERDC noted 'Dr Paterson, the Medical Officer of Health is now in Germany',[4] but he was soon back home to resume his duties. In November, he gave 'an interesting account' at the Victoria Hall on his experiences as a prisoner of war. He had been in the enemy's country at the outbreak of hostilities and first arrested by the police and interrogated before being released after three weeks. He was incarcerated before being 'tardily released' to Holland (the Geneva Convention required doctors to be freed). 'Russ and Hoptroff ... surveyor's men ... are rejoining their regiments,' recorded ERDC in the same month, 'their jobs will be kept open.'[5] In December, the road foreman had 'enlisted in the army'.[6]

A meeting was held at Dr Fielden's home to discuss the call for special constables. These men 'would guard ... special points, such as railway and other bridges, post offices, reservoirs, churches, and other important posts ... This was only a patriotic and loyal citizen movement for the training of those willing to help in the protection of property.'[7] Several men put their names forward at the end of the meeting.

The Victoria Hall was used as a small hospital by the local VAD detachment of the Red Cross, but this later moved into 'Oaklea', a house in Church Road, although it was only capable of treating up to fourteen men at any one time. Dr Fielden made available a room at his house for use as an office by the local Red Cross personnel. A War Depot was also set up on the premises in 1915, with 'upwards of a hundred workers, where sandbags, shirts, pyjamas, and other hospital clothing, also knitted goods ... surgical dressings, splints, bandages of all kinds, etc.'[8] were produced.

Various fundraising efforts and collections soon started and continued throughout the duration of the conflict, and 'the children bring their pennies and half-pennies each Sunday'. Annual hospital parades continued, albeit with Boy Scout bands providing the accompanying music. There were regular concerts and entertainments at the Victoria Hall, including ones by the D'Oyly Carte and Covent Garden Opera companies in 1918. Special parcels were sent to every local man serving annually at Christmas and were always much appreciated. Two teams of players of the Old Bracknell Wanders raised nearly £4 from a game of football (£300 in today's money). Special events were held for the children of men at the front, or for soldiers home on leave. The committee of the Working Men's Club unanimously voted 'that all soldiers and sailors are to be admitted free membership of that Club during the period of the war, where there is also a splendid rifle range ... where they can improve their shooting.' Royal Flying Corps men, based at Ascot, were regular visitors to the club from 1916 onwards.

Lists of men being called up or volunteering were regularly published, but so too were the names of those wounded and being treated at home or abroad. Eric Roe was the first Bracknell man to be killed, at the village of Soupir in northern France on 14 September. Working as a messenger boy at the post office after leaving school, Eric had joined the army in 1909 at the age of 16 as a drummer boy in the Grenadier Guards.[9] By the end of October, 'it was noted that no less than nine ex-telephone messengers from the Bracknell Post Office are serving with the Colours'. The following year, the number of postal deliveries was reduced by a half, due to the shortage of staff. Alfred Davis died from tuberculosis in November 'after lingering for some time'. He was 18 years old, 'one of the earlier members of the Bracknell Boy Scouts',[10] and had also joined the Berkshire Territorials.

In September, it was reported:

The Brewery House near the station has been lent for six months, and this has been fitted up as a home for Belgian Refugees. Several families have already arrived and been settled in this house. Furniture has been provided, partly by purchase, partly by loan, and a sum of money has been promptly and generously contributed, sufficient to maintain them for the period for which the house has been lent.[11]

'Oaklea', a private house in Church Road, was used as a convalescent hospital during the war. With only eight bedrooms, it was the smallest hospital in Berkshire.

1915

Pubs had been able to open all day before the outbreak of war, typically opening their doors at 6 a.m. and not closing until 10 or 11 p.m. Now their hours were reduced to prevent drunkenness. Servicemen on active duty were not to be served during the day. The change in opening hours was soon followed by shops, which closed earlier in the evenings. Grocery prices were already starting to rise as people began stockpiling food, and there were some shortages of basic foodstuffs.

Early in January, the 5th Battalion, West Kent Regiment arrived in Bracknell, and nearly 1,000 men were billeted in local houses. While their presence had been anticipated, there had previously been two 'false alarms' over the arrival of a unit requiring accommodation. Their presence must have caused great upheavals but was appreciated, with the *Reading Mercury* reporting:

> It is pleasant to be able to say that their departure will be viewed with universal regret ... We have been brightened up by their visit and interested in what we have seen of their work. On each Sunday there has been a Church parade at 9.45, and afterwards the men, headed by their excellent band, have marched

around the town. A good many of the men have also attended the Sunday evening Service, and a few have been singing in choir. The Victoria Hall has been open every day as a Soldiers' Club and Recreation Room where the Soldiers could sit and read papers and play games.

Two months later, 200 Royal Engineers were found accommodation overnight, and more than 1,000 men of the South Wales Borderers for four nights in May.

A month later, 'Kitchener's Army [battalions formed exclusively of volunteers] has been operating around Bracknell ... On Wednesday night and Thursday, they held Bracknell station bridge and goods yard as strategical points. They showed much enthusiasm and their training is evidently progressing rapidly.' A Parliamentary Recruiting Armoured Car visited Bracknell in March, with several local men signing up to fight. More recruiting took place in the town in May, June and August. By the end of April, eighty men from Bracknell were already serving overseas.

Local Scout troops held mock battles during the course of the year, 'defending' strategic buildings in the area.

Bracknell Cricket Club delayed publishing its fixture list by two months, but then reported its 'finances are in a serious condition'. Some members of the committee were also away fighting. They decided to abandon matches but continue practices, only maintaining the ground 'as far as the committee find necessary'. The Royal Forest Agricultural Association decided to limit their competitive activities to a ploughing match later in the year, but had to abandon even that in June.

From May, spirits, wine and beer were heavily taxed. Meat and fish prices were going up, and bread prices fluctuated wildly, but on a more optimistic note, there was less crime. Some businesses catering for male clientele were struggling or closing down, notably tobacconists and hairdressers.

There was a major fire at Thomas Lawrence's timber yard in the High Street at the end of May:

> The Bracknell brigade were soon on the spot, quickly followed by the Wokingham and Ascot brigades. The fire, however, quickly attained large dimensions, and efforts were made to preserve the surrounding buildings. The timber yard is in the midst of houses and offices, the business premises in the High Street running back nearby, and had there been much wind, a huge conflagration must have resulted. Fortunately, owing to the splendid work of the brigades and many willing helpers, the fire was confined to the yard, the offices and a large shed being preserved intact and the engine shed nearly so, the roof being damaged.[12]

During the war, the timber yard cut sleepers to be shipped to France from trees felled in the area between Martins Lane and Swinley.

In August, cards started appearing in the windows of families with members serving in the forces. News and details of missing men was slow – Henry Hollingsworth was reported missing in September 1914, and only confirmed killed nine months later. In the same month, the Berkshire Yeomanry led an assault at Gallipoli resulting in several injuries to local men, including Major Edward Gooch of Cooper's Hill. The wife of Corporal Michael Fox was allowed to visit him in hospital in France, and wrote a glowing report of praise on the work of medical staff there. Sidney Harvey died from a shrapnel wound to the head, leaving a widow and six children. Local lads Harry Hearne and Charles Longhurst were among those who sailed for Egypt in October, the latter having managed to enlist at Reading whilst only 15.

In the early stages of the war, the authorities had relied on volunteers to fight, but it soon became clear that larger numbers of men were required. The Derby Scheme was introduced late in the year, allowing men to register ahead of conscription, along with boys aged 15 and over. This involved ERDC in compiling a local register with the assistance of local volunteers, most of whom were women. George Littledale, of Wick Hill House, and George Douglas, a local builder's foreman, were among those on an Appeals Tribunal, to assess the cases of men contesting their call-up. In November, 'a recruiting office ... opened at Bracknell. The office is in one of the smaller rooms of Victoria Hall ... Several recruits have been attested each day.' Two weeks later, it was noted that:

> whilst no figures can be given, the response in Bracknell has far exceeded expectations, and there can be few, if any, eligible who have not been attested. Many of the local firms have no eligible men on their staff now unregistered. The Post Office have no eligible men who have not either been attested or rejected. With large numbers already serving, Bracknell and district may be said to have responded magnificently during the war.[13]

A month later, the British Automobile Traction Company (later to become Thames Valley) started running a bus service between Reading and Sunningdale Station that came through Bracknell.

1916

All single men were now being called up, according to their age, but soon married men were following. Appeals slowed down the system of call-ups, and the local newspaper regularly reported on those attempting to claim exemption and the result of their appeal. William Hunton, the auctioneer at the cattle market, was called up, appealed successfully, had the appeal overridden, and then successfully appealed again. Lawrence's Stores tried to block the call-up of any more of their staff, sixty of their workforce of 100 having already joined the military. ERDC won a provisional exemption for their highways surveyor, but lost an appeal for 'the only man at the Sewage Works who has a knowledge of the whole drainage system'. By 1917, several of the town's master bakers were serving overseas. The remaining bakers agreed to share their customers between them for the duration of the hostilities, in the hope that the returning men would be able to resurrect their businesses after the war.

Overnight blackout regulations were introduced in light of the Zeppelin raids that had begun twelve months earlier in parts of the country. Holy Trinity fitted curtains ('this will involve considerable expense') to comply with the new blackout rules, but a church in Reading employed a cheaper option by painting the insides of their windows! Lawrence's Stores and corn merchants Drake and Mount were both fined for showing a light.

Although publicans complained of losing trade, more women were reported to be drinking. Many of them were now working on farms, replacing the men away fighting; a photo of Edith Gale from Peacock Farm was used in national publicity.[14] Communal kitchens sprang up to assist the women, providing meals at the end of the working day.

Bracknell Cricket Club faced a dire position at their AGM in February:

> The financial statement ... showed a balance of £10 at the bank, but there was £27 outstanding for a year's rent on the ground. After a long discussion, it was resolved that the landlord be offered the club's properties and assets, valued at £60, but which would probably fetch not more than a third of this sum at the present time. A resolution was carried that the club be wound up.[15]

On 27 March, a local writer recorded in her diary: 'Day of wild rumours (locally). Our navy defeated! Big battle in North Sea for 3 days! Germans landed in Scotland. All troops mobilized. Nothing in papers.'[16] It was all a false alarm. Another rumour spread widely in Bracknell that Bullbrook School was to be turned into a military hospital. 'We can assure the parents and scholars that there is no sort of foundation for this rumour,' announced the authorities.

British Summer Time was instituted in May, moving the clocks forward by one hour to maximise working hours in the day, particularly in agriculture. ERDC introduced a scheme to pay for the storage of furniture for men being called up, their wives often going back to live with their family. When Lawrence Trodd and Bert Wood were killed towards the end of the year, ERDC paid for the continued storage on behalf of their widows.[17]

The area around Bracknell was heavily wooded, with many trees now being cut down for the war. 'Whole acres of Swinley and parts of the woods round Chavey Down have been denuded of trees, and lorries and wagons of all descriptions form a constant steam into Bracknell station, thousands of tons having been dispatched from there.'[18]

More news, purporting to come from the fighting front, was published in early July. An eyewitness account gave an account of the first day of the Battle of the Somme:

At 7.30 our colonel blew the whistle, and the line advanced. It was splendid; looking right and left, one could see a single even line 'charging' at the walk. We were the first line over. Their artillery had been smashed by ours before, but oh! The machine gun fire we came under was hell itself, and we suffered.[19]

Five Bracknell men were killed on this day, with many more wounded. The press reports continued to record this as a great victory well into July, but also listed 'Berkshire Casualties in Great Push'. These continued to the end of September, almost filling an entire page at times. A month earlier, readers were informed that 'no representative of this locality has so far been reported as having been lost or wounded in the great fight off Jutland'.[20]

A fire at Skimped Hill destroyed a shed containing carts belonging to butcher Henry Collins, but prompt action by the police and members of the Bracknell Fire Brigade prevented the blaze from spreading to adjoining buildings. Three weeks later, 'a fire which broke out at Messrs Lawrence's Stores Ltd which ... might easily have had far more serious consequences. As it was, the damage caused by smoke and water is very considerable, and is estimated at from £5000 to £6000'– between £300,000 and £360,000 in today's money.

A Canadian Forestry Corps Company had started extracting timber around Rapley Lake in May, which was causing damage to Bagshot Road within three months. As ERDC no longer had any vehicles available for repairs (they had been given up for use in the war effort), they were forced to hire some from the firm of Thomas Lawrence. Material for the work was shipped to the old brickworks sidings at Ascot West station. John McNeil, a Canadian soldier, was arrested for being drunk and incapable in the shop of hairdresser Walter Denby in the High Street. He had been in Bracknell for forty-eight hours, and the police had received several complaints about his behaviour. He was handed over to the military authorities. Timber was also being extracted on Swinley Road, Long Hill Road, and around Caesar's Camp.

There was local excitement at the end of September when three men were found asleep at the side of the road near The Royal Foresters Hotel. A special constable sent to investigate 'soon discovered that they were foreigners'. They were German prisoners who had escaped from Deepcut a few days earlier, 'and with the assistance of men from the Royal Flying Corps who were passing at the time ... removed them to Ascot Police Station'. Two further Germans were captured the following day afternoon:

> The local police, with many zealous assistants, scoured the woods, where they were believed to be, and eventually succeeded in locating them, through a keeper named Thomas Brickwell, who found them in a small wood at Hawthorndale, Warfield [now part of the Syngenta site]. They surrendered to him quickly ... and taken in a police motor-car to Wokingham, where they were handed over to the military authorities.[21]

A film about the Battle of the Somme was being shown to British audiences for a week in October, the nearest screening being in Reading cinema. *The Times* newspaper reported:

> Crowded audiences ... were interested and thrilled to have the realities of war brought so vividly before them, and if women had sometimes to shut their eyes to escape for a moment from the tragedy of the toll of battle which the film presents, opinion seems to be general that it was wise that the people at

The Canadian Forestry Corps worked in various locations in east Berkshire, felling and extracting trees. This included Swinley Forest, with the timber being despatched from Bracknell railway station.

home should have this glimpse of what our soldiers are doing and daring and suffering in Picardy.

A cinema van visited the town from time to time, organised by the War Aims Committee, displaying pictures of propaganda material.

Two thirds of Britain's food was imported, and by the end of the year, German U-boat activity was taking a huge toll on incoming ships. At home, prisoners of war were being used to do agricultural work, while schoolboys were drafted in to help at harvest time.

1917

Food supplies began to dwindle, and voluntary rationing was introduced – 4lb of bread, cakes and puddings, 2½lb of meat (including bacon, sausages, game, poultry and tinned meat), and ¾lb of sugar per week. This was one of the key factors in the popularity of the newly launched Women's Institute, whose cake-baking demonstrations used vinegar instead of baking powder as a raising agent, and jam preserved with salt rather than sugar. However, one butcher in the High Street continued to get meat deliveries most weeks to turn into sausages – no questions asked about the source. A local Food Committee ensured rationing was adhered to, food was sold at reasonable prices, and no black market operated. Four such cases appeared before the magistrates in 1917.

Sidney Hobley (born 1903) spoke of his feelings about rationing:

> Mother used to send me to the shops in Bracknell and everything was gone under the counter. It all sold for the highest price. You used to see the butchers' boys with legs of lamb and joints of beef going to the big houses, and all we could get was bones to boil up for soup. But once Lloyd George brought in rationing it was alright.

The price of paper had risen by 800 per cent since the start of the war and newspapers were reduced in size with no space for adverts, and only the most important news being published. Allotments were still rare but their use was encouraged, and more parks and public land were being turned over to food production.

There was bitterly cold weather in February, with heavy snowfalls and severe frosts: 'Skating has been in full swing on "Englemere" ... Priestwood Schools are closed on account of the small attendance early in the week, and on Thursday, Bullbrook children were sent home on account of failure of the water supply, all services being frozen up.'[22]

Dr Paterson was called up to work as a doctor in the army, but ERDC ensured 'the necessary steps *are* being taken with a view to securing his exemption from service'. They also supported a request for exemption for the Highway Surveyor James Treadwell.[23]

Two more Canadian Forestry Corps men appeared before Berkshire magistrates at Windsor at the end of April:

> Privates John Macdonald and Cornelius Hansen ... quartered at Rapley Lake Camp, were charged with being drunk at Easthampstead Road, Winkfield, on April 29th.
> P. C. Smith of the Berks Police, said at 8:50pm on Sunday evening, he saw the two prisoners outside The Horse and Groom. They were trying to force their way into the house ... They were drunk and very disorderly ... Landlord Edward Hawkins saw them about fifteen minutes earlier, but refused to serve them a drink, and locked the door ... The prisoners said they got drunk at Bracknell, but they did not remember the names of the houses they went in. They had had about 15 pints of stout each. Macdonald said they started from camp at 2 o'clock, and went into three houses at Bracknell. They slept outside one house until it opened again. P. S. Griffin said they were absolutely mobbed when they took these men into custody. They were mostly in a semi-intoxicated condition. The magistrates required Supt. Jannaway to communicate with the Commanding Officer of the Corps, with a view to Bracknell being put out of bounds.[24]

The Working Men's Club were also fined for serving alcohol to military personnel outside the allotted hours. The following month, William Prior of The Bull was summoned for selling alcohol to a Canadian who was already drunk. There was conflicting evidence from the police and other people who saw the man in question. The case was dismissed but Prior was cautioned 'to be more careful in future', and ordered to pay costs.

On an evening in June, an aeroplane made a planned landing in the grounds of Ramslade House. 'A great crowd gathered to see the machine and aviators, who, after a short stay, rose again beautifully into the air and sailed away, the people giving them a great cheer.'[25]

In July, fifty-four wounded South African soldiers 'suffering principally from arm and leg wounds ... arrived by train at Bracknell station' from a military hospital in Richmond, 'where they were met by seven carriages and brakes' and taken to Binfield House, where the owner gave them tea and entertainment. News on their visit travelled fast, as 'at every point along the route on the return to Bracknell station, women, girls and children came out and waved their welcomes to our African friends'.[26]

Although the cricket club had folded, a 'newly-formed Bracknell Ladies' Cricket Club played their first match ... with a Wokingham team ... A very close and well-fought game resulted in a win for Wokingham by two runs.'[27]

The local branch of the Workers' Educational Association continued to hold regular meetings. The subject for October was 'The Reconstruction of Europe'. The following month started with 'Will this war end war?' with a discourse on war and peace in Europe over the previous 100 years. Other topics covered included 'The Netherlands: The Cockpit of Europe', and 'Poland'. A lantern lecture was also given in the Victoria Hall entitled 'Italy's Share in the Great War', by an officer recently returned from the Italian front.

Bracknell received some refugee children from London who were evacuated to escape the Zeppelin raids. The local superintendent of police compiled a list of builders to repair any air-raid damage that might occur locally.

The funeral for John Firman Quick, another casualty of the war, took place in November:

> The deceased, an old soldier, rejoined the Army at the outbreak of war, and has been serving in the Army Service Corps, attached to the Remount Depot at Arborfield Cross (where horses were trained for war conditions before being shipped to France). After returning from his home in Bracknell on Monday, he reported himself sick, and after examination by the registered doctor, expired almost immediately. He was accorded a military funeral, the body being conveyed to the cemetery by Army wagon from Arborfield, an officer and about a dozen of his late comrades following.[28]

He was soon followed by another soldier, Joseph Mills, who died of kidney disease:

> He had contracted muscular rheumatism in the trenches in France and returned to the UK for treatment before dying in hospital near Leeds. Born in Bracknell, he worked for Messrs Lawrence and Sons as a butcher, High Street, from the age of 14, until he joined the Army. He left a widow and two children.[29]

A couple of weeks later, Portsmouth Ladies' Football Club played a team of men from the Bracknell Down Saw Mills on the ground behind the Downshire Arms. 'The men played with their hands behind their back ... After a very exciting game, the ladies won by six goals to five ... The proceeds were in aid of the local Red Cross funds,' although the organiser appeared before the Wokingham magistrates a few months later over a technicality in the ticket sales, and was fined.

1918

Food rationing began in January 1918 affecting meat (none was available in Bracknell for several days), butter, margarine, lard, tea and sugar, while prices of some other foods were pegged. Later in the year, poultry, cheese and jam were also rationed.[30] Shopkeepers were required to display their prices prominently to mitigate charges of profiteering, but food was available in Bracknell in most cases. There was a talk on the growing of herbs at Victoria Hall. Thefts from allotments became more frequent, and bulk buying and hoarding of sugar was reported. A 'food economy kitchen' was set up where schoolchildren were served with soup for the nominal price of 1d. By its third day, 170 children were attending. Gas supplies to the town were interrupted during January (a testing time as several inches of snow fell on the 17th), and there were complaints of 'an inadequate supply and poor quality of gas' at the end of the month. Appeals were made to people to save water and conserve fuel supplies (coal prices had already been fixed). But by September, there was enough food for afternoon tea to be given to all schoolchildren in the town, an annual event that had been suspended for four years.

The war took a turn for the worse in late March when the Germans launched a major offensive, pushing the Allies back 20 miles, but a daring attack on Zeebrugge the following month (in which Edward Gilkerson from Binfield Road lost his life) restored British morale. By May, a British soldier reported, 'The Huns ran so fast we could not keep up with them.'

The Women's Army Auxiliary Corps was set up and an appeal made for volunteers for a Home Defence Force. Meanwhile, ex-soldiers at home set up a 'Comrades of the Great War' movement to recreate the links forged during the fighting, while those at home opposed to the war held pacifist meetings.

A snowstorm in mid-April 'worked considerable damage to telephone and telegraph wires in the district, and greatly interfered with telephone communication generally'[31]. Two boys from Priestwood School were hit by lightning when sheltering from a storm under a tree in July; one was killed while the other was badly injured but eventually recovered.

At the end of July, an 'influenza epidemic' was being reported in the country, and although it started to recede in August, a far more virulent form began to emerge in September. There were reports of two people being taken ill in the morning and dead by evening in Bracknell.[32] Another circular from the Local Government Board arrived on the desk of the clerk to ERDC regarding 'precautions to be taken in connection with the influenza epidemic'.[33] Consideration was also being given to the 'housing of the working classes' with new three-bedroom houses being proposed.

Walter Callingham put his plant nursery on the Bagshot Road up for sale. Part of the site of the nursery is now occupied by Elizabeth Close.

By the end of October, rumours about the end of the fighting were rife. On the 28th, Ludendorf (the general in charge of the German Army) resigned, and there was talk of the Kaiser abdicating.³⁴ A UK diary entry for the 29th recorded: 'Austria breaking from Germany. Wishes separate peace – accepts all P[resident] Wilson's terms,'³⁵ and on the 31st, 'Turkey out of the war.'³⁶ There were rumours of revolution in Germany on 6 November, and in the German Navy two days later. The armistice was signed on 11 November. The news was received in Bracknell about eleven o'clock, and spread rapidly. 'Groups gathered together, discussing the news, and the street was soon gay with flags.' A Thanksgiving Service was held in the church in the evening, which was attended by a 'large and representative gathering'.³⁷ Services were also held at all the other churches in the town.

Roy Coles was 5 years old when the war ended. He later recalled:

> Another strong memory is of Armistice Day in 1918. Opposite us in the High Street was a jeweller by the name of Poynter and a saddle-maker called King. These two, between them, got hold of some fireworks and on Armistice Day ... they had a firework display in the middle of the High Street.³⁸

Oaklea Auxiliary Hospital was closed on 22 November, the patients being evacuated on that date. During the conflict, it had treated almost 300 in-patients and 'a considerable number of out-patients'.

Although the fighting had ceased, men would not return home for several months, and the usual collections ensured presents and 'goodies' were sent to them for Christmas. ERDC pressed for the early release of their employees, especially Pearson (the road foreman) and Russell (from the sewage farm).³⁹ Edward Sargeant was already home. Wounded no fewer than four times during the fighting, and having received the Military Medal for bravery, he received a bad injury to his hand at a home base and was invalided out of the army in May 1918. A week before Christmas, he was married, the first wedding of an ex-solider.

There had been a government of National Unity during most of the war, but a general election was held in December, with soldiers overseas voting by post. The coalition government won a landslide victory.⁴⁰

1919

Although food supplies were slowly recovering, new ration cards were issued in 1919, with farmers warning of a limited harvest due to lack of manpower, a situation repeated the following year. The price of meat and milk continued to rise.

The year started with a meeting in the Victoria Hall 'to consider what will be the best form of memorial to those of the parish who have fallen in the war ...

two or three forms had been suggested – a cottage hospital or home ... a recreation ground, or some kind of memorial at the top of the High Street'.[41] Each scheme had its own supporters. 'It was suggested in regard to the hospital scheme, that the neighbouring parishes of Easthampstead, Binfield, and Warfield should be asked to join.' Charles Wilson, the local solicitor, attended a similar meeting at Easthampstead two days later to gauge their feelings. Although there was some support for the proposal, Lady Haversham from South Hill Park 'then made a most feeling speech', effectively scuppering the idea.

The next meeting was held two months later. A committee appointed at a previous meeting reported that the proposed cottage hospital scheme appeared to be too expensive to adopt, but that suitable land at a reasonable price could be obtained for the proposed recreation ground (this was where the top end of Deepfield Road now meets Park Road). 'After some discussion, the recreation ground scheme was adopted.'

Life returned to 'normal' very quickly, with local football competitions restarting in February and national leagues following in August. The local hunt resumed in April, and athletics, horse racing, bowls and cricket competitions soon after. At the end of May, 'there was a good attendance at the Working Men's Club ... when a meeting was held to consider the possibilities of reorganising football in

Peace Day was celebrated across the country on 19 July 1919. In this photo, the local parade has reached the top of the High Street.

the district for the next season ... It is hoped to re-construct the Old Bracknell Wanderers Football Club as the premier club in the district.'[42]

A meeting of demobilised sailors, soldiers and airmen was held at the Working Men's Club 'for the purpose of forming a local branch of the Comrades of the Great War ... The subscription is 1s per annum' (about £1.80 in today's money).[43] This was one of several organisations set up by war veterans, all of which later merged to form the Royal British Legion.[44] By October, the newly formed club had arranged for 'a hut for the club to be brought down from London, and re-erected at Bracknell' on the newly purchased war memorial ground.

Prisoners of war were the first men to return after the end of hostilities, but it would be June before the last of the Royal Berkshire Regiment landed back on British soil. Meanwhile, firms were pressing for their former employees to be allowed back. Annual regimental reunion dinners were held for many years. The employment of disabled men also became a major issue, with the Reading newspaper carrying up to two columns each week with details of men seeking work. One local story made the national newspapers in 1928. John Charles Leisk was born in Liverpool in 1906. Some twenty years later, when he was found living rough near Caesar's Camp, 'the hair on his head was a foot long, he was clothed in rags and tatters, and presented a pitiful sight'. His appearance 'had frightened children and females'. He appeared before the Magistrates Court in Wokingham, charged with miscellaneous petty thefts, and also with begging in Ascot. He already had convictions in Wolverhampton (for stealing a bicycle) and Andover (for begging), and had already twice been found wandering around the country and returned to his home; when asked why he kept leaving, he replied, 'No work.' The Chairman of the Bench at Wokingham told him:

> There is no work for you in Easthampstead woods. The Bench are going to do what they consider the kindest thing ... We shall send you to Oxford prison for a month and write to the Discharged Prisoners' Aid Society and ask them to send you home to your mother. You will have some good food ... and you will be kept clean.[45]

Things did not improve for John, as ten years later he was in Belmont Road Workhouse in his home city.

By 1929, ERDC were growing increasingly concerned about unemployment in the area. The number of tramps increased across the country that year; in Easthampstead they rose by 50 per cent in twelve months. The Stock Market crash in 1930 only exacerbated problems. Leonard James Carter of Reading committed suicide by crawling in front of a train near Bracknell station, while several men 'of no fixed abode' appeared before the Wokingham magistrates for petty crimes committed in Bracknell.

Although plans were drawn up to build houses to overcome the post-war housing shortage, many projects remained on the drawing board. ERDC built some new homes in Binfield Road, near the junction with Shepherd's Lane. The Ministry of Labour set up a Branch Employment Office in the town 'for work connected with the resettlement of His Majesty's Forces in civil employment, and unemployment insurance'. The office was operational by mid-July, when employers were being urged to make known their vacancies.

Although hostilities ceased with the Armistice on 11 November 1918, the First World War did not end officially until the Treaty of Versailles was signed in June 1919. On 19 July, Peace Day celebrations were held across the country. In Bracknell, the celebrations started with a short church service at 12:30 p.m.:

A luncheon was given to all the local men who have served in the war, over 200 being present ... In the afternoon, the children were entertained in the Victoria Hall, and there was a parade through the streets. A sports programme and tea was followed by a concert ... and dancing and a bonfire completed the day's enjoyment.[46]

ERDC employees received pay at the Sunday rate for the day.[47]

Two minutes' silence was held across the country at 11 a.m. on 11 November to mark the Armistice. A few days earlier, Bracknell Congregational Church had unveiled their war memorial, a list of nine men who made 'the supreme sacrifice', and a further thirty-five who 'served with the colours'. When the church was demolished in 1968 as part of the regeneration of the High Street, the memorial was moved to St Paul's United Reformed Church in Harmanswater.

1920

The *Reading Mercury* reported: 'Motor omnibuses pass through Bracknell from Reading to Ascot.' A service to Maidenhead was proposed later in the year.

Ex-soldier Arthur Belcher used a razor in an attack on his wife, leaving her in a serious condition. He had been expelled from their home in Bagshot Road the previous evening, when Mrs Belcher had returned home from an event at the Victoria Hall with another man who Belcher attacked, before turning his attention on his wife. He disappeared after the incident and was found at 10.30 the following morning, hiding in a disused shed on Mill Lane, brought before the Wokingham magistrates and charged with attempted murder, and remanded into custody. The evidence was heard a couple of weeks later when Belcher was committed for trial at Reading Assizes.

'The Comrades of the Great War' was one of the forerunner organisations that became the Royal British Legion. The local branch was formed in 1918, and within twelve months had raised enough money for a clubhouse. (Photo courtesy of Albert Brant)

The lease was signed for the Comrades clubhouse in April, and work began to re-erect the building, a construction of part brick and part corrugated iron. On the second Sunday in July, the newly formed group (which now had more than 400 members) held an event to remember their fallen comrades, a commemoration that became an annual event. A procession started from the police station, with the local Boy Scouts' band in attendance, with a service being held at 3.30 p.m. in the new clubhouse. A pleasure fair visited Bracknell later in the month, and donated its takings on the last night from the swings and roundabouts to the Comrades Club. Sir Doveton Sturdee, described as 'one of England's foremost Admirals', visited Bracknell in August to formally open the premises.[48] 'Many local dignitaries and prominent residents also attended the event.'

At the start of August, '27 happy little boys and girls from the Cottage Homes left Bracknell by the 8 o'clock train for Tankerton near Whitstable for a month's holiday, provided by kind-hearted subscribers. These little people had never seen the sea, and were looking forward to a great time.'[49] They were accompanied by Mr and Mrs Crews, the Master and Matron of the home.

Bracknell Wednesday Football Club re-formed the same month. 'A suitable ground has been kindly placed at the Club's disposal in Bull Lane.'[50]

Lawrence's Stores began a summer sale that lasted the entire month of August.

At the end of September, a field gun 'presented by the War Office to Easthampstead District Council has just been fixed on the triangle opposite Old Bracknell House, and is a source of much interest to the parishioners'.⁵¹ Across the nation, the War Trophies Committee was endeavouring to foist redundant German ordnance on towns and villages that wanted a memorial to the fallen. These were not universally popular, and more than one village awoke to find their new acquisition in the local duck pond!⁵²

In October:

> a public meeting was held at the Comrades' Hut ... to consider the advisability of reviving the Bracknell Choral Society, when a large number interested in music attended ... and a resolution unanimously carried. The Comrades' committee offered free use of the hut for rehearsals, along with use of their piano.⁵³

A week later, there was a 'large attendance' at another meeting at the Victoria Hall 'to consider the question of reviving the Bracknell Cricket Club'. The initial expenditure was put at about £200 to purchase a pavilion and ground-keeping equipment, and an annual income of £150. The old cricket field on the High Street was available, the current tenant:

Redundant German ordnance was distributed to local councils as memorials to the war, but were far from popular. Locally, a field gun was placed in front of Old Bracknell House.

placing no obstacle in the way, and ... offering the use of adjoining fields in connection with the annual sports in August. A representative committee was elected, including many of the old members, and also those of Easthampstead Cricket Club ... Within a few minutes, £120 was subscribed towards the initial outlay[54].

Two other organisations in the town were mentioned in December: 'The 1st Bracknell Girl Guides Troop is gradually gaining new members and progressing admirably under the guidance of Miss St Quentin', while 'arrangements are in hand for an exhibition of boxing at an early date. It is being arranged by local sportsmen, provided suitable accommodation can be found.'

1921

A meeting was held in January:

to receive ... the report of the War Memorial committee and to sanction the purchase of three acres of land adjoining the Comrades' Hut, Park Road, for a recreation ground. A further appeal would be made so a memorial with a list of names of the fallen might be erected there as well.[55]

Later in the month, the Comrades:

gave a tea and entertainment at the Club House to the widows and orphans of their fallen comrades, about 125 in total. Motors were provided to fetch and return the children from Easthampstead, Binfield, Warfield, and Winkfield. After tea, 'Old Father Christmas' presented each child with a gift from his bag. In the evening the place was packed and the Easthampstead School children repeated their programme, given earlier in the day, consisting of part songs, dances, etc. The boys in a nigger burlesque brought the house down. The Comrades hope to make this an annual event.[56]

The Comrades also visited the Working Men's Club for a games tournament, but 'proved a poor match for their cleverer opponents and were hopelessly beaten by 17 points to 3'. The tournament included billiards, whist, cribbage, darts, shove-halfpenny, draughts and dominoes.

Lawrence's Stores were again holding a massive sale in February. 'Practically the whole of this company's stock, valued at over £55,000 [*£1.8 million in today*'s money], is being offered at enormous reductions, and in all their showrooms ... there are numberless big bargains to be had.' The firm was struggling as a result of the war.

The Effect of the First World War and its Aftermath

Old Bracknell Wanderers still had a reputation for 'rumbustious' play and disorderly behaviour by their supporters. As a result of the referee's report on their match against Bear Wood in March, they were 'cautioned and ordered to post warning notices'.

The war memorial inside Holy Trinity Church, a wooden board containing a list of the fallen men, was dedicated on 20 March (Palm Sunday).[57] Several appeals had been made in the parish magazine for relatives to put forward names for inclusion, and these were painted on the panels of the board in alphabetical order, with several more being added subsequently. 'The Comrades of the Great War paraded and marched to the church, headed by the Ascot Brass Band.'[58]

There are fifty-seven names in total, and the effect on the town can be judged from their pre-war professions:

Silas Brown was the manager of the Home and Colonial Stores in the High Street.

Stanley Coates, Albert Court and George Fish were all grocer's assistants.

Harry Hollis worked in his father's tailors shop.

Edwin Holloway worked in his father's greengrocers shop.

Albert Jordan worked at a fishmongers in the High Street.

John Pinnell worked in his father's bakery.

George Almond was a shop assistant in the Stanley Road Stores.

Gilbert Barber was a clerk in the post office; Stanley Ewins and Sidney Harvey were postmen.

Ernest Blay, Alfred Davis and Albert Searle worked for local corn merchants.

Richard Legg worked in the brewery trade.

Christopher Elwick, Harry Fletcher and George Rance worked as gardeners at local 'big houses'.

Arthur Jenkins, Thomas Johnson, George Matthews and Arthur Richardson worked in the local brickyards.

Charles Olyott, Frederick Rance and Frank Sargeant worked locally in the building trade.

Lawrence Trodd had won several prizes for sprinting at the annual sports meetings. He was also caught up in the betting scandal that saw his father fined in 1910.

Albert Searle was the Boy Scout who welcomed Princess Victoria to the Art Exhibition in 1911.

Samuel Bowyer (garden nursery at Windlesham), Albert Butler (London), Ernest Gambriel (Hereford), Walter Hope (Hereford), John Olyott (ironmonger in Nottingham) were all Bracknell born, as were Ronald Gregory, William King, John Merrett.

Luke Baker, Herbert Norman, Eric Roe were Bracknell natives, already serving in the armed forces when war broke out. Frederick Butler was on the Reserve List, having formerly served with the army.

In addition, William Gilkerson (who worked in the Lawrence Stores and played football for Old Bracknell Wanderers), Charles Langley (the first Boy's Prefect at Priestwood School), and Terence Faulkner (the bugle player at the funeral of Alfred Davis in 1914) are among those listed on the Easthampstead war memorial.

The Bracknell Cricket Club resurrected their Athletics Sports meeting in August. Despite a hiatus of eight years, and a record number of entries, the event ran like clockwork before a crowd of more than 5,000.

1922

The president of the Working Men's Club unveiled a roll of honour in April in the club lounge, 'in memory of those members who gave their lives for their country, or served in H. M. Forces during the Great War'. This Roll of Honour has now disappeared.

In July, it was reported that, on a point of law, the Hind's Head was allowed to stay open all day when the market was in operation, being the nearest establishment to the market venue.

The Bracknell Athletic Sports again took place in August, with photos from the event appearing in the press for the first time. Local runner Bill Cottrell, who had won the British Army Three Mile Championship in the morning, 'rushed from Aldershot to take part, winning by half a lap from his nearest rival'. The cricket club had also formed a boys' team. 'Under proper tuition, the boys have become promising material. Four matches have been played, including Ascot (twice), Warfield and Priestwood, and on each occasion they have proved greatly superior in all-round cricket, winning all matches easily.'[59]

The Scott McComb family purchased Starch Copse, having bought the adjacent Lily Hill estate ten years earlier. They now planted the woodland with 'a large quantity of hardy-hybrid rhododendrons from the Waterer Nursery in Knapp Hill', many of which are still thriving and flowering magnificently a century later. The estate was sold to Bracknell Development Corporation in 1955.

Wreaths from the Comrades Club were prominent at local churches on Armistice Day, as well as at the newly erected war memorials at Winkfield and Ascot.

1923

Dame Nellie Melba was one of the most famous opera singers of the period, and the first singer of note to be heard on the radio. 'Thanks to the enterprise of Lawrence Stores the public have, free of charge, been able to "listen in" to her performance at Covent Garden.'[60]

The ERDC minutes for 22 March record the following: 'An application was received from the committee of the British Legion for permission to erect a Memorial at the junction of the Binfield and Wokingham roads, and this was agreed to, provided no interference to the Council's sewers and appliances results.' Frederick Finch Mackenzie of Ramslade House, a former army man, was concerned there was no public memorial for Armistice Day commemorations, so organised and paid for one out of his own pocket.

The final of the Fielden Cup, a competition started four years earlier, was played at the Old Bracknell Wanderers ground in Larges Lane in May. The home side had narrowly failed to reach the final, having lost to Bear Wood in the semi-final – but only after four replays! Bear Wood and Winkfield then played out another drawn game, with extra time failing to separate the two sides. In the end, the winners were decided by a toss of the coin, and Winkfield, the better side on the day, proudly took the trophy home. Profits from the competition were used to help finance the Royal Victoria Nursing Home in Ascot.

There was a record attendance at the Bracknell Athletic Sports in August, where local man Bill Cottrell again won the 3-mile championship 'with ease'. As well as the sports, there was a display from the Army School of Physical Training Staff from Aldershot, which included horizontal and parallel bars, high vaulting horse tricks, fencing and quarter-staff displays. There was disappointment for Cottrell the following year when, having been chosen to compete in the Olympic Games in Paris in July, he suffered 'an accident' and had to withdraw from the British team.

The Comrades of the Great War was one of four organisations formed for ex-servicemen after the conflict. These all merged in May 1921 to form the British Legion, becoming the Royal British Legion on its fiftieth anniversary in 1971. An exhibition was held in its premises in October, the former Comrades Club, of 'rare French, American, British and Canadian war posters … The proceeds were devoted to the purchase of furniture for the club.' Three months later, 'a very successful whist drive was held … when about 150 were present. Considerable interest was taken as the proceeds were in aid of a new piano which the club is badly in need of.'[61]

Until now, the area that is the Harmanswater estate was simply a woodland of pine trees. Ralphs Ride was mentioned at the time of the Windsor Enclosure Act in 1813, but when the land changed hands a century later, it was being advertised as 'about 76 acres of fir wood, known as Harman's Water'. However, in 1923, the *Reading Standard* carried an advert: 'Messrs Robins and Wright Bros have now sold the whole of the frontage on the west side of Ralph's Ride, Bracknell. A few more plots are available on the east side at £40 per acre' – £1,700 in today's money. The first properties were built within eighteen months. By 1927, the sanitary inspector at ERDC noted that 'Ralph's

The war memorial originally stood at the junction of Wokingham Road and Binfield Road, and was unveiled on 25 October 1924. It moved to the top of Skimped Hill Lane in 1957, and to its current position in 1971. (Photo courtesy of Stewart Willis)

Ride was the only part of the Council's area which had no water supply. It was so scattered an area ... that a scheme for the supply would prove very expensive.' A mixture of residents lived in the area – labourers, people of an artistic nature, retired people of various financial means, and Madam Leana, 'a scientific palmist'. Men returning from the war received a gratuity ranging from £5 to £30 (£200 to £1,200 in today's money), depending on their length of service. With so many trees, serious fires were always a risk. In 1933, 'a fire broke out at Ralph's Ride ... and fears were expressed for the safety of the adjacent bungalows. The Bracknell Fire Brigade were soon on the scene and prevented the flames from spreading.'[62]

1924

A small library opened at the Victoria Hall. It was staffed by WEA volunteers, contained just over 150 books, and was open for only one hour per week (on Saturday evenings). It moved to the Congregational Church schoolroom ten years later.

Lawrence's Stores were advertising again in May:

Having lately purchased the entire contents of a number of houses ... and not having the necessary room to exhibit same in their show-room, we have secured the use of Messrs Hunton & Sons auction room in High Street, Bracknell, to display these goods for one month only from April 28th. All goods purchased will be delivered free within a twenty mile radius.

Bracknell's war memorial was unveiled 'in the presence of a large gathering' on 25 October by General Lord Rawlinson, Commander-in-Chief of the British Army in India, in front of a large crowd assembled for the event. The high-profile dignitary triggered a photo and brief report of the event in the *Daily Mirror* newspaper, as well as the *Reading Standard*, which carried photographs of the occasion.[63]

With the erection of a war memorial, Bracknell drew a line under the conflict. The fallen were still publicly remembered on an annual basis, but life was moving on.

8

Life Goes On

'Bracknell never altered in those days ... you seemed to know everybody whenever you came home after being away,' remembered Bess White, who was born in 1905 and grew up near the railway station.

'High Street properties had shops on the ground floor with gardens behind, backing onto open fields. The shopkeepers generally lived above the shops themselves. All the shops delivered to people's homes, with shop boys travelling by foot or bicycle, or sometimes horse and cart. 'We used to have about four good grocer's shops ... You could rely on all of them and the little bakers and all ... the baker came round regularly; the milkman came with his can.' Len Donne recalled: 'My father first worked for a shop in Bracknell – May & Sons, a corn straw and hay merchant. They were in the High Street and the warehouses were in Stanley Road ... My father used to drive a horse and cart and deliver the goods.'[1]

Bess White continued: 'Jimmy Matthews the greengrocer ran a small shop with only room inside for one customer at a time, while fresh bread straight from the oven could be bought at the back door of Pinnock's the bakers ... There were two very good laundries ... both off Broad Lane.' The East Berks Laundry (founded in 1928) stood on the corner of Broad Lane and Martins Lane, while the Forest Laundry site (1939) is now Poplar Close.

The coming of the railway allowed the village to grow quicker than the surrounding ones. Ron Morris, born just after the war, could recall:

> Cattle being driven up to the market ... The cattle sold there were then driven along Church Road to the station and sent off by train ... It was a very busy time on the farm coming up to Christmas, when all the poultry, geese and ducks were killed for the Bracknell Market Christmas Fat Stock Show. I can remember picking the birds in the kitchen in the evening and there were two or three inches of feathers on the floor.

Occasionally a cow would escape down the High Street, chased by the drover and young children, providing some excitement. In another incident with livestock: 'I remember one day a load of sheep – you know how sheep go – one came in and they all came in the shop and they scattered everything in the International Stores. We lads had some fun trying to herd the sheep out!' Lily Hill Poultry Farm (at the bottom of Allsmoor Lane), and Hollywood Poultry Farm (probably on Ralphs Ride or The Warren) contributed to the local egg production. Milk in churns from the local farms would arrive daily at the railway station by 6.30 a.m., either collected by a lorry or transported by pony and cart (the boys driving the carts would then engage in races back to their respective destinations). Other than market day, Bracknell was very quiet. 'We walked to school, I suppose it was about a mile and a half, we used to go home mid-day and walk back again. There was no transport much in those days, the roads were very quiet, no traffic hardly, just a horse and cart and suchlike and a few cycles.'

As well as the railway and regular bus services, many local garages and firms offered private hire vehicles for outings, excursions and services to local events. Keene's 'Cody' Bus Service, based in Binfield, ran from The Hind's Head to an Olde English Fayre being held in Hurst in 1925, while Jarvis and Sons from Reading offered outings to Southsea, Bognor, Eastbourne, Cheddar Gorge, Bournemouth or the British Empire Exhibition (with elephants, model railways and butter sculptures) at Wembley in 1924, with pick-up points in Wokingham, Bracknell and Ascot, during the August Bank Holiday weekend. Other operators could transport you to Hindhead, Kew Gardens, Burnham Beeches or Warwick Castle (via Stratford-on-Avon), 'with rugs provided and passengers set down at their homes on return'. Sporting events were not forgotten – Harper's Rover Coaches De Luxe would take you to the racing at Goodwood or Epsom. Travel was, of course, much slower – a charabanc trip to Portsmouth might travel at 20 mph, with passengers having to get out and walk when they reached the uphill sections of road! Not to be outdone, the Southern Railway Company offered cheap tickets to London on Saturday afternoons, while in 1927 the Thames Valley Traction Company offered a daily service between Reading and London, stopping at Sindlesham, Wokingham, Bracknell, Ascot, Sunninghill, Sunningdale, Egham and Staines. This service was running hourly by 1930.

There were limited opportunities for women to work, especially after they were married. This was especially the case during the depression years as unemployment rose:

> My mother did not go out to work until we were about twelve, and then she only used to go a few hours a week to do some housework for a lady. The 1930s were a pretty quiet time here really. There was quite a lot of unemployment during the depression years and it was hard for poorer people.[2]

Len Donne was in his early twenties by then, but stayed in Bracknell apart from seeing service in the Second World War. Life was hard for many people such as Len, who often lived in very basic conditions with very little money:

> Mum and Dad slept in the front bedroom, girls in back bedroom and my brother on the sofa in the living-room. We slept on paillasses filled with straw and went to bed at five o'clock in the winter ... I was often hungry as a child. I have sat out many a time in Harry Gale's fields and eaten swedes and turnips. And whenever the farmer put cabbages out for the cows, my mother used to send us out to get them.

Life in the surrounding countryside was dominated by the large estates and houses and the seasonal round of agriculture and social events, such as shooting. Easthampstead Park, South Hill Park and Lily Hill provided employment for many local people as house servants, farm workers, gardeners and gamekeepers. Albert Cheney of Bay Road recalled:

> It was all Lords and Ladies and Majors and Generals round here in those days ... South Hill Park – Lady Haversham, Mrs Lucena was at Westwick, and Ramslade was Colonel MacKenzie ... They used to ride into Bracknell to do their shopping, they used to have a carriage and a pair ... old coachman would sit up there.

The big regional event was Ascot week:

> Ascot week was quite an event. The schools used to close because of the traffic. People used to turn out to watch the traffic because it was so dense then. For that week it was like it is in modern times, but that was an unusual sight then. Children with their notebooks taking all the numbers on the cars. And if they'd had a good day, the racegoers used to throw handfuls of money out to the crowds from the old open charabancs.[3]

'Gypsy camps were a familiar sight around the outskirts of Bracknell,' wrote Eileen Briggs, reminiscing on her childhood in Bracknell. 'Strings of washing would be hung up to dry on a line tied up between two trees. Ponies were tethered nearby, grazing on the grass verges. Well-fed dogs would always be roaming around with them.'[4]

Stanley 'Figgy' Billing, born in 1924, remembers the town in the 1930s:

> I used to go out with old Billy Gale on Saturday mornings in a pony and trap with the milk. He had a milk round in Bracknell. I used to hold the horse while

he went to the houses. Otherwise the horse would wander about, as there was plenty of grass in Bracknell in those days.

Ron Morris also helped with milk deliveries:

> I used to get up at five-thirty every morning, winter and summer, and milk the cows by hand. I had my breakfast at seven o'clock and then I was out with my uncle around Bracknell with the milk. The night's milk was always taken to Bracknell Station and sent to Hounslow on the six o'clock train.

1924

Viscount Cecil of Chelwood, 'one of the greatest authorities on the League of Nations, addressed a largely-attended meeting at the Victoria Hall'[5] in November. The League had been set up in 1920 in an attempt to avoid another global conflict but ultimately failed in its objective. It was replaced by the United Nations in 1946. A League of Nations branch was set up in the town. Within three years, a visiting speaker was warning of the threat of war again – 'France was mobilising ... and resentment among former enemies caused by feeling they had not been given a fair deal.'[6]

A few days before Christmas, 'the scholars of the Church of England Schools, Bullbrook' gave two ambitious performances of an operetta, *The Wishing Cup*, at the British Legion Club, with proceeds going towards funds for war widows and their children. Although dense fog led to a disappointingly small audience on the first evening, 'the whole production went admirably'.[7]

1925

The year started with the River Thames 'overflowing its bank at several points ... and large tracts of country ... are under water. The road between Binfield and Bracknell was flooded for a quarter of a mile to a depth of over a foot.'[8]

No sooner had the waters subsided, than Lawrence's Stores was subject to a break-in. The robbery was big news in the little town. 'The affair has created a sensation in Bracknell, where the police investigations are being followed with the closest interest.'[9]

Messrs Wright Bros. of Reading were offering 1-acre plots of land for sale at The Warren estate off Bog Lane. Most of the houses built there were wooden bungalows until the area was developed in the 1980s as Bracknell expanded. They also had a rabbit warren available in Bracknell for Angora rabbit breeders: 'Only 27 miles from London ... why not take up this very profitable hobby?'

The Home Counties 1-mile cycling championship was part of the Cricket Club Athletic Sports in August. So many entries were received that two heats needed to be held. The pre-meeting publicity announced that 'some of the best light-weight tug-of-war teams in England will pull for the valuable trophy presented by the Marquis of Downshire'; the event was won by a team from the Metropolitan Police.

1926

The General Strike, lasting nine days, took place in May but without any comment on its effect in Bracknell in the local newspapers, although one visitor to Bracknell Market tried to blame his bad parking on it! Less than 20 per cent of Southern Rail services ran, but the drivers and conductors of the Thames Valley Traction Company continued working, and bus services were unaffected.

Henry Smith's coal and coke business at Bracknell station was put up for sale, the owner having been declared bankrupt (he claimed the business had struggled ever since the coal miners' strike of 1921).

Another long-serving railway employee retired in November. Alfred Bray had worked for Southern Railway for more than forty-eight years. He had spent over half his working life at Bracknell, where he had been employed variously as signalman, shunter, porter and crossing keeper at Waterloo Road in Wokingham at various times. His son also started work at Bracknell railway station at the age of 14, but 'resigned after indifferent conduct' just four months later.

1927

Ascot Gas Company was about to install three new lamps on the Bracknell streets, bringing the total in the town to seventy-five. An ERDC councillor commented the matter had been agreed three months earlier, and the gas company 'ought to get a move on'. Later in the year, it was decided not to replace the gas lamps with electric ones, the running costs being 50 per cent greater.

Colonel Edwards, chairman of the Bracknell branch of the British Legion, praised the work of the women's section at a garden party, organised by them: 'You show an enthusiasm which is not found in the men's organisation,' and appealed to them to 'get their menfolk to take a little more interest ... Judging from the work done in Bracknell, nine tenths is done by the women's section ... due to the apathy of the men, it is almost impossible to get a quorum at a committee meeting.'

Snow in December was said to be the heaviest for nearly forty years. Eddy Jaggard (born 1922) recalls skating from his home in Binfield Road as far as The Stag and Hounds in Binfield. 'Before there were many cars about, whenever we had a snowfall the snow soon got hard and compacted and you could skate on it.' Mill Pond in Easthampstead, the brickworks at Amen Corner, and Dry Pond on the Crowthorne Road were also popular skating spots (the latter, being shallow, was frequented by beginners).

1928

Although a carrier was still operating a daily service to Reading, this had ceased by 1931. Buses were now running to both Windsor and Sunningdale. A telephone was installed in the police station, the local exchange having had its capacity increased the previous year, although it would be several years before Bracknell got a telephone kiosk. ERDC purchased a tar-spraying machine for road surfacing, but declined a request for road nameplates to be put up.

After twenty-eight years, Dr Fielden retired and left Bracknell. For all but six of them, he had been the District Medical Officer and Public Vaccinator for the Bracknell district, as well as Medical Officer for the Easthampstead Workhouse. 'Over thirteen hundred people ... rich and poor alike, joined together in making a presentation ... He is beloved by all classes and particularly by the poor, to whom he has been so generous in his treatment.'[10] It was felt a public testimonial should be made to Dr Fielden and his wife, 'who has also taken the keenest interest in the welfare of the people', and more than £550 (over £24,000 in today's money) was subscribed, 'the contributors being people of humble station and people of means'. The presentation took place in the Victoria Hall, although only the organisers were able to be present as 'there is not a hall large enough in Bracknell to accommodate all those who wished to attend'.[11] But within a few years, Fielden and his wife moved back to Bracknell, at town with so many happy memories for them.

Although not rosy, the cricket club's finances had improved slightly, due in part to an anonymous donor who had gifted them almost £1,000 in today's money. Two women's races were included in the Athletic Sports in July for the first time.

A representative from the Canadian National Railways, with practical farming experience as well, visited Bracknell to give a presentation at the Victoria Hall. 'He can tell you all you want to know about going to Canada, working in Canada, and opportunities in Canada for men, women, and boys (were girls not wanted?). He also has particulars on Assured Farm Employment, Assisted Passages, and £3 fares.'[12] A farmer from Saskatchewan was also in town twelve months later.

The Olympic Games took place in Amsterdam. Local man Frank Angel represented Britain in the heavyweight division of the wrestling, having won the UK Championship earlier the same year.

Having been disbanded a few years earlier, the fire brigade was reconstituted, jointly funded by Warfield, Winkfield and Easthampstead parish councils. Binfield turned down a request for contributions, stating they were adequately covered by the Wokingham brigade. A fire engine was purchased, and a garage supplied until a purpose-built fire station opened in Rochdale Road three years later. The telephone for them was at The Hind's Head, with a siren located at the Slyfield Sawmills, but if they received a call during the night, a runner would be sent to wake the firemen. In a test turn-out at 11.30 p.m. one evening, they were on the road within seven minutes. ERDC took over responsibility for the service in 1938, before the National Fire Service took over three years later. An old resident recalled the equipment being stored in a small room next to The Crown, while Dick Harvey, a firefighter from the early days, remembers: 'Before the war there weren't many fires. We used to go for months and months without a call-out.'[13]

The new brigade's first shout came in November when a fire at Hunton's printing works was discovered an hour after midnight on a Tuesday morning. 'Although

A fire engine had been purchased for the town in 1928. It was stored in a garage until a purpose-built fire station opened three years later. (Photo courtesy of Albert Brant)

the fire was under control very quickly, a considerable amount of damage was caused to machinery, etc.' The response to the fire was delayed when it was discovered the fire hydrant was buried under 9in of 'road material ... mud and stones'.[14]

Badminton had become a popular sport, with 3,500 clubs in the country boasting 120,000 members. The first reference to a club in Bracknell came in December when they beat the Battle Club of Reading by nine rubbers to nil. Other organisations were springing up, including the Bracknell Mummers (who regularly performed in Victoria Hall, and raised funds for the unemployed in the early 1930s), a motorcycle club (who staged races in a field beside Binfield Road), and a hockey club with members from Bracknell, Warfield and Winkfield.

1929

ERDC had a problem with rubbish, or rather with disposing of it. The owner of the current tip site had been prosecuted for burning rubbish too close to the highway. The council identified another site as a temporary measure, noting the amount of rubbish they were dealing with had gone from 800 to 2,000 tons in three years. Many complaints were made about the collection of refuse the following year. ERDC had a new contractor:

> and there was always this trouble when the work changed hands ... In some cases widowed ladies and maiden ladies living in houses were unable to get their maids to carry the bins out of doors and so put twopence near the bins for the dustman to fetch the bin out. The new men had not yet discovered where the twopence was hidden.[15]

The cricket club's Annual Sports, a major event in the calendar before the war, were held for the last time, having failed to generate as much interest and support as in earlier times. The event made a profit of just £10 (£440 in today's money).

Frederick Hunton, the long-time auctioneer at Bracknell Market which he had instigated, and 'one of the oldest auctioneers in the country',[16] died at the age of 86. He was still working until a fortnight before his death. He had held several posts in the community at Holy Trinity Church, Bracknell and District Cricket Club (latterly he had been their president), a trustee of the Victoria Hall, the Priestwood School Council, and The Royal Forest Agricultural Association.

Work started on Church House, a hall for Holy Trinity Church, which opened in July the following year, as well as repairs to the roof of the church itself.

July also saw Bracknell Bowling Club win their first county championship in the fours event, which they retained the following year and narrowly failed to win for a third time in 1931.

Life Goes On

1930

The committee of the Bracknell and District British Legion Club invited tenders for the erection of proposed new premises in February. Although still based at the Comrades Hut in Park Road, the club by now had '250 very active members'. The building was paid for by local businessman Harold Footman on the understanding that only local men were employed, and local materials were used in its construction.

The new facility opened in November, although not in time for Armistice Day:

> The splendid new club house of the Bracknell branch of the British Legion was opened in the presence of a large number of Legionnaires and friends by Admiral Sir Dudley St Chair (late Governor General of New South Wales and founder of the branch) ... Members, with delegates from twelve neighbouring branches, paraded with their banners in front of the old club in Park Road and, headed by the band of the Maidenhead British Legion, marched via the

Opened in November 1930, this replaced the Comrades Hut erected eleven years earlier. It was regarded as the finest Legion in southern England until its demolition to make way for the town centre redevelopment. (Photo courtesy of Albert Brant)

High Street to where the new building stands in Stanley Road ... In a short address Admiral Sir Dudley St Chair congratulated the branch on having what he considered was the finest club house in England for a British Legion branch of its size, and said they were all very grateful to Mr Footman for the extremely generous and practical way in which he had shown his interest in the club.

The Union Jack was hoisted by Mrs Footman and Sir Dudley then unlocked the door of the building with a golden key, a replica of which was presented to Mr Footman as a memento ... Tea was served and a concert organised by members, their wives and friends was held in the new club's delightful concert hall in the evening.[17]

There were more complaints about the water supply in Bracknell: 'The water which came through the taps contained "living creatures" ... and a large quantity of reddish solid matter ... The supply was perpetually being cut off and sometimes the pressure was very weak and water came through with grit and earth.'[18] The Wokingham Water Company replied that any shortage was entirely due to 'the large amount of water wasted and illegally used ... for gardens and non-domestic uses'. The ERDC Medical Officer of Health said the problems generally occurred in the summer when water levels were low in the reservoirs. The living organisms were mosquito larvae. 'You should disinfect it with whisky' was his light-hearted reply to a councillor who complained he was afraid to use the tap for a drink. Later in the year, residents were warned about 'the excessive charges made by the Water Company' which were blamed on 'a clerical error by a late accountant', while their 'continued evasion' on the water supply was causing irritation to ERDC; 'I think we need to nail them down to an agreement to maintain an adequate supply during the summer months.'[19] Water shortages occurred again the following summer.

The formation of a civil parish of Bracknell was mooted to ease the bureaucratic nightmare of the current system of working out rates for the town, which fell in three different parishes – Easthampstead, Warfield and Winkfield. The latter parish were upset by the plan as they would be losing income from the reorganisation, and Easthampstead were said not to be keen on the idea either.

1931

If you thought nothing much ever happened in Bracknell, 1931 was the year of two plane crashes and an earthquake!

Nationally, there were more discussions about the number of pubs and whether some should be closed down. Renewal of the drinks licence for The Crown was refused on the grounds of the number of pubs in Bracknell High Street. It was

The post office opened in 1934 on the site of the old Crown Inn and lock-up. It closed in 2015 when the facility moved to W H Smith in Princess Square.

demolished the following year, along with the old lock-up next door and an old forge, to make way for a new post office (which opened in 1934).

A local branch of the St John's Ambulance Association formed in April, mainly due to the effect of the extra traffic in the area when racing was taking place at Ascot, with sixteen men volunteering their services. Although it would be another three years before they acquired their first ambulance, they became the first division in the county to operate a twenty-four-hour voluntary ambulance service in 1935.

Joseph Harmsworth, a postman for almost fifty years, retired. The ERDC Rating Officer, Mr Gorrman, was fired after irregularities were found in the books; he was later jailed for six months. The publican at The New Inn, Alfred John Collinson, was fined £10 for 'driving while intoxicated'.

An earthquake centred on Dogger Bank in the North Sea occurred at 1:26 a.m. on 7th June, with the effects felt in western parts of Europe as well as Britain. It remains the strongest earthquake recorded in this country, measuring 6.1 on the Richter Scale. Damage was reported in Yorkshire and other locations in eastern England, and even in Berkshire there were reports of cracks in buildings. Local residents spoke of the violent shaking of their houses.

Children and adults headed off on a day trip to the south coast on two trains, organised by local shopkeeper Joe Smith and other local businessmen. This became an annual event until his untimely death in 1956. On one occasion, a young girl went missing in Sussex but was found by the local police and brought home by car the following day. Joe was very active in the town, being president of the Royal British Legion, and taking over the Prince of Wales pub in the High Street in 1951.

In September, films with sound ('talkies') were able to be shown at the Victoria Hall. Films were only shown on three evenings a week, but still continued 'to draw big crowds' for several weeks.

Later in the month, Bracknell hit the national newspapers:

> An aeroplane crashed into a tree at Bracknell on Saturday evening, and remained there, but the two occupants were not hurt and managed to reach the ground by sliding down one of the wings and dropping the remaining six feet. The machine, which belonged to Messrs. Phillips and Powis, at Woodley Aerodrome, had left Woodley in the afternoon, piloted by Mr. Glen Richardson, a student, whose home is in Glamorganshire, and who had just learnt to fly. He was alone in the machine and lost his way. He came down at Arborfield and telephoned to the aerodrome, from which Commander C. W. Croxford, one of the instructors, went to assist him. Commander Croxford flew the machine with Mr. Richardson as passenger, but he took the wrong direction, eventually a landing was made in a field near Broad Lane, Bracknell. It was in taking off again that the machine struck a tree.[20]

The second crash occurred just before Christmas when an RAF plane crashed into a field in Shepherd's Lane. The pilot, who had lost control of the aircraft, and his mechanic both jumped to safety.

To finish an eventful year, anyone standing at the top of High Street would have seen an 'enormous meteor'[21] that passed over Lisbon in Portugal earlier in the day.

1932

A rugby club was formed in March, augmented by staff from Lambrook School. Their pitch was near The Foresters, London Road, with a team from Woolwich being their first opponents.

The Lawrence Stores also held another giant sale in April, when the doors had to be locked at midday due to crowds, but the business finally closed for good three months later. Thomas Lawrence's son, Sidney (who faced bankruptcy proceedings in 1933), maintained the stores had been losing at least £3,000 per year since 1921 (over £100,000 in today's money) due to higher wages, rates and taxes, all of which had increased after the war.

An open-air swimming pool opened on the corner of Broad Lane and Martins Lane. It was operated by ERDC, and followed similar facilities in Reading, Wokingham, Maidenhead, Pangbourne and Theale. Entry was the equivalent of

Located at the corner of Broad Lane and Martin's Lane, the outdoor swimming pool opened in 1932. It closed in 1977 and Quadrant Court now stands on the site.

The Regal Cinema was located on the corner of Station Road, opposite The Red Lion, and opened on 26 November 1932. After a chequered career (it was a bingo hall for a time), it finally closed in 1982.

50p, allowing access all day, and with a heatwave in August, it proved extremely popular. The facility included two pools with a fountain between them (later removed), diving boards of various heights, a slide, and a flat roof for sunbathing (only officially available to those aged over 16). As the roof was coated with tar, it was very hot and very sticky! There was also a shop (now Ballcock and Bits plumbing merchants).

Unemployment continued to be a problem. Six Bracknell men returned from potato harvesting in Jersey in June after five weeks away. They had worked daily from 7 a.m. until 9.30 p.m. for 5s per week (£12.20 in today's money). Accommodation and arrangements were 'very primitive' but the farmer 'on the whole treated the men fairly well'. 'It was better than hanging about doing nothing at home.'[22] Various schemes were discussed to help those without a job, with a suggestion that those in work should donate 2d per £1 of their pay. ERDC discussed using the unemployed for labouring jobs.

BCC were planning to 'dispense with Bracknell Register Office' – the nearest was in Windsor. ERDC wrote to object, and the office was retained. Plans to change the district's boundaries, and merge them with Windsor Rural District, also met with opposition from all concerned.

Bracknell now had a purpose-built cinema that stood opposite the Red Lion, described as 'spacious, well-lit, artistically decorated, and with excellent seating'.[23] It opened on 26 November, having been floodlit for the previous few nights. Independently owned, it was taken over by the Union Cinema chain in 1936, and Associated British Cinemas the following year. There was a full house on the first night, with almost 400 patrons watching *The Man Who Played God*, a film that featured a then little-known actress named Bette Davis. Two of Queen Victoria's granddaughters were in the audience.

1933

A 4-acre playing field at Priestwood School was officially opened in January. An appeal was made for funds for facilities and equipment, which was raised quickly (with the aid of a grant from the Carnegie Trust) and a pavilion and changing rooms were opened five weeks later.

An 'old landmark' was disappearing in Bracknell as the engineering firm W. J. Cole and Sons demolished a chimney stack in their yard to make way for more storage facilities. 'The chimney had belonged to Bracknell Brewery, and may have been built in 1865, the date found on one of its bricks. The well of spring water is in the yard, also the original tank and pump that was used to deliver the water for brewery purposes.'[24]

Old Bracknell Wanderers won the Ascot and District League title (for the second time in their history) by the smallest of goal difference margins.

Dr Fielden's son, Flight Lieutenant Edward Fielden, was appointed Chief Air Pilot and Extra Equerry to Prince of Wales in October. Apart from a break during the Second World War, he continued to serve the royal family until his retirement in 1969, a year after receiving a knighthood.[25]

1934

There were heavy frosts at the start of the year, with skating taking place at Englemere Lake. Despite foggy conditions, an ice hockey match was played there as well.

Huge numbers of eggs were produced in the district, with an egg packing station opening at the corner of London Road and Larges Lane, dealing with up to 129,000 eggs per week. This figure was more than three times the number sold at Bracknell Market just five years earlier. Eggs were collected from producers within a 10-mile radius every day and brought to the packing station, where they were graded, tested for freshness, and packed to be sold by auction at the market. The scheme continued until the outbreak of war.

The death was reported of Mrs Sarah Limmer at the age of 96. She had been on board the first train from Bracknell to Reading, and was also present at the opening of Holy Trinity Church. Asked for her opinion on modern life, she replied, 'The old times were better than today.'

Colonel Mackenzie of Ramslade House died in July. As well as being responsible for Bracknell's war memorial, he was an ERDC councillor, the president of the local Conservative Association, a former president of the Royal Forest Agricultural Association, had a strong association with the Royal British Legion, was a magistrate at Wokingham, chairman of the council of the Broadmoor Lunatic Asylum, and a member of the council of the Holloway Institute. He had also been High Sheriff of Berkshire in 1904. The funeral was held at Holy Trinity, after which he was buried in Larges Lane cemetery. His grave is stopped by a large angel, similar to the one on Bracknell's war memorial.

1935

In February, a football match was arranged between Old Bracknell Wanderers and the unemployed to raise funds to help them. The Wanderers won by four goals to three.

A cycling group in the town, Bracknell Wheelers, organised weekly rides travelling as far as the south coast and Dorset. In May, they set off for a night ride around London to view arrangements for forthcoming King's Silver Jubilee celebrations. In Bracknell, the event was celebrated with a lunch for pensioners at the Victoria Hall (volunteers took meals to those unable to attend). At 2 p.m., a thanksgiving service was held at the war memorial field, and four commemorative trees planted. This was followed by a carnival procession, starting in Park Road and continuing along Church Road and Station Road, and up the High Street back to Park Road. There were so many floats and participants, the procession took fifteen minutes to pass, and completely filled the High Street. Afterwards, Victoria Hall, Church House and the Royal British Legion hosted a children's tea, with each child receiving a commemorative mug. There was a darts tournament, tug-of-war and fancy-dress competitions, sports and a gymkhana. The King's speech was broadcast at 8 p.m., and a bonfire and fireworks rounded off the day.[26]

There were references to two new tennis clubs in the town, one associated with the cricket club, the other at Skimped Hill, which had hard courts.

1936

King George V died on 20 January. A service for him was held at Holy Trinity five days later, and another at Christ the Scientist Church on the 29th. A Bracknell man was one of the soldiers that accompanied the gun carriage bearing the coffin on its journey to Windsor.

A new ambulance for the town was presented by the Marquis of Downshire at the Victoria Hall in February, and a waiting room opened at the railway station a few weeks later. The bowling club purchased the freehold of their ground, while 'Studlands' (now known as The Old Manor) became a 'high class residential club and hotel'.

With an eye on developments in Europe, Britain began preparing for another possible conflict. ERDC formed an Air Raid Precautions Committee, which met for the first time in March, although meetings were not as frequent as those of an Office Accommodation Committee. By May they had identified that decontamination units, street wardens and mobile units would be needed, as well as air-raid squads and sub fire stations 'for each hamlet'. A full-time officer would be needed (but who would pay for him?) They were also requesting '30 masks and 4 suits for experimental purposes'. Two months later, the local branches of the St John's Ambulance and Red Cross reported that all their volunteers had received training; in contrast, the fire brigade and British Legion had made no progress.[27]

The film being shown at The Regal cinema on 11 December was halted for the broadcast of King Edward VIII's abdication speech broadcast.

1937

The New Inn on the High Street was being rebuilt when a fire started in the builders' debris in its yard. Although there was some damage, it was prevented from spreading to the Thomas Lawrence timber yard next door.

The coronation of George VI was celebrated on 12 May. Trains ran between Reading and Waterloo for twenty-four hours, starting at 3 a.m. Locally, the celebrations started at 10.30 a.m. with a bicycle polo match at the football ground in Larges Lane. Pensioners sat down to lunch at midday, while a service was held at the War Memorial Recreation Ground at 2.30 p.m. A procession through the town was led by the band of 4th Queen's Own Hussars, and was recorded as being 'one of the most spectacular seen in the town'.[28] The King's speech was broadcast before some sports took place. Local schoolchildren received a mug, while 15-year-old Hilda Slade was crowned Coronation Queen. Just after 6 p.m., the Chavey Down gymnastics team gave a demonstration, and the day concluded with a bonfire and fireworks at 9 p.m., brought forward an hour due to rain starting.

Fire destroyed a machine room and store at the Timothy and Sandwith factory in Warfield Road. The company manufactured tailor's chalk and garden chemicals.

The firm of Timothy and Sandwith, known locally as the 'chalk factory', stood in Warfield Road, behind The Old Manor. It manufactured tailor's chalk and garden chemicals. A motorist passing early in the morning on 5 July saw flames and alerted the local fire brigade. 'The fire practically destroyed a store building and machine room ... The building was reduced to a shell ... Prompt action by the firemen prevented the blaze spreading to other parts of the factory.'[29]

Later the same month, it was announced that the Royal Berkshire Regiment would make a tour of the county:

> The Band, and a detachment of officers, N.C.O.s, and men will be conveyed by bus to various towns, and march past the respective Mayors and Chairmen of Urban District Councils, returning to barracks at Reading each evening ... The county tour concludes on Friday [16 July], when the detachment goes to Bracknell and Ascot. This idea of visiting various towns, and thus enabling Berkshire people to see the men of their county Regiment, is a commendable one. The Royal Berkshires are sure to be given a right royal welcome everywhere.[30]

1938

New lighting was installed in the High Street. Work began on widening the road between Wokingham and Bracknell. Disputes over other land needed for the widening resulted in the County Council having to use Compulsory Purchase powers, which slowed progress. By the end of November 1939, this was one of only two road schemes still in progress in the whole of Berkshire.

Bus services to Maidenhead now only ran on Saturdays, 'because for some years the service was operating at a loss'. The service between Bracknell and Bagshot was also withdrawn as it 'operated unremuneratively, but that if building development took place along the route, the possibility of operating a service would be considered.'[31]

With the prospect of war looming, preparations and precautions began to be made. Public meetings about air-raid precautions were 'poorly attended', but lessons on anti-gas training were 'filled almost to capacity'. Gas masks were supplied in November, but not anti-gas protective clothing ('in the event of a gas attack the A.R.P. services in the district would be completely immobilised')[32]. Another appeal for ARP wardens was made a few months later. Planning started on evacuations schemes for the area, with ERDC tasked with compiling a list of available housing. By February 1939, ERDC were discussing air-raid precautions and food control, while military manoeuvres were carried out locally 'in the summer'.

An estate of nearly 100 new houses was built in Bullbrook on land that was previously part of Barn Farm; this is Deepfield Road. Despite the changes and expansion that had taken place, Bracknell still had 'a charm about the whole district which makes for restfulness and peace'.[33]

One of the government schemes to alleviate unemployment in the 1930s was the provision of low-cost loans to the major railway companies to undertake construction works. The Southern Railway took the opportunity for electrification of existing routes. Electric trains already ran from Waterloo as far as Staines. By the end of October 1938, the first electric train was tested between Waterloo and Reading. Steam trains on the line were superseded on 1 January the following year, with two trains per hour instead of the one that ran previously, and the travel time to London was reduced by around ten minutes. Passenger numbers trebled within ten years.

1939

ARP exercises were held at Ranelagh School and Victoria Hall in February, and a siren installed at the police station; this was tested at 1 p.m. on the first Monday of each month. The fire bell alarm system was also moved from The Hind's Head to the police station, and bells also installed at firemen's houses. Exercises were also held in Warfield, Winkfield and Binfield. Another full exercise for all ARP units in the area took place the following month, although bad weather made it impossible for aeroplanes to take part as was originally planned. This was followed by a blackout practice in early May, covering an area from Maidenhead to Liphook, and Reading to Guildford. There was 'enthusiastic co-operation from households, shopkeepers, motorists, and the railway companies'.[34]

The Ministry of Health earmarked the area for 5,000 evacuated children, and the Bracknell branch of the League of Nations Union Committee appealed for anyone able to provide temporary housing for refugees. The ERDC chairman expressed 'reservations over the accommodation for the teachers and scholars of St Paul's School, London'. The Clerk of ERDC 'reported at length on Civic Defence measures which local authorities were required to carry out'. But not everyone was happy with the preparations. 'At the back of my own mind is the fact that a considerable amount of this defence work is utterly useless,' said Captain Jackson, the chairman of ERDC at their annual meeting after planning for war had been given priority over normal council duties for five months. 'Since September, the clerk and ... the remainder of the officials have been doing Government work ... who is going to pay?' A report to BCC in July stated:

While the numbers of wardens are generally sufficient and casualty services personnel adequate, there are two important defects both relating to Bracknell proper. We have only enough volunteers for one shift for staffing the report centre, and we require more clerks, more telephonists, and more messengers. The first-aid post at Victoria Hall requires another 30–40 volunteers in order to provide three full shifts.

The controller also complained that space for the staff was constricted, adding: 'Unless decent conditions are given, I cannot be responsible that the report and control centre, and therefore the A.R.P. services, will function efficiently.'[35] In August, the Reading Co-op were running a front-page advert in the newspapers, advising the population to 'store a week's food'.

Seventeen-year-old Frank Chaney, who played at centre half for Old Bracknell Wanderers Football Club, had a trial with Wolverhampton Wanderers (who finished second in the league that season). He took part in a game with the 'Wolves' junior team in April and 'came through with credit, and it is likely he will arrange terms for next season's games'. Sadly for Frank, the war intervened and his dream of playing professional football was ended.

By July, the Victoria Hall had been earmarked for a first-aid post. Air-raid wardens could be found in Easthampstead Road, Stoney Road, Stanley Road (off the High Street), Bullbrook, Ranelagh School, the library, Ramslade House (by now converted into flats), and Brook Drive (off Ralphs Ride). Another blackout exercise was held in August.

Everyone held their breath as the political situation worsened.

9

Second World War and the Coming of the New Town

'Bracknell then was a small market town where the farmers brought their animals. Market Day was Thursday and Wednesday was half day closing in the High Street,' remembers Joyce White:

> Cows and sheep were brought in from miles around and sold at the market, along with chickens and rabbits ... Chickens were kept by quite a lot of people. I remember going with my grandfather to Bracknell station to collect our own day-old chicks, little balls of yellow fluff in a round, corrugated cardboard box with holes in the side – they had travelled from Essex.

Joyce has a keen memory and can still name all the shops in the High Street from her childhood:

> Mr Mason's the cobbler, through the window could be seen the shoes being mended ... Snell's was a little dark shop with lovely wooden counters; it became Bracknell's first laundrette. Achille Serre on the opposite side of the street was a cleaners – if it rained while shopping, you could borrow an umbrella and return it next visit. Turner's the bakers was nearly opposite The Old Manor, bread baked on the premises and a tea room always busy, especially on Market Day. Gale and Jordan was a butcher and fishmongers. Young's was an outfitter and stockist for Ranelagh School uniforms. Mrs Twickle's sweetshop. Frisby the shoe shop, Youens the cycle shop ... The Spinning Wheel, a shop that sold toys and sweets, it also had a tea room. Poynter's the jewellers had a big clock seen from most of the street so you always knew the time.

Joyce continues:

> The Flower Show was held each year in the cricket field. This was a big event of the summer when the local gardeners showed the best of their crops and flowers, and hoped to win a prize. I used to enter the children's classes, also those for rock cakes, and scones ... Ascot races weren't held during the war of course. When they started again the schools in the surrounding districts closed for the race week in June as there were too many cars on the road – much too dangerous to go to school. A lot of this time off school was spent sitting by the roadside taking car numbers. We filled pages over the years – it was great fun at the time ... A favourite walk was to the bridge that echoed. Many a cuckoo sound has come back to me. This bridge was replaced by the Twin Bridges we know today; the old bridge still stands, filled in under the embankment, between the two newer ones.
>
> There were two doctors in Bracknell. Dr Hick had his surgery in a green corrugated hut in Station Road. You sat on wooden benches to wait until your turn, no appointment system. Dr Turner had his surgery in Church Road in his house, a bit more comfortable. It was said he was drunk a good deal of the time, so you took your pick!
>
> I suppose the highlight of the year was Joe Smith's outing for all the local schoolchildren. We were given sixpence and an orangeade. We boarded a special train for a day at the seaside. On arriving home tired and sunburnt, flags were flying and a band playing, parents and friends cheering.

Even during the war, 'there was always food if you had a shotgun,' remembers Roy Saunders. Chickens and pigs could be kept and killed, pheasants and rabbits were readily sourced from the surrounding fields. 'People saved rather than spent. They did without and they borrowed and lent amongst each other. They queued, they juggled their ration points and their coupons, and they dug for victory, growing more vegetables and potatoes than ever before.'

1939

Shortly after 11 a.m. on 3 September, Prime Minister Neville Chamberlain announced that Britain was at war with Germany again.[1] Unlike the First World War, much planning had been done prior to the Second. Two days earlier saw the start of the evacuation of more than 1.5 million people (over 50 per cent were children) from urban areas likely to be bombed. Nationally, a Committee of Evacuation had been established in May 1938 and 'the project ... was planned like a military exercise'. Trains full of evacuees arrived at Reading, Windsor,

Wokingham, Bracknell and Theale stations with arrangements already in place to deal with their occupants, the whole exercise running 'efficiently and smoothly'. Children arriving at Bracknell were taken to Ranelagh School for 'distribution'.[2] Thirty arrived in the first batch, but more would arrive during the London Blitz in 1940 and 1941, sometimes sleeping on the floor of Church House overnight until billets could be found for them.

The grant of 8s 6d per week (about £20 in today's money) to look after an evacuee was considered inadequate, and the government would later be urged to increase the amount. Assessments were made periodically to the amount households received for billeting costs, a system that was open to fraud in some cases. The extra youngsters in the area put pressure on schools. In some places, half the pupils attended classes in the morning, while the remainder were taught in the afternoon. Ranelagh School catered for 180 pupils in 1939; by 1946 the number had risen to 308. With a few exceptions, locals and the new arrivals did not mix. At Easthampstead School, the evacuees were called 'Newts' by the locals, who in turn named them 'Carrot Crunchers'. Within twelve months the ERDC area was accommodating 638 refugees and 672 evacuees. It was not just children who moved to Bracknell – Elsie Suddaby, a well-known soprano singer, moved from Hampstead and remained in the town for some twenty years.

ERDC voted to give the chairman and vice chairman emergency powers for the duration of the conflict, and the clerk was given the authority to issue death certificates for civilians who died 'due to war operations'. Two outdoor council staff on the reserve list were recalled (others would follow). Halls and large houses were commandeered for troops, with Ramslade House, Church House and the 'Forest' housing RAF personnel at various times, while Victoria Hall was given over to the Red Cross. Lynwood Chase (now an estate of the same name) was used by the 1st United States Volunteer Cavalry, and Warfield Park accommodated the Doncaster and Cheshire Regiment in the grounds, as well as more Americans in the mansion itself. Nissen huts in the grounds of Easthampstead Park housed both British and foreign troops.

Within a week, blackouts were in place overnight; among those fined for displaying lights after blackout was Easthampstead Rural District Council at their office in Church Road! The 1939 Register was taken on 29 September 1939. The information was used to produce identity cards and, once rationing was introduced in January 1940, to issue ration books. Information in the Register was also used to administer conscription and the direction of labour, and to monitor and control the movement of the population caused by military mobilisation and mass evacuation.[3] Local newspapers in Berkshire were reduced, with the *Wokingham, Bracknell and Ascot Times* merged into one publication of just four pages. Petrol rationing was introduced, and significant increases in income tax announced. Food control committees were set up, the local one being under the auspices of

ERDC, but the number of forms the population were required to fill in led to numerous complaints. An extra fire engine was allocated to Bracknell (the town having got a motorised one four years earlier) that now had to cover Sandhurst as well, and a fire bell installed at the fire station in Stanley Road (which was now manned at night).

Local authorities were granted powers to requisition buildings for wartime use. Dr Fielden's home and surgery, the former Forest Hotel, was taken over as a hospital for evacuees, the owner saying that 'no obstacle would be in the way'. An ERDC report on it noted:

> Thanks to the generosity of local people, a large amount had been saved in the provision of furniture and equipment for it ... A great number of ailments and illnesses had been reported among the evacuees ... there were also cases of dirty and vicious habits, which made it undesirable to billet people concerned in private houses ... Notifiable diseases would be transferred to Maidenhead [which had an isolation hospital at St Mark's].

In exaggerated headlines, the *Windsor, Slough and Eton Express* declared: '50% of evacuees are untrained and verminous.' The facility at the 'Forest' had seven beds (all in use) and was in desperate need of more. It had been suggested it could take forty to fifty beds on one floor, and this figure 'could be increased if necessary'. Windsor Rural District Council were also offered use of the facility, but prevaricated about the cost to them. By December, the Ministry had given sanction for stays up to fourteen days, and four other authorities were contributing to the cost of running the facility. Mr Walter Elliott, the Minister of Health, included it on his two-day tour of Berkshire, although he was surprised to find it empty of patients on his arrival, the last occupant having been discharged a few days earlier. At the end of October, the local Medical Officer of Health reported that the committee set up to oversee the use of 'The Forest' had not used its powers: 'The hospital ... was carrying on to full capacity, but proper arrangements for equipment and payment of staff not been made. Nobody at the hospital had yet been paid.' The committee responded – they could not spend government money on it as no official recognition for it had yet been received. An ambulance train was also stationed at Bracknell until 1941.

Local people performed extra duties during wartime. Albert Youens owned a cycle shop in the High Street and was one of Bracknell's air-raid wardens, as was greengrocer William Wooding, businessman Harold Full, Henry Wall and his wife Gladys, plus bank clerk Eric Styles and his wife Marjorie. Linda Wilkinson of Church Road and secretary Ruby Essex were telephone contacts for the local ARP unit, which had its depot at 'High Elms', the former home of Thomas Lawrence. Tailor Lally Warner, postman William Flower, estate agent Alan Hambling, and decorator Horace Purnell doubled as firemen, while sawmill foreman Reuben Elliott and Maxwell Heron, now in his seventies, were special constables (volunteer policemen). Harry Wheeler worked at the corn stores in Station Road and was also an ambulance driver, while Kathleen North juggled bookkeeping with nursing duties. Sisters Hilda and Winifred Kingham both performed volunteer driving duties and their brother was involved in food distribution administration.

The Royal Forest Agricultural Society decided 'to abandon this year's show', but Fielden Cup football matches continued, with the local newspaper reporting: 'Football, with certain modifications, will continue in Bracknell and district during the winter ... but probably there will be fewer teams. Bracknell and Binfield Darts League also resolved to continue, provided at least six teams continued to play.' The matches started in mid-November. Bracknell Cage Bird Society met to decide what to do about the war and unanimously agreed to 'carry on'. The Garth Hunt continued to meet as well. The first of a series of twelve lectures on 'The European Situation' attracted a large number of WEA members to the Congregational Schoolroom. Owing to the illness of the appointed tutor, Mr A.C.L. Bullock (Lecturer of History at Merton College, Oxford) took her place.

As well as individuals, some schools, colleges and other organisations were evacuated too. St Paul's School in Hammersmith moved to Easthampstead Park, where it became solely a boarding school for the period of the war. Playing fields and some other facilities were borrowed from Wellington College,[4] but the boys and the teachers from the two schools remained entirely separate. Dutch and Polish soldiers were also based at Easthampstead Park in Nissen huts (these were erected near Bracknell Crematorium in South Road), plus Canadians nearby. Old residents remember the Dutch would often walk into Bracknell in their spare time. The army's presence attracted a German Junkers bomber on 4 October 1940, which dropped a stick of bombs down the main drive, the last one hitting the lodge at the main gate and damaging it without exploding. A Wokingham postman arrived just in time to see the plane approaching and had evacuated the occupant of the lodge into his van. Fifteen-year-old St Paul's schoolboy Geoffrey Trewinnard was on air-raid duty at the time.[5] Two specialist counter-intelligence units were trained at Easthampstead Park, and handled over a dozen double agents in France in the final year of the war. The Dutch were still there as the war ended, training before going to fight in the Indonesian War of Independence, the country still being a Dutch colony.[6]

There were GIs in Bracknell, too. American troops stayed on Cabbage Hill prior to D-Day, much to the delight of the farmer at West End Farm who was able to sell them a lot of milk! On a less happy note, there were fights in Binfield between the Americans and Canadians. A US bomber crashed on the grass runway of the RAF training airfield behind Winkfield church in October 1943, although the entire crew escaped without injury.[7] Although there are stories of

ST. PAUL'S, LONDON'S FAMOUS DAY SCHOOL, EVACUATED TO BERKSHIRE: BOYS AT WORK IN THE GARDENS—THE SCHOOL HAVING DECIDED TO GROW ITS OWN VEGETABLES.

People were encouraged to grow their own food to help mitigate the losses of ships carrying food being sunk by the enemy. Here a group from St Paul's School in Hammersmith, who had been evacuated to Easthampstead Park, are cultivating land behind Easthampstead Church. (Photo courtesy of Mary Evans Agency) a Messerschmitt crashing at Easthampstead,[8] no record of this incident has been found (this may have been confused with the Messerschmitt that crashed at the Cavalry Exercise Ground in Windsor Great Park in September 1940).

The governors of the Ranelagh School had 'made provision for the partial accommodation of the boys from the London School of Building, the Clapham Technical School for Women, and for a group of girls from the Notre Dame Girls' School'.[9]

As a result of 'successful competitions held at the Bracknell British Legion Club, some six or eight parcels are being forwarded weekly to local members of the Forces serving overseas. The parcels ... are an ingenious collection of articles, comprising many little, "luxuries".'[10] By the end of the year, 120 parcels had been sent.

It was reported that that the War Memorial Recreation Ground had provided facilities for the large number of evacuees since September, but 'mishaps to the seats, swings, and goalposts had occurred'.

1940

As one writer recorded, 'The winter of 1940 was one of the coldest of the century. It was also a secret ... the news being suppressed for fear it would be of use to the enemy.' The *Reading Mercury* finally revealed in understated tones: 'It was very cold indeed in early January.'

Bracknell's first war casualty was postman Walter Benstead on board HMS *Exmouth*, sunk by a German U-boat in January while escorting a merchant ship north of Scotland.[11] Pilot Officer Kenneth Worsdell, whose parents lived locally, sustained facial injuries after a crash at Peacock Farm in March, the engine having seized though a lack of oil over Binfield. He would die later in the year when his plane crashed in Surrey in bad weather.

An all-party coalition government was formed in May, headed by Winston Churchill. Anthony Eden, Secretary of State for War, called for volunteers to form a Local Defence Volunteers militia (later renamed the Home Guard). Local volunteers were required to register at the ERDC offices in Church Road, and the unit was based at Ranelagh School. The Girls Training Corps was also based there. Teenage girls up to the age of 20 were given training in both domestic and wartime activities, as well as assisting with air warden duties. Later in the year there was an appeal for volunteers to assist the Labour Reserve in case of air-raid damage. The Royal Sea Bathing Hospital in Margate, which used open-air treatment for patients suffering from tuberculosis, evacuated to South Hill Park.

In June, the grocers Teetgen and Company (their store was demolished to make way for the telephone exchange) were fined for not collecting and stamping the ration books of their customers.

As Bracknell was seen as not being vulnerable to attacks, there were no public air-raid shelters, although some shops had a notice in the window offering shelter if one started. The Congregational and Baptist churches also considered whether they could make shelters available, but the cellars of the 'Forest' were ruled out. Leaflets were distributed to householders, describing how to make a shelter in the home. There were calls for shelters to be provided in schools, but BCC decided to only supply them for schools close to factories or other vulnerable targets. A plan to use the cellars of the New Inn on the High Street 'if sufficiently strengthened' was not implemented. A shelter was eventually erected at the recreation ground in Park Road (only to be locked and 'out of use' in the summer of 1942), with another near the railway station.

Joyce White remembers 'being rushed to the Air Raid Shelter in Station Road while out shopping and the siren went'. But as a local resident later summed up the conflict, 'generally speaking, we never knew much about the war in Bracknell'. A tree trunk with barbed wire lay in the road, to be pulled across the bottom of the High Street in case of invasion, while a flat board on a pole near the war memorial would supposedly change colour if gas bombs were dropped. Pillboxes were built after the fall of France in June 1940 when the threat of a German invasion seemed imminent. One stood on London Road, almost opposite The Royal Foresters, and another on Wokingham Road near its junction with Jocks Lane. There was a raised gun emplacement on the north side of Holly Spring Lane, covering its junction with Park Road, Bay Road and Jig's Lane, with another small battery, comprising one gun and a searchlight, in the corner of a field in Bull Lane. Searchlight detachments were also stationed at Caesar's Camp and Jigs Hill (now part of the Whitegrove estate), and a demolition practice site was built near Wishmoor Cross in Swinley Forest in the run-up to D-Day.

Stan Willis remembers the times when London was bombed in 1940:

> The siren was going on all the time and was disrupting our school lessons. So our headmaster at Priestwood School decided that we boys in the top class took it in turns to stay in the playground with a bucket of water and a stirrup pump, and if we saw any German planes passing over towards London, we had to blow a whistle so the schoolchildren could get in the corridor of the school (no shelter was available), and if a bomb fell we had to try to put the fire out. God help us if it did! Every night they passed over Bracknell on the way to London and back. We laid in bed listening to the hum of their engines, the gun batteries blasting away, and the searchlights trying to get them in their sights. We had no shelters to go to. Sometimes when it was really bad, we hid under the kitchen table or under the stairs.

German planes also passed over the town on the way to bomb Coventry in 1940.

Bracknell itself escaped with practically no bombing at all, but on one particularly bad night 200 bombs fell between Bracknell and Ascot. Warfield Hall, then the home of Tommy Sopwith (designer of the Sopwith Camel plane used in the First World War) was targeted. Eight bombs were dropped in a line between Westley Mill (north of Binfield), and Fairclough Farm (near The Plough and Harrow) in November 1940; all missed the target but a large crater was left beside Warfield Road. Three bombs also fell near Lambrook School on the penultimate day of 1940, but there were no casualties; Wellington College was not so lucky, being hit by four bombs a couple of months earlier, with the headmaster being killed. Eileen Briggs recounts how 'the whole of the sky was lit up like day with flares'. The number of bombing raids decreased dramatically in 1941, with none at all in the following two years.

British planes returning from raids over Germany would jettison unused bombs over the woodland between Bracknell and Ascot if they needed to conserve fuel, an area very sparsely populated. Colin Reynolds was living with his parents in a wooden bungalow in The Warren during the war, and recalls the night he woke

Damage caused by a bomb dropped at Fairclough Farm near The Plough and Harrow on Warfield Road in November 1940. The intended target was Warfield Hall, the home of aircraft designer Tommy Sopwith. (Photo courtesy of David Morris)

up just as an incendiary bomb passed through the pillow and mattress next to his head, setting fire to the floor. Reports of a parachutist seen near Caesar's Camp led to an extensive search of the area by the authorities, but nothing was found.

Roy Saunders's childhood home at the start of the war stood on the east side of Jig's Lane:

> a stream ran along the bottom of the garden. In the autumn of 1940 [overnight on 26 September], there was some bombing in the area. Three bombs fell around the house, one across the road at the front in farmer Anderson's Holly Spring Farm field, one at the side of the house where Harvest Ride is now, and one on the opposite side of the stream ... We had to move out whilst the bombing raid was on, up to the Council Offices (ERDC) for shelter.

Roy's father was clerk to the council and a shelter had been built there. Another resident remembers:

> On the corner of the road [opposite the Sports Centre] ... was a huge concrete water container for forest fires as the area was all woodland. Further back was a very large camouflaged Nissen hut which I believe was an ammunition store used during the war as it was surrounded by sandbags [there were 'hundreds of ammunition stores along the Bagshot Road to Nine Mile Ride in Nissen huts' according to another source] ... At the junction of Bagshot Road and Harmans Water, there was a camp of black Nissen huts for Italian POWs. I was five, and used to watch the POWs with their yellow circles on coat backs and trouser legs, being marched under guard to Lily Humphry's shop at the garage.

From their first arrival in the UK in 1941, Italian POWs presented one way of alleviating labour shortages, particularly in agriculture:

> After the Italians were repatriated, the Nissen huts were taken over by squatters (as the locals called them). They were in fact Londoners who had been bombed out and had nowhere to live. They were eventually given housing by Bracknell Corporation Housing Department. There were also similar huts down what is now Woodmere [opposite the Harmanswater shops], along the edge of the mound.[12]

A representative from the *Times and Weekly News* recorded what he saw at an air-raid precautions practice (based at Binfield):

> The main first aid station was then visited at the Church House, Bracknell ... Here were received all the more serious casualties from ten other first aid

points and, when these had been redressed they were dispatched to hospital. Dr. Turner was also in attendance at this point ... Here was also a small detachment of the St. John Nursing Association under the supervision of Mrs. Green who also kept the record of casualties for this detachment. Bombs were dropped at Bracknell Station and the International Stores, High Street. Both of these raids were carried out with high explosives. The St. John Ambulance Brigade under the control of Mr. Green was rendering able assistance in bringing in cases that were more serious in a number of private cars and also a specially fitted out lorry belonging to Messrs. Drake and Mount for stretcher cases, and also the regular ambulance was put into active service. A call was made upon the Fire Brigade during this raid.

A local fund was launched in August to purchase a Spitfire. In September, more refugees arrived but 'it is hoped there will not be a need for compulsory billeting'.[13] Three Bracknell men were reported as being prisoners of war.

In November, a tank and lorry collided on Wokingham Road, with the lorry coming off decidedly the worst. Old Bracknell Wanderers played a football match against a team made up of members of the Warfield Home Guard, beating them by six goals to three. Despite the blackout restrictions, weekly dances resumed at Church House, although to radio music rather than a live band, but the Ranelagh School orchestra were able to provide the accompaniment on one occasion.

1941

More petty crime appeared in the newspapers. Coal was stolen from the stocks at Bracknell railway station in January, and the Baptist church had three collection boxes pilfered in March. An unnamed butcher was fined £10 for displaying meat for sale without a licence, and fined again a month later for selling mouldy meat. The unscrupulous trader was cautioned again in October for 'diddling' the ration scheme 'by keeping meat refrigerated for months'. Two samples of 'inferior milk' were recorded in Bracknell the following year.

Evacuees, including teachers and helpers, still continued to arrive. Church House opened its doors on Tuesdays and Fridays as a rest room for evacuees and refugees. The same venue received a six-month licence for a stage play. Local facilities were also used by other evacuees billeted locally, with those in Ascot coming to Bracknell for swimming lessons at the pool in Martins Lane. Fundraising for local hospitals continued, and Poppy Day in November raised a record amount. Raising funds for the war effort became a major part of daily life, with 'War Weapons Week', 'Wings for Victory Week', and 'Warship Week'. Joyce White recalls: [14]

On several occasions I placed pennies edge-to-edge on the pavement in Bracknell High Street. These were collected for the soldiers I was told. The usual parades of servicemen were held. I remember Mr Greenaway the blacksmith with his terrier Judy. She was harnessed to a little cart with a money box attached and collected money at these parades and on other occasions.[15]

The Regal Cinema was permitted to open on Sundays, the first film to be shown being *Pennies from Heaven* starring Bing Crosby.

The Air Training Corps (ATC) was formed in 1941 to prepare cadets for joining the RAF.[16] A Bracknell squadron was established the following year at Ranelagh School; it still meets twice a week at their premises off Gibson Drive. An official inspection in March reported: 'Visited the Light Anti-Aircraft Regiment HQ at Bracknell and find they need no vehicles from us at the moment.'

Food shortages were becoming acute by April, with food wardens responsible for its distribution appointed. An application for a catering establishment in the High Street was turned down by the division office for the Minister of Food. About 100 people donated blood when the Women's Voluntary Service visited Bracknell. Gas mask practices were held at the local schools. Civilian clothing was rationed (soap would be rationed the following year). Although petrol had been rationed since the start of the war, it was noted there were many cars at the Newbury races.

Clocks had not been put back an hour at the end of British Summer Time in 1940. Now they were put forward another hour (double summer time), effectively putting Britain on the same time as the rest of western Europe.

In May, a serious fire at the St Andrew's Works of builder John Sargeant in Wokingham Road (where The Weather Vane pub is now) caused severe damage to the premises and its contents.

In September, Dr Fielden's grandson was reported as having been shot down and killed, but this was later amended to 'officially missing'. The funeral of William Hunton, the auctioneer at Bracknell Market, was held at Holy Trinity. He was also the secretary of Bracknell Athletic Sports, and had played cricket for Berkshire in his youth.

The sick bay at 'The Forest' was now to be used as a clearing house to accommodate boys evacuated from Brixton. Bert Bridges remembers being there, describing Bracknell as 'a beautiful compact and cosy village ... We didn't mix, we were tolerated but not accepted.' Many evacuees were homesick or failed to settle in their new surroundings, with many cases of bedwetting being reported, but others thrived, treating it as 'a big adventure'. Many coming from abject poverty in London came to a healthier environment, with some allocated to hosts determined to make life as pleasant as possible for them under the circumstances. Bert also remembers a 'riotous football match against the inmates of the Easthampstead Asylum [Church Hill House]'.

The second National Service Act was passed a week before Christmas, requiring all men and women between the ages of 18 and 60 to perform some form of national service, including military service for those under 51. The Schedule of Reserved Occupations was abandoned, and 'only individual deferments from the draft will be accepted'.[17]

The year ended with a barrage balloon, which had broken loose from its mooring behind the Congregational Church, being shot down in flames by a British plane, the charred remains landing on the railway embankment. Eileen Briggs was at school and 'missed this bit of excitement'.

1942

Home Guard membership became compulsory in February. A target of £30,000 was allocated to Bracknell for Warship Week, the money to be raised from whist drives, concerts, competitions (for both adults and children) and a dance. The effort was rewarded when ERDC were presented with a certificate to mark the community's 'adoption' of HMS *Derwent*, a Hunt-class destroyer.

Bracknell Cricket Club held their AGM at The Red Lion, and vowed to make 'every endeavour to carry on'. In October it was reported that Old Bracknell Wanderers were still playing football matches, although 'struggling to raise a team'. A Junior Football League was formed.

Local casualties were beginning to mount. Ronald Rowley was reported missing in Malaya in March. He had attended Priestwood School as a boy, and worked at Home and Colonial Stores in the High Street prior to the war. He had married a few months earlier. Arthur Skinner, a sergeant in the Royal Marines, was listed as 'missing' (his ship was later confirmed as having sunk in the Mediterranean). Frederick Youens was also missing in Thailand, as was Edward Longhurst in Malaya. Maurice Jay lost his life in Egypt, having received severe burns in action. Sapper Albert Sarney was taken as a prisoner of war in Italy and interred at Wolfsberg, Austria.

Philip Carlini, an old Bracknell resident, can remember two planes crashing over the Bagshot Road (Eileen Briggs also mentions the crash in her book *A Backward Glance*):

> I lived in Bracknell throughout the war ... My grandparents were in service ... at the large white Manor House called Firlands and ... had a cottage within the grounds, so I spent most of my time there. It is now a housing estate, still called Firlands ... Two aircraft crashed, killing off the crew. One crashed on Firlands property which caught fire ... the other aeroplane crashed on the opposite side of Bagshot Road ... We youngsters formed up with the RAF from Ramslade

as one crew man was missing. Sometime after he was found in Copper North's potato patch as the haulms were high and it was difficult to see the last man.

The crash occurred on 20 July. Two Douglas A-20 Havocs belonging to the RAF's 605 Squadron took off from Ford, Sussex. The flights were giving air experience to three Canadian servicemen ground crew who were based nearby, in readiness for the unsuccessful Dieppe raid the following month. An inquest into the casualties was held at the St John's Ambulance Room in Bracknell four days later, and a verdict of 'Death by misadventure' returned.

Several RAF personnel stationed at Ramslade gave evidence, including one who had seen the crash happen:

> I heard the noise of two aircraft approaching from south, flying in close formation at approximately 2,000 feet. The aircraft appeared then to go into a tight left hand bank together, and proceed on this until they had turned 90 degrees from their previous path. When I first noticed the planes, they were flying side by side. During the turn, it appeared that the plane on the outside had lost way and was endeavouring to regain formation. At the time of the collision, the outside plane appeared to be passing under the leader. I was surprised to see that the machines had actually collided, the result being that the plane attempting to regain formation partially disintegrated and commenced to spin to earth, followed by the leader. Among the debris that fell was a parachute partially opened, falling slowly as though insufficiently weighted; the object attached to the parachute appeared to be the parachute pack.

The three Canadians, William Barnett, George Palmer and John Orviss, all from Toronto, were buried at Brookwood Military Cemetery near Woking, as was one of the pilots (his parents visited Bracknell a few months later to see the spot where their son had lost his life).

To keep young teenage boys occupied and out of mischief, Bracknell Boys' Club was formed in September, meeting at the Congregational Schoolroom. Indoor games, a library, stamp collecting, first aid, a swimming club, football and physical training were provided. No doubt all activity would have stopped late in the afternoon on 10 September when a partial solar eclipse was visible from Bracknell.

The Ministry of Food formalised the establishment of 'communal feeding centres', later renamed British Restaurants, in 1940. They were run by local government or volunteers, and helped those who were unable to provide food for themselves. A British Restaurant at Bracknell was approved in September, but then rejected before it could open.

Across the country, Armistice Day services were cancelled in large centres of population, but the ones in smaller places such as Bracknell went ahead. Due to

Second World War and the Coming of the New Town

a bureaucratic muddle, 8-year-old Betty Hiscock at The Blue Lion received her call-up papers!

1943

With the police and authorities concentrating on war matters, crime continued to increase. A Virginia Water man was convicted of gross indecency with two schoolboys in Bracknell. There were local shortages too, with a lack of razor blades in the town. Later in the year, there was a national dearth of leather for shoes. Meanwhile, ERDC were concerned about plans to move the bus stop outside the post office in the High Street, and the painting of telegraph poles in black and white to avoid people walking into them in the blackout!

There was a shooting in the High Street in April. Three Free French Forces members were drinking in The New Inn for three hours. When they started causing a disturbance, a Canadian soldier ejected one of them. Two shots were fired, one of the Frenchmen (Emile Le Carr) fell, while another (Eugene Laot) ran up High Street and escaped, although he was later apprehended and identified by witnesses. Laot was remanded to Kingston Assizes. The gun was found

Ramslade House was commandeered by the RAF and was the headquarters of the 2nd Tactical Air Force. Part of the planning for D-Day was carried out here. After the war, it was used as an RAF Staff College.

in bushes when railings near the police station were being removed. Railings around graves at Holy Trinity were also removed as part of the campaign to 'recycle' metal for the war effort, but ERDC complained the stumps left were 'unsatisfactory'.

'Wings for Victory Week' in Bracknell during May had a target of £180,000. Money was raised from a procession, dances, concerts, whist drives, Home Guard manoeuvres, an unarmed combat demonstration and an exhibition organised by Ranelagh School. The final sum raised was almost £30,000 more than the goal set.

News reached his parents that Harold Hutson, reported missing for sixteen months, was a POW in Japan. Earlier, it was learned that Lieutenant Eric Adie had suffered a similar fate.

Ramslade House had been requisitioned by the War Office in 1940, and by now had become the headquarters of the Second Tactical Air Force.[18] From June 1943, they were planning and preparing for the D-Day Landings in Normandy twelve months later.

Although children were missing from schools in earlier years to help with the harvest, it was noted that sixteen boys were now absent for two weeks from Bullbrook School to assist in potato lifting. Eileen Briggs recalls school team races being held opposite along Bay Road, with cars waiting for the races to finish before proceeding.

A serious fire at the Regal Cinema in November destroyed the roof and many seats. It was thought to have started with a discarded cigarette butt catching alight a curtain at the Station Road exit, and was discovered at 1.15 a.m., by which time the roof was well alight. The blaze took two hours to put out with the use of extension ladders, a recent addition to the fire service.

1944

Almost £20 was raised at The Running Horse pub for the Red Cross in January, bringing the total to £57 in six months (about £1,800 in today's money). There was some good news on the horizon with the promise of a pound of oranges being available on ration books 'soon'.

Residents were advised to test their gas masks, an exercise that could be done at the Royal British Legion during February. Aluminium strips blew into Bracknell on strong winds; these were radar-jamming strips dropped by the Luftwaffe over London to confound the city's defences. The British deployed the same tactics over Germany. The Regal Cinema was reopened by local soldier Reg Gibson, at home while recovering from a serious leg injury sustained in Italy, as the guest of honour. Roy Saunders remembers the haste to get it open again after the fire; it was an important facility to many during the war, and its temporary loss would have been felt keenly.

Incendiaries fell near Ralphs Ride on 23 January, one being close to the railway line. This was probably the bomb that Janet Verlander remembers dropping in the garden of her childhood home in Martins Lane. More were dropped in woodland about a mile south of Bracknell exactly a month later, but none of them found their target of the military vehicles, equipment or ammunition dumps set up ahead of D-Day, hidden under the trees. The remains of tanks, built to store water in case of fire, can still be seen here today. The whole of Swinley Park had been sealed off from the public during the war, and ERDC were still attempting to get gates and fences removed to reinstate access in 1951. Some of the military equipment was buried rather than removed, and a couple of local historians are still recovering items left over from this period.

By now, Bracknell only had one doctor left to serve the population, the other having been called up. Alexander Nutley, the former manager of the fish department at Gale and Jordan's in the High Street, died of illness in Italy, leaving a wife and young son. Christopher Cummings, a former pupil at Bullbrook School, was killed. Grace Wooff of Stanley Road lost a brother, while Ted Cheney and Stanley Rowden were prisoners in Germany. But Frank Cox, formerly a manual worker at W. J. Cole in Station Road, was awarded the Distinguished Flying Medal.

In March, there was no coal to heat Bullbrook School, so pupils were taken on 'brisk walks', given a meal, and then sent home. The local fuel overseer had no coal to allocate but managed to find some for them, much to the disappointment of the pupils. The bus service was very poor, leading to overcrowding; ERDC took issue with Thames Valley Bus Company. A lecture to fire guards was given in Victoria Hall by a man who had performed a similar role during the London Blitz. There was more disappointment for local children when Lord John Sayer's Circus failed to get to Bracknell due to an accident. As a slight recompense, Bracknell's 'adopted' tank halted briefly in the High Street.

'Salute the Soldier' week was held in May. Three quarters of the £200,000 target was raised in just five days. Gibson, who had now had his leg amputated, took the salute.

The Normandy landings, better known as D-Day, took place on 6 June. Corporal Dick Brooker of Station Road was one of the first ten paratroopers to land in France – a surprise to his wife, who was unaware of his involvement. With the war now turning in favour of the Allies, censorship was eased and reports on D-Day and subsequent actions started to appear in the press, with observations on Germans retreating in France logged in September. ERDC started planning for tasks post-war, including housing and a health centre. Many of the town's properties were overcrowded, while others did not have a mains water supply, and several roads were not connected to the sewers. There was also 'a deplorable situation' in Harmanswater and Ralphs Ride where bungalows had been springing up 'in situations most unsuitable for health and general wellbeing of inhabitants'. They also pressed for the early return of two of their staff considered vital. The 'Forest' was assessed for new council offices but found to be 'impractical at this time'.[19] Meanwhile, dances, darts matches and youth club football matches continued at home.

The blackout was eased in August, being replaced in September by a partial 'dim-out', and evacuations were suspended. From June, London had been hit by a new weapon, the V-1 Flying Bomb, nicknamed 'the doodlebug'. One of these passed over Bracknell in October, heading west and coming down in Earley.

The Home Guard stood down at the beginning of December, with a parade and farewell dance at the cricket ground a week earlier. The year ended with a report that ERDC would expedite the purchase of land at Skimped Hill Lane for post-war housing.

1945

There was now a feeling that the end of the war was in sight, and some evening rail services to London resumed in the second week of January. But just before 1 a.m. on the 15th, a second plane crash occurred in the Bracknell area. A Mosquito aircraft, returning to base at Blackbushe from an operational flight over the Prum area of Germany, came down near modern-day Woodenhill in Great Hollands. The official report stated:

> It would appear that the aircraft was under control while gliding in an attempt to make a belly landing. Witnesses state that the aircraft passed low overhead, and are certain that the engines were not under power. It is thought the crash was due to either shortage of petrol, or faulty manipulation of fuel cocks.

The pilot, Lloyd Joseph Berry of the Royal Canadian Air Force, and navigator, Walter Brown of the RAF, were both killed. Roy Saunders remembers the crash site being cordoned off 'because live ammunition was exploding'.

By March, ERDC were able to dispense with the town's air-raid siren (it was later used as the fire siren). Plans were being drawn up for evacuees to return home a month later. Although many had gone back the previous year, others stayed on as the faster electric trains meant it was possible for families to visit the Bracknell area on day trips. VE Day on 8 May was greeted with relief, with a party for 200 children held in Binfield Road the following day. The local newspaper reported that 'V.E. Day was celebrated with sober restraint in east Berkshire,'[20] although this does not square with the burning at the stake of an effigy of Hitler at Wokingham! Celebrations continued for a few weeks – the Home Guard held a reunion at the Royal British Legion on 14 May, Deepfield Road's VE party took place four days later, with another in Searle Street the day after. On the 23rd it was the turn of Mount Pleasant, who held a party in the St John's Ambulance Hall. A victory dance at took place at the Royal British Legion on the 28th, where the raffle prize was a bunch of bananas. The Bagshot Road VE party took place on 13 June at Westwick Hall, with one for Broad Lane and Martin's Lane at the end of the month. The Binfield Road party was held in fields behind the council houses. There was a whole rash of post-war weddings. A 'Welcome Home Fund' was started for returning servicemen, with a dance raising £25; the figure raised passed £2,000 by Christmas.

ERDC noted that 'a considerable quantity of chemical weapons are still stored at Swinley Park. Residents should keep respirators and recognise gas warnings.'[21] The stored material was to be removed 'in the near future'.

A general election was called for 5 July, although it would be three weeks before the results were announced. A mock election was held at Priestwood School a few days before the event to teach the children how to vote. Local elections took place later in the year on 1 November.

Things started to return to normal, even though fighting still continued in the Far East. Street lighting was restored in mid-July. ERDC gave an extra bank holiday to their staff, and hoped businesses would reciprocate. Although 250 men, making 10 million bricks per year, had been working at the brickyards in Bracknell, Swinley and Wokingham before the war, these were now lying idle. The senior section of St Pauls' School at Easthampstead Park was closed, although the junior section remained there until 1947. VJ Day was announced on 15 August and the war was finally over. The party planned for London Road was held in Bullbrook School due to inclement weather, Stanley Road held their celebration in Church House, but the Albert Road event took place outside in the sun. A huge party was also held in Bay Road for everyone from Bullbrook in mid-September.

Not everyone celebrated legally. Two Pioneer Corps soldiers, unable to get into the cinema, which was full, went for drinks with a WAAF instead, and then attacked her while walking her back to her billets on Bagshot Road. They were each sentenced to twelve months in prison. Two Canadian soldiers, from the Blackdown Camp in Hampshire, attempted to rob Humphrey's Garage on Bagshot Road.

Rail services returned to pre-war timetables, although there were complaints that they frequently ran thirty minutes late. Newspapers had more pages now, with wide margins as paper became available again, and with adverts appearing by November. Organisations and societies, dormant during hostilities, were now being resurrected. New Year's Eve saw the revival of one of Bracknell's most popular functions, the Fireman's Ball at the Victoria Hall.

Fire engines rushed to Ramslade House on 19 October, only to find it was a false alarm, the fire practice call for the on-site unit having somehow been put through to the Bracknell brigade.

Women Labour Party members met with the clerk of ERDC at the end of November to find out the council's post-war plan for housing. The 'Forest' and 'Holly Bank' (a large house in Church Road) were to be de-requisitioned 'soon'.

Twenty-nine names of local men would be added to the Roll of Honour in Holy Trinity Church, casualties of the second global war.

1946

Although the war was over, rationing continued for several more years. Long queues formed outside local shops when deliveries of certain foods were expected. As in the rest of the country, black marketeering was rife.

Local military equipment was gradually being cleared, with ammunition from local storage taken to Easthampstead Park for removal. The air-raid shelter on the recreation ground was demolished.

Old Bracknell Wanderers was reconstituted in January and played their first game, away against Broadmoor patients, winning 6–0. A women's tennis tournament at 'Holly Bank' in Church Road was held in the summer as sport slowly resumed.

ERDC expressed concern that houses still requisitioned were not being used, and that ammunition was still arriving at local dumps in the area. Victoria Hall, which had been commandeered by BCC for ARP, was back in use by the local community, with the East Berkshire Waltz Championships being held there in June.

The Royal British Legion held a 'Welcome Home' meal and entertainment for 150 men and women (including two First World War veterans). The menu consisted of celery soup, roast chicken, fruit salad with mock cream (made from caster sugar, vegetable oil, margarine and water), cheese and biscuits. A £5 gift voucher was also given to all the attendees. A second meal was held three months later for a further 140 men and women, another 140 entertained in October, and a fourth event held in March the following year. In all, nearly 600 people were thanked for their war services.

South Hill Park was sold for just over £25,000 to Joseph Horn for conversion into high-class flats. He had run a similar concern at Ramslade House prior to the war before it had been requisitioned, but the new venture ran into financial difficulties and the property was back on the market five years later.

Victory Day was celebrated across the country on 8 June. Events in Bracknell started with lunch served to 160 elderly residents at the Royal British Legion, with 'another thirty or so' meals taken to those who were unable to attend. Meanwhile, a children's fancy dress took place in a shed at Bracknell Market, as heavy rain spoiled the plans for it to take place on the London Road Recreation Ground. The weather also forced the cancellation of the children's sports, but the Baby Show for under-2s took place under cover.[22]

In early August, plans were announced for twenty-two new houses in Skimped Hill Lane.

Planning for the rebuilding of London began in 1944 with the publication of the Abercrombie Plan for the city. This proposed a ring of eight satellite towns within 50 miles (80km), each with a population of up to 60,000. These would be built on greenfield sites, with neighbourhoods comprising low-density housing, shops, primary school and a pub. Stevenage was the first of the New Towns, designated in 1946. This was followed by Crawley, Hemel Hempstead and Harlow (1947), Hatfield and Welwyn Garden City (a garden city founded in 1920) in 1948, and finally Basildon and Bracknell in 1949. Newton Aycliffe (1947) and Peterlee (1948), both in County Durham, and Corby (1950) in Northamptonshire were also earmarked, along with East Kilbride (1947) and Glenrothes (1948) in Scotland, and Cwmbran (1949) in Wales. The BCC County Planning Officer presented the Abercrombie Land Plan to ERDC in October. The proposal for the town was the arrival of 25,000 new residents, along with 'light industries'.

1947

There was 'slow progress' on the houses at Skimped Hill due to a shortage of labour. It was emphasised the houses would not be pre-fabs 'as it is a valuable site' although the ERDC minutes refer to 'aluminium bungalows' being built. There was no house available for the incoming Roman Catholic priest at St Joseph's, but he was eventually housed in a hut behind the fire brigade station. Squatters did occupy the empty army huts at Easthampstead Park, which had lain empty for more than six months. The army turned off the water supply in an attempt to force them out, but the council sanitary inspector restored it two hours later. Polish soldiers also tried unsuccessfully to evict them just before Christmas, and ERDC took over the site soon after to safeguard local residents from further harassment. Squatters also occupied the huts in Warfield Park; here plans were put in place to make forty-two of them habitable for a temporary period of five years. One family allocated a hut had been living in a bell tent in Owlsmoor.

One anonymous former resident recalls her time there:

> There were three entrances to the park. The main one and only one for vehicles came out in Jig's Lane, just past Strawberry Hill [now Warfield Park Farm Drive]. This was the one we used when going in to Bracknell, or to Bullbrook School. The one used most often came out in Hayley Green where there were two grocers, one each end of the council houses ... The third entrance is the one still in use for the mobile home park, at Chavey Down [at the top of Long

Hill Road where it meets Lock's Ride]. We were not allowed to use this as it was MacLaren's private entrance [Archie MacLaren, former cricketer, bought Warfield Park shortly before the war started].

There were three different types of hut: most were wooden and considered the best. There were two or three made of corrugated tin in a curved shape, very hot when the sun shone down on them and noisy in rain. Some on the corner where the two drives met were made of some sort of concrete and were very cold. One of these was twice the size of the others and locked. Someone picked the lock and it had obviously been a canteen – there were long tables in it. We used this for parties. Inside, all the huts were basic, just one long room with tiny windows along each side and a door each end. There was a tortoise stove in the middle and two gas mantles for light hanging in the centre. The two ends remained dark. There was a sink in one corner with a drain but no water or toilet. We divided the room into three with curtains – a bedroom with three beds, one for my parents, one for the boys and one for the girls, a main room and a kitchen. There was a copper and gas cooker in the kitchen.

Water had to be collected by the bucketful from what had been the shower block. There was just one tap working. We had a large earthenware crock we kept filled with water. We owned a tin bath, but the effect of filling buckets, carrying them across the park, filling and heating the copper then filling the bath was too much to do too often. It was impossible to do this very often and the water was usually cold by the time the youngest ones got in. We would often travel to some of our relations to have a bath and John, my younger brother and I often spent weekends with different aunts.

The toilets were in a block in the middle of the camp, one for each family. The doors had locks but we children soon found that all the locks were the same. In the winter we held on as long as possible before making the trek to the toilets and by the time we had put on hats, coats and boots, we would get there just in time. The toilets had the oddest flushing system. There was no chain to pull but at regular intervals water would flush through from end to end. The older children told us that the water would suck us away if were on the toilet when it flushed, and this would scare us silly.

Some local people called us squatters and gypsies, but most mothers took great pride in keeping children and houses clean despite the difficulties.

The park was a marvellous playground for children, with freedom to roam. There was a group of wellingtonias behind our hut which towered over all the other trees and we were allowed to roam as long as we could see those trees. They could actually be seen for miles.

Our family had one of the few gardens behind our hut and we kept chickens and had a dog, Nigger, a mongrel. My father bought day old chicks from

Bracknell market and we kept them indoors in a box until they were big enough to go outside. Nigger would lay down and let them climb over him.

There were blackberry bushes behind the huts for jam each autumn and an old, very big oak tree, claimed by the girls for playing mothers and fathers. There were trenches dug the other side of the huts with steep banks around them, claimed by the boys for games of soldiers, though we used them for sledging when it snowed. There was also a tower of some sort where we played 'Moonlight, Starlight' at night. This consisted of one player standing by the tower with a torch switched off while the rest would hide. They would call out 'Moonlight, starlight, bogey won't be out tonight' then try to reach the tower before the 'bogey' switched on the torch and shone it on them.

The children went to different schools but all played together at home. We had no radio, no cars, no shops, so our time was spent outside whenever possible. If it was wet, we played around in the shower block, or played board games indoors.

We moved to Warfield Park in the spring or summer of 1946. That November we had a large bonfire and firework party. There weren't many fireworks or much food but it was the first firework display most of us had seen and we had fun. We also all joined together for a Christmas party that year in the canteen the men opened, with Father Christmas and presents for everyone.

We spent the winter of 1947 here, and this winter has made me realise how the adults struggled to cope. The water and toilets must have been frozen – I know for a time no one could get in or out of the park. I can't remember there being a shortage of food but I know we were very cold. We went to bed in our clothes, with overcoats over the blankets and macs over these because the roof leaked. Once the way was cleared to get out, John and I were taken to relatives because we both had chest problems. I was annoyed that I had to go to school while Ruth and Eddie stayed at home.

We moved out, the first to be rehomed, probably because of John's and my health problems in February 1948 and the council was beginning to make improvements. They were laying on water, building toilets outside each hut, and breeze block partitions inside.

The winter of 1946–47 was 'very harsh'. Snow began falling in late January and fell somewhere in the country for almost two months, which 'led to thousands of people being cut off by snowdrifts'. Disruption of coal supplies to power stations led to daily power cuts lasting five hours.[23] Snow remained uncleared in the High Street for several weeks. Bullbrook School closed for two weeks due to a frozen sanitary system, while Ranelagh School ran out of wood for their heating, with pupils being asked to bring two pieces with them so teaching could continue! A funfair at the Royal British Legion was postponed due to a blackout and cold weather. Towards the end of February, there were also fears of a food shortage as supplies were cut off and vegetables were frozen into the ground. Finally, the weather relented but a rapid thaw caused floods, only to be followed by 'the worst storm in fifty years in south Berkshire', although Bracknell escaped with just two fallen trees and a few missing roof tiles. Albert Brant's abiding memory of the winter was the floods that followed – 'sheets of water as far as the eye could see. And of course it flooded at The Bridge and Jocks Lane, it always flooded in those spots.'

Winter finally gave way to spring with Holly Spring House opening its garden for charity at the end of April. There were two small heath fires at the beginning of May, but a major blaze at Easthampstead Park two weeks later destroyed part of the roof and upper floor, with water damage to the lower floors.[24] Appliances from Wokingham, Bracknell, Ascot, Reading, Maidenhead, Slough, Crowthorne, Sonning, Henley and Windsor all attended and took five hours to bring it under control, hampered by poor water supplies. By August, there were 'many heath fires, with firemen almost working full time', and twenty-four outbreaks were recorded during the last week of the month.

Bracknell Dramatic Club, which had stopped in 1939, restarted in June.

German youth leaders visited Bracknell in July, where they were given 'a cautious welcome'. They explained that 'Germany has no meat, and only one pound of fish per month.'[25]

Berkshire was to receive one of the New Towns. Plans to build at White Waltham had been dropped, due to high-grade agricultural land there and the lack of a railway station. Didcot was also considered but was again ruled out due to the productive agricultural land around it and its distance from the capital, and Goring, Frimley, Thatcham, Romsey and Thame were also examined and eliminated. ERDC held a private meeting lasting two hours with the ministers of Town and County Planning and Health, BCC, and the two London boroughs of Brentford and Chiswick, and Southall (where the housing situation was described as 'appalling').[26] The press was not invited, and no press statement was issued.

The secretary of the local branch of the Royal British Legion was quoted as saying: 'I think it will be better for businesses and that we shall get a lot better Public Services. It will spoil the rural district, though not so much perhaps as people believe.' An old resident of the town was not so enthusiastic: 'Bracknell is an old rural village, and it would be a shame to spoil it by introducing smoky factories.' The vicar at Holy Trinity sat on the fence:

> The prospect of development on the scale suggests calls for careful thoughts from the point of view of those who will be responsible for those coming to the district. It would be a delightful opportunity which ought to be made the most of. On the other hand, it could equally destroy the present amenities.

A statement from ERDC finally confirmed: 'There will 20,000 Londoners for Bracknell at an early date. It will not a dormitory town, but self-supporting with suitable industries. Meadow Way, the areas between Park Road and Wick Hill, Broad Lane, and Bay Road are currently available without undue pressure on existing services.'[27] The local press reported a 'buzz' among locals in the town's pubs, while the Licence Trade Organisation called for 'sufficient pubs in New Towns'. In September it was reported that ERDC had 'accepted' 670 houses for the New Town. By the end of the year, £10 million of government money had been allocated for the town's expansion, and ERDC agreed to a Bracknell Development Corporation to plan and execute it. While officially everything had been agreed, Jim Pocknee of Bracknell Development Corporation (speaking in 1981) observed: 'I am sorry to say the majority of ERDC were against it ... and they fought and fought against it.'[28]

Meanwhile, Leslie Kirby was having a run-in with the local council over his home on Ralphs Ride. He had initially submitted a planning application for a caravan on the site, but had been told it was 'too big' and been advised to build a house on piers instead. But this was rejected by ERDC in October after work had already begun and he was told to demolish it. 'I shall defend my home as one who is called to the Services defends his country.' The story of Briar Patch, as he named his bungalow, escalated as the months passed.[29]

August was hot and sunny and the driest on record. Many wells in the area dried up, 'but the council came to the rescue,' remembers Albert Brant. 'After the refuse collections were finished for the day, they placed a large galvanised metal tank in the back of a dust cart ... filled it with water, and piped the water down into the well.'

The current council offices were deemed to be 'too small'. There were rumours that the 'Forest' was to become a civic centre, although its dilapidated condition, traffic noise, and a proposed road widening might mean its demolition instead. There were complains about 'noisy' dances at Victoria Hall, possibly due to a lack of restriction on liquor sales on the premises.

The Armistice Day service in November was due to be held at Holy Trinity, but the vicar refused to invite the local non-conformist ministers on 'a matter of principle'. The Royal British Legion labelled his actions 'petty', and the service was held on their premises in subsequent years, although the vicar refused to attend them.

The year had started with bad weather, and looked like ending in a similar vein with a blizzard in mid-November. To make matters worse, an outbreak of fowl pest meant very few chickens were available for Christmas. It had certainly been an eventful year for Bracknell.

1948

Those living in the Nissen huts (named The Avenue) at Easthampstead Park formed a Residents' Association. They cited those living in 'slums', similar huts in Warfield Park. These had been divided into three rooms with walls built of breeze blocks, but often the two end rooms were so damp, they could not be used. The site had lavatories without doors, and sinks that were not connected to a drain. Cllr Bowyer, chairman of the Housing Committee, was attacked for not visiting either site as he 'had more important things to do'. A disabled serviceman who was making rugs in his Warfield Park Nissen hut, against regulations stating no industry could be conducted on the site, won a temporary reprieve.[30] ERDC were inviting tenders in 1950 'for the conversion of the Officers' Mess ... into seven units of accommodation'. The huts continued to be lived in until 1960.

There was opposition to proposals for a National Health Service. Doctors were concerned about 'central totalitarian powers decreeing where they should work, and medical details being recorded on patients' certificates. Costs for patients would rise from an average of £14 per annum, to £14 per month,' they warned. The start of NHS on 5 July generated no local comment, the *Wokingham and Bracknell News* only recording it 'generally runs smoothly'.

ERDC workers moved in to begin the demolition of 'Briar Patch'. Chicken houses and garage workshops were taken down, and crowds gathered to watch. A police sergeant was stationed on the site during the afternoon, and furniture removed the following day. A removal van plus workmen from Southern Electricity Board arrived, but left without doing anything. The saga took a new twist when a telegram arrived from Surbiton: 'Hold house and home at all costs. Have petitioned Attlee [the Prime Minister], Bevan [Minister of Health but with also a strong interest in housing], and the King.' The case had appeared in the national press and was raising awareness and support in some quarters. A telephone call to ERDC from Lewis Silkin, the Minister of Town and Country Planning, stopped work, with him stating, 'I feel an impartial review of the case would be desirable.'[31] An enquiry was held in Church House in May. Leslie Kirby, the owner, was reported to have built a house, sold it, moved away, moved back again, built and sold a smallholding in Binfield in 1943, before starting on the current house. ERDC stated that Ralphs Ride, which had no sewers, was 'plagued by illicit buildings'. Kirby countered: they had taken two years to make a decision. He had been offered a Nissen hut which was 'unfit to live in'. After consideration, the Minister agreed to the demolition but with a six-month stay of execution. In October, Kirby returned from a holiday (his doctor stating he was 'on the edge of a nervous breakdown') to find one room of the property burnt out in an arson attack 'by an enemy'.

At the ERDC AGM, the council were told they had 'bitten off a little more than they can chew' by agreeing to the potential increase of population to 25,000.

Second World War and the Coming of the New Town

Foreign soldiers were accommodated in Nissen huts erected in South Road (now the site of Bracknell Crematorium). The huts were taken over by homeless people after the war until houses were found for them. Note the water tower in the background.
(Photo courtesy of Paul Wilkie)

Despite warnings of 'you're selling your birthright', the motion to permit a Development Corporation to run the expansion was passed by thirteen votes to five. Councillors from Brentford and Chiswick, and Southall, soon visited the site of the proposed New Town.

Bracknell Lawn Tennis Club was established, playing on three courts in the grounds of 'Holly Bank', a large house in Church Road. There were just twenty members initially, but 'tireless work and dedication' from the founders soon bore dividends, and the club joined the Berkshire Lawn Tennis Association the following year, and the county leagues soon after. They continued to use the Hollybank courts, and later made use of Jocks Lane court facilities for the next twenty years as the club increased in size. In 1973 an opportunity arose to switch to their present location in Lily Hill Park, although the cost of building new courts caused the club problems. Among the first purchases on the new site was a terrapin building, used as a club pavilion. In 2001, a modern, 'chalet-style' clubhouse with facilities replaced the temporary building, which was opened by former top British player Mark Cox.[32]

Bracknell Youth Hostel opened in the 'Forest', the former hotel and home of Dr Fielden, at the top of the High Street.[33] It had a capacity for forty visitors, with fifteen accommodated on the first night, including a Norwegian from Oslo. It was soon providing lodgings for overseas visitors who had arrived in Britain for the Olympic Games being held in London for two weeks in August, although it was never full until 1951.

In August, representatives from BCC, ERDC, New Windsor Borough Council, Thames Conservancy and the Metropolitan Water Board met government minister Lewis Silkin and agreed 'in principle' to the New Town. Local councillors soon visited Chiswick housing estates to see what might be built in Bracknell. The vicar of Holy Trinity now stated he was 'wary of a New Town'. Meanwhile, sites were being marked out at Skimped Hill for fifty Orlit houses, a construction method using precast reinforced concrete,[34] for 'key building workers for New Town', while another forty were 'under construction'.

Local builder Joe Brant was in court over unpaid rates; he would become a familiar figure in the local court in the coming years, battling against the development corporation, ERDC, and anyone else he considered to be imposing inconvenience or bureaucracy on himself or the wider population of the town.

Firemen tackling a blaze in the bar of Farley Hall Hotel on Wokingham Road were faced with the hazard of bottles of whisky, gin and rum exploding.

Thick fog enveloped Berkshire for five days at the end of November, 'the worst ... for forty years'.[35] In true British fashion, sports continued, even though spectators were unable to see what was happening on the pitch!

Maps illustrating proposed development areas were shown to ERDC. Asked for comments by the local press, they responded with 'no comment at present',

Work started on these post-war houses in 1946, although progress was slow due a lack of materials, so some were built of Orlit, a construction method using precast reinforced concrete.

as these had only arrived on the morning of a council meeting. The area under consideration covered the Wokingham Road/Jocks Lane junction, north to Priory Road (now Priory Lane), to the boundary of Warfield Brick and Tile Works, Bay Road/Jigs Lane/Holly Spring Lane/Park Road crossroads (skirting Holly Spring Farm), London Road/Allsmoor Lane junction, south to Crown lands, west to Bay Road, north to the edge of South Hill Park, Jennett's Hill (passing south of East Lodge), Peacock Farm, Amen Corner crossing, Longshot Lane and Jocks Lane. The plans would involve the loss of Rectory and Manor Farms, which produced 2 tons of wheat per acre (against a national average of 18 cwt), along with 700 acres of Peacock Farm, 100 acres of Home Farm (now an estate of the same name), the whole of Old Bracknell, plus other farms, but leaving Crown and common land untouched. It had been 'drawn up in Whitehall with no knowledge of the local area'.³⁶ Binfield Parish Council decided to save their objections for the public enquiry. BCC, who had objected to initial plans for a New Town in the county at White Waltham, now dropped their opposition in favour of Bracknell. By November, it was reported that building work was to start earlier than previously reported 'due to the housing situation in London'.

By December, ERDC had come down in favour: 'If the area was good enough for the Romans ...' Lewis Silkin announced the New Town order would be issued 'soon', explaining that Bracknell was 'capable of expansion from 5,000 to 25,000 into a well-balanced, self-contained community'. There was 'adequate drainage, the sewage plant was sufficient, and agricultural land was not of the highest quality, with only a limited amount under cultivation'.³⁷ The Berkshire Executive of the National Farmers' Union expressed their opposition to the taking of good farm land in 'the strongest possible representation', providing returns to counter the claim of 'poor land'. They were also critical of the lack of time: 'There is not enough time to prepare our report,' while the district organisers stated: 'Farm workers of Berkshire are disgusted.' The chairman of Berks Agriculture Executive Committee said: 'We have never been consulted in any way,' and a Farmer's Fighting Fund meeting at Victoria Hall vowed to take the fight to four MPs and the House of Lords. The vicar of Warfield weighed in: 'We must remember sympathetically the needs of people who are looking for new houses.'

The future of Bracknell, a market town of some 5,000 residents, was still to be decided, but the community had already been split by the proposal. The disruption and trauma it would bring would take many years before finally being resolved. Joyce White sums up the end of an era:

> The Bracknell of my childhood had fields everywhere ... I left school the year the 'New Town' was started. The construction huts were being put up in readiness for the first of the houses. The last line of the song ... sums it up I think – 'Fings ain't what they used to be.'

Postscript

The origins of Bracknell as a place have been lost in the mists of time. The poor soils to the south did not encourage early settlement and its position is more an accident of tracks in the landscape. The laws of Windsor Forest and the dangerous lands to the south and east limited it further. The turnpike road gave a route to London, but it was the arrival of the railway that transformed it from an agricultural settlement to an industrial one, surrounded by several brickyards. Bracknell's population expanded massively between 1861 and 1911, with the town centre extended and workers' cottages built on Priestwood Common. Bullbrook was annexed early in the twentieth century.

It is difficult to discern the history of Bracknell when so much has been lost. Gone are many of the old buildings and much of the High Street. Most of the houses on London Road and Wokingham Road have disappeared, while those in Church Road were swept away. Stanley Road, Rochdale Road and Searle Street have gone completely, while Station Road barely survives. But look carefully and there are still a few survivors – Holy Trinity Church, The Old Manor, The Bull, The Red Lion (now renamed Blue's Smokehouse) and the Station Hotel (more familiar as The Market Inn). Some of the 'big houses' still exist, albeit adapted to life in the twenty-first century – Wick Hill House and Coppid Hall have been split into apartments, while Priestwood Court is now The Admiral Cunningham hotel. Smaller homes can be glimpsed in Binfield Road, Park Road, Broad Lane and Bay Road in Bullbrook.

But what the new Bracknell has gained is a planned layout with many green spaces. The vision of communities in the early estates is still discernible with local shops, school, church and community centre, even if the local butcher and hardware shops have now been replaced by bookmakers and takeaways. There are multiple green spaces including South Hill Park and Lily Hill Park (both formerly private houses), The Elms Park (land exchanged for the old War Memorial Field), and Braybrooke Recreation Ground (the site of a former brickworks).

All settlements change over time, but those earmarked for wholesale redevelopment change the most. Old Bracknell may have been lost under concrete and paving but it is still there, waiting to be discovered in the pages of old books and newspapers. And if you know where to look, there are still glimpses of a time before the New Town.

At the start of this book, I posed the question: 'Bracknell is a New Town – why do we need a History Officer?' I hope this book provides the answer.

Acknowledgements

I wish to thank the following for their contributions to this book:

Alistair Miles for information about the collection of flints found at Amen Corner.

Richard Brignall, who has made extensive research into the history in Swinley Woods from maps and documentation, and on the ground. I am greatly indebted to him for the information on the Devil's Highway, Wickham Bushes and the Napoleonic redoubts.

Reports from Berkshire Archaeology (mounds near Caesar's Camp, 1963), Bracknell District Archaeology Group (Wickham Bushes in 1975), Berkshire Field Research Group and Reading University (Wickham Bushes, 1983 and 1985), Oxford Archaeology (Park Farm, Wood Lane, Binfield in 1990, The Parks in 2005, and Jennett's Park in 2006/7), permission granted for use of excerpts by Leo Webley, Head of Post-excavation Oxford Archaeology, Oxford office, Thames Valley Archaeological Services (Wickham Bushes in 2005, and Devil's Highway in 2006), and Border Archaeology (water mains work in Swinley Woods, 2015).

Albert Brant, Eileen Briggs, Joyce White, Roy Saunders, Ada Harris and other members of the Priestwood Reminiscence Group.

Bracknell Railway Society, especially the late Mick Hutson, for information on Bracknell station and local railway lines proposed in the 1800s.

Paul Lacey for information on the early buses in Bracknell.

Various members of the Bygone Bracknell Facebook group. Special mention must be given to Philip Carlini for his account of the Second World War plane crash over Bracknell, Walter Spencer for his account on the workings of Swinley brickworks, and Vin Miles and Stan and Stewart Willis for sharing their extensive knowledge of Bracknell in former days.

The following have allowed me to use photographs in this publication:

The members of Bygone Bracknell Facebook group, including:

Albert Brant (Victoria Hall, Binfield brickworks, British Legion, opening of the fire station);

Vin Miles (The Crown, cricket ground);

David Morris (Fairclough Farm);

Paul Wilkie (Easthampstead Nissen huts);

Stewart Willis (Bullbrook and Gough's Lane brickworks, Bracknell College, Congregational Church, Skimped Hill);

Wendy Wright (Hind's Head);

Bracknell Central Library (cattle market, Bracknell railway station);

Colin Hickson (Thomas Lawrence);

Mary Evans Agency (Queen Victoria's visit to Bracknell, Dig for Victory).

Bibliography

Banyard. Michael, *Warfield: A Berkshire Village Between the Wars* (Roselle Publishing, 2000).0
Barty-King, Hugh, *Warfield: A Thousand Years of a Berkshire Parish* (Commissioned by Warfield Parish Council and published privately, 2001).
Bracknell Forest Council Countryside Service, *The Coming of Railway* (Undated).
Briggs, Eileen, *A Backward Glance* (The Book Guild, Sussex, 1998).
Codrington, Thomas, *Roman Roads in Britain* (Society for Promoting Christian Knowledge, 1903 (with later revisions)).
Collins, Diane, *Who Owned South Hill Park* (Self-published privately, 2019)
Currie, Ian, Mark Davison and Bob Ogley, *The Berkshire Weather Book* (Froglets Publications, 1994).
Dancy, Kitty, and Sam Chesterman, *History of Sandhurst* (Self-published privately, 1986).
Ditchfield, P.H., *Byways in Berkshire and the Cotswolds* (Robert Scott, 1920).
Dumbleton, Michael, *Brickmaking: A Local Industry* (Bracknell and District Historical Society, 1978).
Hanson, Allan (ed.), *I Remember ... The reminiscences of seven people of Bracknell* (Bracknell and District Historical Society, 1991).
Hickson, Colin, *Bygone Bracknell* (Phillimore, 1984).
Hodder, F.C., *A Short History of Sunningdale* (St Catherine Press, 2011).
Hughes, George Martin, *A History of Windsor Forest, Sunninghill and the Great Park* (Ballantyne, Hanson and Co., 1890).
Hylton, Stuart, *The Little Book of Berkshire* (The History Press, 2014).
Jaggard, Eddie and Peter, *Mr Garth's Hounds* (Priestwood Books, 2009).
Long, Roger, *Caesar's Circle and Mysteries Therein* (Self-published privately, 2000).
Lord, Roger, *The Crowthorne Chronicles* (Self-published privately, undated).
Lynch, Gerard, *Gauged Brickwork* (Routledge, Second Edition, 2006).
Margary, Ivan D., *Roman Roads in Britain* (Phoenix House Ltd, 1955).
Morris, Reg, *Distant Views from Sunninghill* (Tempus, 1985).
Parris, Henry and Judith, *Bracknell, The Making of our New Town* (Bracknell Development Corporation, 1981).
Prescott, Martin, *The Crow on the Thorn* (Self-published privately, 1973).
Radgick, Andrew, *Bracknell's Great War Fallen* (Grosvenor House, 2014).

Shorland, Eileen, *The Pish (Parish) of Warfield and Easthampstead which include the Old Bracknell* (1967).
Smith, Clifford, *The Great Park & Windsor Forest* (Bank House Books, 2004).
Thompson, E.P., *Whigs and Hunters: The Origins of the Black Act* (Penguin Books, 1975).
Stevens, Mark, *Broadmoor Revealed* (Pen and Sword, 2013).
Weightman, Christine, *Remembering Wartime, Ascot, Sunningdale and Sunninghill, 1939–1945* (Cheapside Publications, 2006).

Newspapers and magazines

Berkshire Chronicle
Berks and Oxon Advertiser
General Evening Post
Hampshire Chronicle
Imperial Gazetteer
London Illustrated News
Newbury Weekly News and General Advertiser
Reading Mercury
Reading Observer
Reading Standard
The Lady's Magazine
Times and Weekly News
Windsor and Eton Express
Wokingham, Bracknell and Ascot Times
Wokingham Times

Directories

Kelly's Directory

Pigot's Directory

Archaeological reports

Border Archaeology
Oxford Archaeology
Thames Valley Archaeological Services
Hansard Parliamentary Report, 1896
Miscellaneous websites including:
www.heritagegateway.org.uk (2020)
ancientmonuments.uk (2020)
historicengland.org.uk (2020)
www.britishnewspaperarchive.co.uk (2020)
www.berkshirehistory.com (2020)
www.workhouses.org.uk (2020)
bracknellrailwaysociety.co.uk (2021)
richardbrignall.com (2021)
berkshirevoiceswwi.wordpress.com (2022)

Endnotes

Chapter 1

1 Bracknell Forest Council, Parks and Countryside leaflet.
2 www.cambridge.org/core/journals/archaeologia/article/abs/xii-observations-on-a-roman-encampment-near-east-hempstead-in-berkshire-by-john-narrien-esq-of-the-royal-military-college-at-sandhurst-in-a-letter-to-henry-ellis-esq-frs-secretary/20074A9D51266AD865E7915E457964DA
3 Hughes, George Martin, *A History of Windsor Forest, Sunninghill, and the Great Park*, p.36.
4 www.heritagegateway.org.uk/Gateway/Results_Single.aspx?uid=247736&resourceID=19191
5 Ibid.
6 ancientmonuments.uk/111136-bowl-barrow-on-bill-hill-bracknell
7 historicengland.org.uk/listing/the-list/list-entry/1007944?section=official-list-entry
8 historicengland.org.uk/listing/the-list/list-entry/1007929?section=official-list-entry
9 www.heritagegateway.org.uk/Gateway/Results_Single.aspx?uid=MBF591&resourceID=1028
10 Thames Valley Archaeological Services report, 1992. archaeologydataservice.ac.uk/library/browse/issue.xhtml?recordId=1054392&recordType=GreyLit
11 Thames Valley Archaeological Services report, 2020. archaeologydataservice.ac.uk/library/browse/issue.xhtml?recordId=1194751&recordType=GreyLitSeries
12 Thames Valley Archaeological Services report, 2015. archaeologydataservice.ac.uk/library/browse/issue.xhtml?recordId=1136334&recordType=GreyLitSeries
13 Thames Valley Archaeological Services report, 2017. archaeologydataservice.ac.uk/library/browse/issue.xhtml?recordId=1164268&recordType=GreyLitSeries
14 Thames Valley Archaeological Services report, 2018. archaeologydataservice.ac.uk/library/browse/issue.xhtml?recordId=1164274&recordType=GreyLitSeries
15 Oxford Archaeology report, 1990. eprints.oxfordarchaeology.com/1191/
16 Ibid.
17 Oxford Archaeology report, 2006 and 2007. eprints.oxfordarchaeology.com/564/

18 Prescott, Martin, *The Crow on the Thorn*, p.11.
19 Codrington, Thomas, *Roman Roads in Britain*, p.239.
20 Ibid.
21 basedinchurton.co.uk/2021/07/16/who-was-bishop-bennet/
22 *United Services Journal*, 1836. archive.org/details/dli.bengal.10689.14046/mode/2up
23 Thames Valley Archaeological Services report, 2006. archaeologydataservice.ac.uk/library/browse/issue.xhtml?recordId=1025203&recordType=GreyLit
24 Prescott, Martin, *The Crow on the Thorn*, p.12.
25 ancientmonuments.uk/114540-wickham-bushes-romano-british-settlement-crowthorne
26 Hughes, George Martin, A History of Windsor Forest, Sunninghill, and the Great Park, p.369.
27 Shorland, Eileen, *The Pish (Parish) of Warfield and Easthampstead which include the Old Bracknell*, p.71.
28 Martin Prescott, *The Crow on the Thorn*, p.11.
29 P. H. Ditchfield, *Byways in Berkshire and the Cotswolds*, p.19.
30 *Berkshire Archaeological* journal, 1933. archaeologydataservice.ac.uk/archives/view/berks_bas_2007/journal.cfm?volume=37
31 Ibid.
32 archive.org/stream/surreyarchaeolog47surruoft/surreyarchaeolog47surruoft_djvu.txt
33 https:/archaeologydataservice.ac.uk/archiveDS/archiveDownload?t=arch-1352-1/dissemination/pdf/Berkshire/12063.pdf
34 Thames Valley Archaeological Services report, 2005. archaeologydataservice.ac.uk/library/browse/issue.xhtml?recordId=1027321&recordType=GreyLit
35 British History Online. www.british-history.ac.uk/vch/berks/vol3/pp85-91
36 heritage.hampsteadnorreys.org.uk/Domesday-Book.html#:~:text=The%20Domesday%20Book%20provides%20extensive,and%20other%20resources%2C%20any%20buildings
37 www.englefieldgreen.org.uk/scr/histlist.php?locid=&bid=64
38 Prescott, Martin, *The Crow on the Thorn*, p.18.
39 www.gatehouse-gazetteer.info/English%20sites/4448.html
40 Shorland, Eileen, *The Pish (Parish) of Warfield and Easthampstead which include the Old Bracknell*, p.85.
41 British History Online, www.british-history.ac.uk/lords-jrnl/vol4/pp602-607
42 historicengland.org.uk/listing/the-list/list-entry/1016331?section=official-list-entry
43 historicengland.org.uk/listing/the-list/list-entry/1017785?section=official-list-entry
44 https://historicengland.org.uk/listing/the-list/list-entry/1017785?section=official-list-entry
45 historicengland.org.uk/research/results/reports/6576/TwoNapoleonicRedoubtsinSwinleyWoodBracknellForestBerkshire_EarthworkSurvey
46 rexurbex.blogspot.com/2013/04/pillbox-to-d-day-training.html
47 historicengland.org.uk/research/results/reports/6576/TwoNapoleonicRedoubtsinSwinleyWoodBracknellForestBerkshire_EarthworkSurvey

Endnotes

Chapter 2

1. historicengland.org.uk/listing/the-list/list-entry/1390338?section=official-list-entry
2. historicengland.org.uk/listing/the-list/list-entry/1390339?section=official-list-entry
3. www.berkshirehistory.com/bios/cduval.html
4. historicengland.org.uk/listing/the-list/list-entry/1390337?section=official-list-entry
5. historicengland.org.uk/listing/the-list/list-entry/1390344?section=official-list-entry
6. historicengland.org.uk/listing/the-list/list-entry/1390340?section=official-list-entry
7. historicengland.org.uk/listing/the-list/list-entry/1390324?section=official-list-entry
8. historicengland.org.uk/listing/the-list/list-entry/1390322?section=official-list-entry
9. historicengland.org.uk/listing/the-list/list-entry/1390336?section=official-list-entry
10. historicengland.org.uk/listing/the-list/list-entry/1390342?section=official-list-entry
11. *Wokingham Times*, 20 April 1943.
12. historicengland.org.uk/listing/the-list/list-entry/1390330?section=official-list-entry
13. Hanson, Allan (ed.), *I Remember ... The reminiscences of seven people of Bracknell*, p.39.
14. historicengland.org.uk/listing/the-list/list-entry/1390334?section=official-list-entry
15. historicengland.org.uk/listing/the-list/list-entry/1390323?section=official-list-entry
16. historicengland.org.uk/listing/the-list/list-entry/1390335?section=official-list-entry
17. historicengland.org.uk/listing/the-list/list-entry/1390325?section=official-list-entry
18. historicengland.org.uk/listing/the-list/list-entry/1390350?section=official-list-entry
19. historicengland.org.uk/listing/the-list/list-entry/1390352?section=official-list-entry
20. historicengland.org.uk/listing/the-list/list-entry/1390351?section=official-list-entry
21. historicengland.org.uk/listing/the-list/list-entry/1391324?section=official-list-entry
22. historicengland.org.uk/listing/the-list/list-entry/1390353?section=official-list-entry
23. wokinghamblacks.blogspot.com/
24. Thompson, E.P., *Whigs and Hunters: The Origins of the Black Act*.
25. *Hampshire Chronicle*, 27 May 1797.
26. Hughes, George Martin, *A History of Windsor Forest, Sunninghill, and the Great Park*, chapter xxvii.
27. historicengland.org.uk/listing/the-list/list-entry/1016333?section=official-list-entry
28. www.richardbrignall.com
29. www.blha.org.uk/wp-content/uploads/2020/02/BOAN97.pdf
30. *Reading Mercury*, 4 May 1795.

Chapter 3

1. www.hungerfordvirtualmuseum.co.uk/?view=article&id=23&catid=9
2. *General Evening Post*, 24 November 1810.
3. *Berkshire Chronicle*, 10 October 1829.
4. Bracknell Forest Council, Lily Hill Park: The Making of an English Landscape
5. *Reading Mercury*, 23 February 1829.
6. *Morning Advertiser*, 5 January 1818.

7   'The Bracknell of Jonathan Gwynn, carrier from 1822 to 1851'.
8   *Windsor and Eton Express*, 10 September 1825.
9   *Windsor and Eton Express*, 30 April 1825.
10 *Berkshire Chronicle*, 13 September 1828.
11 *Berkshire Chronicle*, 21 December 1829.
12 *Reading Mercury*, 15 February 1830.
13 *Reading Mercury*, 12 September 1831.
14 *Berkshire Chronicle*, 3 March 1832.
15 *Berkshire Chronicle*, 28 November 1835.
16 www.workhouses.org.uk/Easthampstead/
17 *Berkshire Chronicle*, 6 June 1868.
18 *Reading Mercury*, 8 September 1838.
19 *Reading Mercury*, 27 April 1839.
20 *Reading Mercury*, 17 August 1839.
21 *Reading Mercury*, 15 February 1840.
22 *Reading Mercury*, 12 June 1841.
23 *Windsor and Eton Express*, 9 July 1842.
24 *Reading Mercury*, 9 September 1843.
25 *Windsor and Eton Express*, 16 August 1845.
26 *Reading Mercury*, 29 November 1845.
27 *Windsor and Eton Chronicle*, 28 November 1846.
28 bracknellrailwaysociety.co.uk/
29 *Reading Mercury*, 18 July 1846.
30 *Reading Mercury*, 10 April 1847.
31 *Reading Mercury*, 12 May 1849.
32 *Reading Mercury*, 10 November 1849.
33 *Reading Mercury*, 16 October 1852.
34 bracknellrailwaysociety.co.uk/

Chapter 4

1   *Reading Mercury*, 4 July 1857.
2   *Reading Standard*, 16 July 1859.
3   *Reading Mercury*, 29 October 1864.
4   *Windsor and Eton Express*, 11 May 1861.
5   *Windsor and Eton Express*, 3 May 1862.
6   *Berkshire Chronicle*, 3 May 1862
7   *Berkshire Chronicle*, 14 March 1863.
8   *Reading Mercury*, 12 March 1864.
9   *Reading Mercury*, 3 September 1864.
10 15 April 1865.
11 Stevens, Mark, *Broadmoor Revealed*, p.134.
12 *Reading Mercury*, 16 June 1866.
13 *Berkshire Mercury*, 18 May 1867.
14 *Reading Mercury*, 29 August 1868.

15 *Reading Mercury*, 24 October 1868.
16 *Berkshire Chronicle*, 21 August 1869.
17 *Reading Mercury*, 30 July 1870.
18 *Berkshire Chronicle*, 8 April 1871.
19 *Reading Mercury*, 27 July 1872.
20 *Berkshire Chronicle*, 25 April 1874.
21 *Reading Mercury*, 28 November 1874.
22 *Berkshire Chronicle*, 17 July 1875.
23 *Berkshire Chronicle*, 22 December 1877.
24 *Reading Mercury*, 8 June 1878.
25 *Reading Mercury*, 17 August 1878.
26 *Reading Mercury*, 18 January 1879.
27 *Reading Mercury*, 11 December 1880.
28 *Reading Mercury*, 26 February 1881.
29 *Berkshire Chronicle*, 20 August 1881.
30 *Reading Mercury*, 25 June 1887.
31 *Berkshire Chronicle*, 10 December 1887.
32 *Reading Mercury*, 26 January 1889.
33 *Reading Mercury*, 23 March 1889.
34 *Reading Standard*, 21 August 1891.
35 *Reading Mercury*, 23 January 1892.
36 *Berkshire Chronicle*, 21 March 1896.
37 *Reading Mercury*, 15 July 1893.
38 *Reading Mercury*, 2 September 1893.
39 *Reading Observer*, 14 October 1893.
40 *Reading Mercury*, 14 July 1894.
41 *Reading Mercury*, 18 May 1895.
42 *Newbury Weekly News and General Advertiser*, 13 June 1895.
43 *Reading Mercury*, 5 October 1895.
44 *Berkshire Chronicle*, 31 October 1896.
45 *Reading Observer*, 28 November 1896.
46 Ibid., 12 December 1896.
47 Ibid., 19 December 1896.
48 Ibid., 28 December 1896.
49 Ibid., 11 December 1897.
50 *Reading Mercury*, 20 March 1897.
51 *Reading Mercury*, 26 June 1897.
52 *Windsor and Eton Express*, 21 August 1897.
53 *Berkshire Chronicle*, 3 December 1898.
54 *Reading Chronicle*, 22 April 1899.
55 *Reading Mercury*, 2 December 1899.
56 *Reading Mercury*, 3 March 1900.
57 *Reading Mercury*, 17 March 1900.
58 *Reading Mercury*, 26 May 1900.
59 *Reading Mercury*, 18 August 1900.
60 *Berkshire Chronicle*, 19 January 1901.

61 *Reading Standard*, 14 December 1901.
62 *Berkshire Chronicle*, 26 January 1901.

Chapter 5

1   Dumbleton, Michael, *Brickmaking: A Local Industry*, p.16.
2   *Windsor and Eton Express*, 15 November 1818.
3   Briggs, Eileen, *A Backward Glance*.
4   *Windsor and Eton Express*, 9 April 1825.
5   jaharrison.me.uk/Brickwork/TLB.html.
6   Dumbleton, Michael, *Brickmaking: A Local Industry*, p.7.
7   Ibid., p.12.
8   api.parliament.uk/historic-hansard/commons/1896/jun/02/swinley-woods-windsor-forest#S4V0041P0_18960602_HOC_73
9   Smith, Clifford, *The Great Park and Windsor Forest*, p.347.
10 Dumbleton, Michael, *Brickmaking: A Local Industry*, p.16.
11 *Windsor and Eton Express*, 14 April 1906.
12 Michael Banyard, *Warfield; A Berkshire Village Between the Wars*, p.71.
13 *Reading Observer*, 6 November 1920.
14 Bygone Bracknell Facebook group.
15 *Reading Observer*, 6 November 1920.
16 *Berkshire Chronicle*, 8 February 1879.
17 *Reading Mercury*, 29 July 1899.
18 *Reading Observer*, 24 December 1904.
19 *Berkshire Chronicle*, 11 March 1905.
20 *Reading Mercury*, 2 January 1915.
21 *Berkshire Chronicle*, 30 January 1897.
22 *Reading Mercury*, 25 May 1901.
23 *Reading Observer*, 6 February 1904.
24 *Reading Mercury*, 28 February 1914.
25 *Reading Standard*, 12 April 1935.
26 Bygone Bracknell Facebook Group.

Chapter 6

1   *Reading Mercury*, 16 February 1901.
2   *Reading Mercury*, 14 September 1901.
3   *Reading Mercury*, 15 March 1902.
4   *Reading Mercury*, 28 June 1902.
5   *Reading Mercury*, 7 June 1902.
6   *Reading Mercury*, 9 May 1903.
7   search.lma.gov.uk/scripts/mwimain.dll/144/LMA_OPAC/web_detail/REFD+LMA~2F4040?SESSIONSEARCH
8   *Reading Mercury*, 8 August 1902.
9   *Berkshire Chronicle*, 16 August 1902.

Endnotes

10 *Reading Mercury*, 13 September 1902.
11 *Berkshire Chronicle*, 6 September 1902.
12 *Reading Standard*, 23 May 1903.
13 *Reading Mercury*, 31 January 1903.
14 *Reading Mercury*, 31 October 1903.
15 *Berkshire Chronicle*, 6 February 1904.
16 *Windsor and Eton Express*, 9 April 1904.
17 *Berkshire Chronicle*, 4 February 1905.
18 www.english-heritage.org.uk/learn/story-of-england/20th-century/
19 *Windsor and Eton Express*, 19 August 1905.
20 *Reading Observer*, 27 January 1906.
21 *Reading Observer*, 12 May 1906.
22 *Reading Observer*, 12 May 1906.
23 *Reading Observer*, 19 May 1906.
24 *Reading Observer*, 2 June 1906.
25 *Berkshire Chronicle*, 9 February 1907.
26 *Reading Observer*, 4 May 1907.
27 roadswerenotbuiltforcars.com/how-two-cycling-organisations-founded-in-1878-led-to-better-roads-for-all/
28 *Berkshire Chronicle*, 21 September 1907.
29 *Reading Standard*, 2 November 1907.
30 *Reading Standard*, 29 April 1908.
31 *Berkshire Chronicle*, 23 May 1908.
32 go.gale.com/ps/i.do?id=GALE%7CA176204305&sid=sitemap&v=2.1&it=r&p=EAIM&sw=w&userGroupName=anon%7E1501b4cf&aty=open-web-entry
33 *Berkshire Chronicle*, 14 October 1908.
34 *Berkshire Chronicle*, 21 November 1908.
35 bracknellrailwaysociety.co.uk/history/bracknell-station-was-very-different-100-years-ago/
36 *Berkshire Chronicle*, 8 May 1909.
37 *Reading Observer*, 12 August 1909.
38 *Reading Observer*, 1 January 1910.
39 *Windsor and Eton Express*, 29 January 1910.
40 *Windsor and Eton Express*, 28 May 1910.
41 *Reading Observer*, 21 May 1910.
42 *Reading Observer*, 13 August 190?
43 *Reading Standard*, 27 August 1910.
44 *Reading Standard*, 27 August 1910.
45 *Berkshire Chronicle*, 11 February 1911.
46 *Windsor and Eton Express*, 22 April 1911.
47 *Reading Observer*, 20 May 1911.
48 *Reading Mercury*, 24 June 1911.
49 *Reading Observer*, 8 July 1911.
50 *Faringdon Advertiser and Vale of the White Horse Gazette*, 29 July 1911.
51 *Reading Mercury*, 29 July 1911.
52 Ibid., 19 August 1911.

53 bracknellbowlingclub.com/club-history
54 *Reading Observer*, 13 July 1912.
55 *Windsor and Eton Express*, 23 November 1912.
56 *Reading Observer*, 25 January 1913.
57 *Berkshire Chronicle*, 21 February 1913.
58 *Berkshire Chronicle*, 3 January 1914.
59 *Reading Mercury*, 7 February 1914.
60 *Reading Observer*, 4 April 1914.
61 *Reading Mercury*, 30 May 1914.

Chapter 7

1 *Reading Mercury*, 15 August 1914.
2 Ibid.
3 *Reading Mercury*, 21 November 1914.
4 Easthampstead Rural District Council minutes, 20 August 1914.
5 Ibid., 3 September 1914.
6 Ibid., 23 December 1914.
7 *Berkshire Chronicle*, 21 August 1914.
8 *Windsor and Eton Express*, 11 September 1915.
9 Radgick, Andrew, *Bracknell's Great War Fallen, Volume I*, p.44.
10 *Reading Mercury*, 31 October 1914.
11 *Reading Standard*, 12 September 1914.
12 *Reading Observer*, 29 May 1915.
13 *Reading Mercury*, 27 November 1915.
14 toxicfrog1.blogspot.com/2008/06/
15 *Reading Mercury*, 19 February 1916.
16 berkshirevoiceswwi.wordpress.com/2017/03/27/a-day-of-wild-rumours/
17 Easthampstead Rural District Council minutes, 21 December 1916.
18 *Reading Mercury*, 10 June 1916.
19 berkshirevoiceswwi.wordpress.com/2016/07/01/you-will-be-proud-of-our-boys-when-i-tell-of-the-splendid-way-they-went-over-the-top/
20 *Reading Mercury*, 10th June 1916.
21 *Reading Mercury*, 30 September 1916.
22 *Reading Observer*, 10 February 1917.
23 Easthampstead Rural District Council minutes, 24 May 1917.
24 *Reading Mercury*, 5 May 1917.
25 *Reading Mercury*, 16 June 1917.
26 *Reading Mercury*, 21 July 1917.
27 *Reading Mercury*, 28 July 1917.
28 *Reading Mercury*, 10 November 1917.
29 *Reading Mercury*, 10 November 1917.
30 www.mylearning.org/stories/ww1-food-shortages-and-rationing/710?#:~:text=The%20first%20item%20to%20be,remained%20on%20ration%20until%201920.

Endnotes

31 *Reading Mercury*, 20 April 1918.
32 *Reading Observer*, 9 November 1918.
33 Easthampstead Rural District Council minutes, 24 October 1917.
34 berkshirevoiceswwi.wordpress.com/2018/10/28/white-flags/
35 berkshirevoiceswwi.wordpress.com/2018/10/29/austria-breaking-from-germany/
36 berkshirevoiceswwi.wordpress.com/2018/10/31/turkey-has-given-in-completely/
37 *Reading Mercury*, 16 November 1918.
38 Hanson, Allan (ed.), *I Remember … The Reminiscences of Seven People of Bracknell*, p.20.
39 Easthampstead Rural District Council minutes, 21 January 1919.
40 www.thehistorypress.co.uk/articles/the-1918-general-election/
41 *Reading Observer*, 18 January 1919.
42 *Reading Observer*, 31 May 1919.
43 *Reading Observer*, 22 March 1919.
44 www.britishlegion.org.uk/about-us/our-history#:~:text=The%20British%20Legion%20was%20formed,and%20Demobilized%20Sailors%20and%20Soldiers
45 *Reading Standard*, 7 January 1928.
46 *Reading Observer*, 26 July 1919.
47 Easthampstead Rural District Council minutes, 19 July 1919.
48 *Reading Standard*, 28 August 1920.
49 *Reading Standard*, 8 August 1920.
50 *Reading Standard*, 28 August 1920.
51 *Reading Standard*, 25 September 1920.
52 www.keymilitary.com/article/gift-kept-misgiving
53 *Reading Observer*, 16 October 1920.
54 Ibid.
55 *Reading Observer*, 22 January 1921.
56 Ibid., 29 January 1921.
57 Radgick, Andrew, Bracknell's Great War Fallen, Volume I, p.13.
58 *Reading Standard*, 26 March 1921.
59 *Reading Observer*, 11 August 1922.
60 *Reading Observer*, 26 January 1923.
61 *Reading Observer*, 12 October 1923.
62 *Reading Standard*, 7 April 1933.
63 *Reading Standard*, 1 November 1924.

CHAPTER 8

1 Hanson, Allan (ed.), *The Reminiscences of Seven People of Bracknell*, p.11.
2 Ibid., p.13.
3 Ibid., p.15.
4 Briggs, Eileen, *A Backward Glance*, p.47.
5 *Reading Standard*, 22 November 1924.
6 *Reading Standard*, 26 November 1927.
7 *Reading Standard*, 20 December 1924

8   *Reading Standard*, 3 January 1925.
9   *Reading Standard*, 17 January 1925.
10 *Reading Standard*, 14 January 1928.
11 *Reading Standard*, 14 January 1928.
12 *Reading Standard*, 31 December 1927.
13 Banyard, Michael, *Warfield, A Berkshire Village Between the Wars*, p.61.
14 *Reading Standard*, 10 November 1928.
15 *Reading Standard*, 26 April 1930.
16 *Reading Standard*, 4 May 1929.
17 *Reading Standard*, 22 November 1930.
18 *Reading Standard*, 19 July 1930.
19 *Reading Standard*, 13 September 1930.
20 *Reading Standard*, 19 September 1931.
21 *Daily Herald*, 29 December 1931.
22 *Wokingham Times*, 8 July 1932.
23 *Reading Standard*, 3 December 1932.
24 *Wokingham Times*, 10 February 1933.
25 military-history.fandom.com/wiki/Edward_Fielden_(RAF_officer)
26 *Reading Standard*, 3 May 1935.
27 Easthampstead Rural District Council minutes.
28 *Wokingham Times*, 14 May 1937.
29 *Reading Standard*, 9 July 1937.
30 *Berks and Oxon Advertiser*, 9 July 1937.
31 *Reading Standard*, 29 July 1938.
32 *Reading Standard*, 28 October 1983.
33 *Wokingham Times*, 12 August 1938.
34 *Reading Mercury*, 13 May 1939.
35 Easthampstead Rural District Council minutes, 1939.

Chapter 9

1 www.bbc.com/historyofthebbc/anniversaries/september/war-announced
2 *Wokingham Times*, 8 September 1939.
3 www.nationalarchives.gov.uk/help-with-your-research/research-guides/1939-register/
4 www.eastpark.co.uk/about-us/history
5 Ibid.
6 kennemerbataljon.wordpress.com/1945-engeland-easthampstead/?fbclid=IwAR3vhCx M5ly4bTR1fcyrhc_PNli3E0UDF6Et1Jp9uqiY3or8CFRr2FD4E8o
7 www.bracknellnews.co.uk/news/15323140.tally-ho-farm-is-gifting-the-piece-of-history-back-to-ramsey-county-minnesota/
8 Briggs, Eileen, *A Backward Glance*, p.103.
9 *Reading Mercury*, 28 October 1939.
10 *Reading Mercury*, 25 November 1939.

Endnotes

11 www.cwgc.org/find-records/find-war-dead/casualty-details/2491668/walter-frederick-benstead/
12 Bygone Bracknell Facebook group.
13 *Wokingham Times*, 27 September 1940.
14 Bygone Bracknell Facebook group.
15 Hanson, Allan (ed.), *I Remember ... The Reminiscences of Seven People of Bracknell*, p.43.
16 www.raf.mod.uk/aircadets/who-we-are/our-history/
17 www.parliament.uk/about/living-heritage/transformingsociety/private-lives/yourcountry/collections/collections-second-world-war/second-world-war-legislation/national-service-act-c15-1941-/#:~:text=The%20National%20Service%20Act%20extended,and%20thirty%2C%20and%20childless%20widows.
18 military-history.fandom.com/wiki/RAF_Staff_College,_Bracknell
19 Easthampstead Rural District Council minutes, 11 September 1947.
20 *Wokingham Times*, 11 May 1945.
21 Easthampstead Rural District Council minutes, 1947.
22 *Wokingham Times*, 14 June 1946.
23 www.markvoganweather.com/2015/12/12/a-look-back-winter-of-1946-47/
24 www.eastpark.co.uk/about-us/history
25 *Wokingham Times*, 11 July 1947.
26 *Reading Standard*, 1 August 1957.
27 *Wokingham Times*, 8 August 1947.
28 Parris, Henry and Judith, *Bracknell, The Making of our New Town*.
29 freedomnews.org.uk/wp-content/uploads/2019/05/Freedom-1948-05-29.pdf
30 *Reading Standard*, 26 November 1948.
31 www.youtube.com/watch?v=GbMY5eClq3o
32 bracknelltennis.com/history/#:~:text=Bracknell%20Lawn%20Tennis%20Club%20(BLTC,was%20formed%20'by%20acclamation'%20!
33 *Reading Standard*, 23 July 1948.
34 nonstandardhouse.com/orlit-prc-house-construction-details/
35 *Reading Standard*, 3 December 1948.
36 *Reading Standard*, 22 October 1948.
37 *Reading Standard*, 6 August 1948.